AF554012

A-Z
LANGUAGE AND LINGUISTICS

A-Z
LANGUAGE AND LINGUISTICS

Andrew Patrick

CENTRUM PRESS
NEW DELHI-110002 (INDIA)

CENTRUM PRESS
H.O.: 4360/4, Ansari Road, Daryaganj,
New Delhi-110 002 (India)
Ph.: 23278000, 23261597

B.O.: No. 1015, Ist Main Road, BSK IIIrd Stage
IIIrd Phase, IIIrd Block,
Bangalore - 560 085 (India)
Tel.: 080-41723429
Visit us at: www.centrumpress.com

A-Z Language and Linguistics

First Edition, 2009

ISBN 978-93-80252-01-8

PRINTED IN INDIA

Printed at Mehra Offset Press, Delhi

Contents

Preface

You are reading a topic, or listening to a lecture, taking part in a conversation about a language, and realize that you don't know enough about what is being said to understand. At this moment, you should seek out this guide book.

All the chapters will provide you much information about different aspects of linguistic. Its history begins longer ago than we know, along with its subject matter, and it will continue for as long as that subject matter remains.

Having language is probably associated with wondering about language, and so, if there is one thing that sets linguistics apart from other disciplines, it is the fact that the subject matter of linguistics must be used in the description. There is no metalanguage for language that is not translatable into language, and a metalanguage is also a language.

According to some persons, language is literally all that there is. According to others, it always reflects, what there is. What seems certain is that we should use it prolifically in creating and changing our momentary values and that in seeking to understand language, we are seeking to understand the every cornerstone of the human mentality.

Author

Chapter 1

Language and Linguistics

Talking, shouting, whispering, lying, swearing, telling jokes or tales, in short: communication of all sorts by means of articulate sound is something we are so familiar with that we hardly ever come to think about it as something unique. However, no other creature on this planet shows the ability to communicate verbally in the way we do. Take a minute to think about the immense impact spoken and written language has on your everyday life! You could not possibly do without it in situations where you meet other people, like in school, university, or at the breakfast table.

The examples are innumerous. In this course, we will take a look at the unique features of human language. As you will see when we proceed, the human curiosity concerning language is no modern phenomenon. Language has been examined by linguists and philosophers for several millennia. Therefore, we can look back on a respectable stock of literature on the topic originating from the times of Ancient Greece until the present day. The result is a compendium of linguistic disciplines that are interwoven with the domains of, among others, philosophy, psychology, neurology, and even computer science: a vast and fascinating network of knowledge. To keep you fascinated and to keep you from becoming intimidated, we will start right away with the very principles that make human language so special.

HUMAN LANGUAGE

Language is a highly elaborated signaling system. We call the aspects that are peculiar to it the *design features* of language.

Some of these we find only with the language of human beings, others we have in common with animals. Another aspect of human language is that we express *thoughts* with words.

Design Features of Language

- A principle feature of human language is the duality of patterning. It enables us to use our language in a very *economic* way for a virtually infinite production of linguistic units. How does this principle work?

All human languages have a *small, limited set* of speech sounds. The limitation derives from the restricted capacity of our *vocal apparatus.*

The speech sounds are referred to as *consonants* and *vowels.*

Linguistically speaking, the distinctive speech sounds are called *phonemes,* which are explained in more detail in the chapter on *phonology.* You cannot use isolated phonemes for communication, because phonemes are by themselves meaningless. But we can assemble and reassemble phonemes into larger linguistic units. These are commonly called "words". Although our capacity to produce new phonemes is limited, we frequently coin new words. Hence, our capacity to produce vocabulary is unlimited.

- Displacement

In contrast to other animals, humans have a sense of the past and the future. A gorilla, for example, cannot tell his fellows about his parents, his adventures in the jungle, or his experience of the past. The use of language to talk about things other than "the here and now", is a characteristic of humans. Displacement is thus our ability to convey a meaning that transcends the immediately perceptible sphere of space and time. Although some animals seem to possess abilities appropriating those of displacement, they lack the freedom to apply this to new contexts. The dance of the honey-bee, for instance, indicates the locations of rich deposits of food to other bees. This ability of the bee corresponds to displacement in human language, except for a lack of variation. The bee repeats the same patterns in its dance, whereas humans are able to invent ever new contexts.

- Open-endedness: The ability to say things that have never been said before, including the possibility to express invented things or lies, is also a peculiar feature of human language.
- Stimulus-freedom is another aspect that distinguishes human language from animal communication. The honey-bee must perform its dance, the woodchuck must cry out in order to warn his fellows when it beholds an eagle.

Humans have the ability to say anything they like in any context. This ability is only restricted in certain ceremonial contexts such as church services, etc., where a fixed form is expected to be followed. The possibility to violate this fixed linguistic behavior is then the source of jokes, such as a bride's "no".

- Arbitrariness

Why is a table called "table"? Obviously, the thing never told us its name. And tables do not make a noise similar to the word. The same applies to most of the words of our language.

Hence, words and their meaning have no *a priori* connection. We cannot tell from the sound structure which meaning is behind it. Language is not *motivated,* as we can also put it.

There are, however, exceptions to this rule: language can be *iconic,* which means that there is a direct correlation between form and meaning.

The length of a phrase, for example, could represent a length of time the phrase refers to, like in "a long, long time ago".

Here, the extension serves to visually represent the semantic emphasis. Iconicity in language can be found frequently. We will see this in more detail in the chapter on *semiotics*.

Another example for *nonarbitrariness* are *onomatopoeia.* These are words that seem to resemble sounds. There are many examples for onomatopoetic words, like *splash* or *bang*. Some names for animals are also onomatopoetic, for example, "cuckoo". Still, since animals such as the bird are named differently in different languages, there can be no ultimate motivation for the name.

- The human vocal tract

An elaborated language requires a highly sophisticated speech organ that will enable the speaker to produce the many differentiated sounds. Only humans are endowed with a speech organ of this complexity.

WHAT IS LINGUISTICS?

Linguistics is the scientific inquiry into the human language with all its aspects. *All its aspects*: these are many. There is a specialized branch for each approach to the examination of language.Until the beginning of the 20th century, scholars were occupied with research on the history of languages and the roots of words in ancient tongues. The famous linguist *Ferdinand de Saussure* coined this approach the *diachronic* analysis and moved to the analysis of the system of language, which he assumed to be of greater importance. Saussure stated this in the first decades of this century and thus formed the fundament of modern linguistics.

Diachronic Versus Synchronic View

- Diachrony: Diachronic linguistics views the historical development of a language. Thus, on the diachronic axis we can go back and forth in time, watching the language with all its features change.
- Synchrony

Synchronic linguistics views a particular state of a language at some given point in time. This could mean *Modern English* of the present day, or the systematic analysis of the system of Shakespeare's English. However, no comparisons are made to other states of language or other times.

Modern linguistics, following Ferdinand de Saussure, is primarily interested i the synchronic point of view. Saussure postulated the priority of synchrony: no knowledge of the historical development of a language is necessary to examine its present system. He arrived at this radical viewpoint due to his conviction that linguistic research must concentrate on the *structure* of language. Later, the whole paradigm was hence called *structuralism.*

The Two Axes of the Synchronic view

When we look at the structure of language, we find sentences and words. This is, however, a very rough view. A grammar of a language must be more precise.

- One axis of the synchronic view is syntagmatic analysis. Here we examine the relationships of all elements of a sentence to one another. We ask ourselves exactly what element appears where and under which condition in a sentence. For example, where do nouns appear? Where are auxiliary verbs applied? All word classes show certain syntagmatic relationships. They can be defined by *distribution analysis,* a method that classifies elements according to their appearance within the logical order of a sentence.

Let's have a look at an example: A + crosses + the + street Obviously, a noun must appear in the blank space, for example: a *woman* crosses the street.

- Of course, nouns and verbs are not all the same. They do not fit into contexts freely. Hence we apply *paradigmatic analysis*. In our example, the idea of a sandwich crossing the street is impossible.

As you can see, the elements of language obviously evince paradigmatic relationships. Elements can be substituted by others of the same paradigmatic class, such as street, lane, road, etc. Articles can also be exchanged. Words that belong to the same paradigmatic class thus belong to the same grammatical class. They also belong to the same *lexical field.*

The Various Linguistic Disciplines: Survey

In the following, the branches of linguistics we will deal with in this course are listed. This is only a very rough summary. You will get more detailed information when you turn to the respective chapters.

• Historical linguistics

This discipline is occupied with the examination of the historical development of languages. But apart from this *diachronic analysis*, it also deals with the *synchronic analysis* of certain states of language. In this course, we will have a look at the development of the English language.

• Language acquisition and communication

How do we learn our language? How do the processes of language comprehension and production work? This discipline gives answers to these questions. Also, it takes a look at the role of memory in language and how it is used once we are able to talk. Strictly speaking, it is a branch of *psycholinguistics*, a discipline that emerged from the interdisciplinary collaboration of linguistics and psychology in the 1950's. Research in language acquisition has meanwhile become a strong domain of its own.

• Phonetics

The subjects of phonetics are the *articulation, transport,* and *receival* of speech sounds. Thus, there are three corresponding branches of phonetics: *articulatory, acoustic,* and *auditory phonetics*. In contrast to *phonology,* phonetics deals with the physical aspect of speech sounds. In order to give a correct transcription of speech sounds, there are several special alphabets. The one most commonly used is the IPA which you will find in this textbook.

• Phonology

Phonology is the study of the distinctive sounds of a language, the so called *phonemes*. Phonology examines the *functions of sounds* within a language.

• Morphology

Morphemes are the smallest meaningful elements of a language. Morphology is the study of these meaning units. Not all words or even all syllables are necessarily meaning units. Morphology employs *discovery procedures* to find out what words or syllables are morphemes.

• Syntax

Syntax is the study of sentence structure; it is a part of grammar in the broad sense. There are several ways of defining and examining sentences. We will have a look at various grammars.

- Semiotics

Semiotics is the study of *signs* in communication processes in general. It concerns itself with the analysis of both linguistic and non-linguistic signs as communicative devices and with their systems. We will take a brief look at the theory of signs, with emphasis on the linguistic sign.

- Semantics

Linguistic semantics examines the *meaning* of linguistic signs and strings of signs.

- Pragmatics

Pragmatics is the study of the use of signs and the relationship between signs and their users.

- Text linguistics

The traditional linguistic disciplines regard the text as a peripheral phenomenon, whereas Text linguistics regard the text as a sign of its own. There are various text types and mechanisms that constitute *textuality*. These lie beyond the borders of the separate sentences.

- Sociolinguistics

This is the study of the interaction of language and social organization. There are several models that determine the variation of language in social contexts both on an individual as well as on a social-group scale. Sociolinguistics is also concerned with national language policies.

- Computer linguistics (also: computational linguistics)

This domain is an interdisciplinary area of research between linguistics and information science. There are two main branches.

First, computer linguists simulate grammars by implementing language structures into computer programs. In this context, the term *computer metaphor* became famous. It refers to the notion that the human brain can be simulated by a computer.

Second, computer linguists use the computer as a *tool* for the analysis of language. For instance, large corpuses of text are processed with the aid of especially designed software.

Chapter 2

Language Universals

Nearly five thousand languages are spoken in the world today. They seem to be quite different, but still, many of them show similar principles, such as word order. For example, in languages such as English, French, and Italian, the words of the clause take the order of first the subject, then the verb, and then the direct object.

There even exist basic patterns or principles that are shared by all languages. These patterns are called *universals.*

When the same principles are shared by several languages, we speak of *language types*. There are several examples for universals.

SEMANTIC UNIVERSALS

There are semantic categories that are shared by all cultures and referred to by all languages these are called semantic universals. There are many examples of semantic universals. Let's discuss two of them:

- One semantic universal regards our notion of color. There exist eleven basic color terms: black, white, red, green, blue, yellow, brown, purple, pink, orange, and gray. The pattern that all languages universally abide by, is that they do not entertain a notion of a color term outside of that range. This means, any imaginable color is conceived of as a mixture, shade, or subcategory of one of these eleven basic color terms. As a result, one way of classifying languages is by color terms. The eleven color terms are not in usage equally among the languages on Earth. Not all languages have all basic color terms. Some have two, some three, and some four. Others have five, six, or seven, and some have eight to eleven. Those with two color terms always have black and white, those with three black, white, and red, and those with more have additional basic color terms according to the order in the list given above. This is a universal pattern. The languages which have the same basic color terms in common belong to the same language type. Hence, we find seven classes of languages according to this scheme.

- Another semantic universal is the case of pronouns. Think of what it is you do when you talk to someone about yourself. There is always the "I", representing you as the speaker, and the "you", meaning the addressee. You could not possibly do without that, and neither could a speaker of any other language on earth. Again, we find a universal pattern here. Whenever you do not talk about yourself as a person, but as a member of a group, you use the plural "we". English is restricted to these two classes of pronouns: singular and plural, each in the first, second, and third person. All languages that evince this structure are grouped into one language type. There are other languages that make use of even more pronouns. In some languages, it is possible to address two people with a pronoun, that specifically indicates, not just their being plural, but also their being 'two' people; this is then the *dual* pronoun.
- Other examples are languages that have pronouns to refer to the speaker and the addressee together, called inclusive pronouns. Exclusive pronouns refer to the speaker together with people other than the addressee. However, these are not among the European languages.

Phonological Universals

Different languages may have very different sets of

vowels. If you are familiar with a few foreign languages, you may find it difficult to believe there are universal rules governing the distribution of vowels, but they do exist. Remember our example of basic color terms: A similar pattern could be drawn on the basis of the vowel system. Languages with few vowels always have the same set of vowel types. And if a language has more vowels, it is always the same type of vowel that is added to the set. These vowels may not always sound exactly the same, but they are always created at the same location in our vocal apparatus.

SYNTACTIC UNIVERSALS

Remember the word order of English we mentioned above. Hmhm, you say: that cannot be a universal rule, since you know other sentences from English and possibly from other languages which do not follow this order. You are right, but the order subject, verb, object (SVO) may be defined as the *basic* order of English sentences. In other languages there are different "basic" orders, such as Japanese (SOV) or Tongan (VSO), a Polynesian language.

After an extensive study, one can define two different sets of basic orders that languages follow: First SVO, VSO, SOV and second VOS, OVS, OSV. What is the difference? In the first set the subject precedes the object, in the second set it follows the object. Since the first set is the one which applies to the basic structures of far more languages than the second one does, the universal rule is that there is an overwhelming tendency for the subject of a sentence to precede the direct object among the languages of the world.

ABSOLUTE UNIVERSALS – UNIVERSAL TENDENCIES; IMPLICATIONAL – NONIMPLICATIONAL UNIVERSALS

Of course, not all universals can be found in all languages. With so many tongues spoken, it would be hard not to find any exceptions. Most languages have not even been the subject of extensive research as of yet. However, some rules appear without exception in the languages which have been studied so far. We call these *absolute universals*. If there are minor exceptions to the rule, we speak of *universal tendencies* or *relative universals*. In saying this, we take for granted that exceptions may be found in future surveys among languages which have remained unexplored up to the present day.

Sometimes a universal holds only if a particular condition of the language structure is fulfilled. These universals are called *implicational*. Universals which can be stated without a condition are called *nonimplicational*. In other words, whenever a rule "If ... then ..." is valid, the universal appears in the structure of the respective language.

There are thus four types of universals: implicational absolute universals, implicational relative universals, nonimplicational absolute universals, and nonimplicational relative universals.

The final determination of which type a universal belongs to is dependent on intensive field research.

Chapter 3

The History of English I: Old English

Looking at a living language, one of the most interesting aspects is *language change*. All languages, except for the extinct ones, change permanently. Usually we do not notice the change that takes place during our own time because it happens quite slowly. But if we take a look back over a considerable span of time, language change becomes more obvious. Of course there were no textbooks in the beginnings of language, but fortunately linguists have developed certain methods to trace back words even beyond earliest records. Thus we have knowledge not only of the last 1500 years of English. We can even make an assumption about the very roots of the language.

English is an *Indo-European* language. Indo-European was discovered to be the parent language of most European, Anterior-Asian, and Indian languages. As a rule, according to prototypical features of some of these languages, two main branches are defined in the Indo-European language tree, namely an eastern branch and a western branch. However, scholars have disputes about where the divisions within the Indo-European language family are to be placed. For example, in examining languages other than the prototypical, it has been found that not all languages can be classified into one of the two main branches, the eastern and western branches, of language families.

How do we recover features of languages which are so old that no speakers live to tell us about them? Historical linguistics deduces that an abundant occurrence of features in a daughter language, the presence of which cannot be explained by language universals or by the assumption of them having been borrowed, or adopted, from another tongue, is likely to have been inherited from the parent language.

Thus, by inferencing from widespread phenomena on a mother tongue from which these phenomena came, linguists trace back languages. In Indo-European languages, for example, obvious correlations can be found.

The Latin and Sanskrit words for "hundred", namely L. "centum" and S. "satem", can be traced back to a common root. Since these two languages were considered to be the most prominent examples for the respective branches, the whole branches were named after them.

Also, former scholars believed that they should make judgements about the various languages. Sanskrit, Latin, and Greek were commonly believed to be of a higher quality than the modern languages.

Often scholars argued that these languages were more "pure" and praised their "perfection" and "clarity". Today we consider such notions to be outdated. There is no room in linguistics for the approval or disapproval of a language. If we look for the origin of a word, we call this the word's *etymology* (etymon = Greek for "root").

Within the Indo-European family tree and among the centum languages, we find language families like the Germanic, Celtic, or Latin families. Some authors refer to the early Germanic language as "Proto-Germanic". The Germanic language family is again split up in the West-, East-, and North-Germanic groups.

While the Scandinavian tongues derived from the North-Germanic language group, Anglo-Frisian and Modern German came from the West-Germanic group.

In the case of English, interaction with other languages was very important during its history, as we will see. Hence, many influences from foreign sources can be found in Modern English, while the family tree does not suggest these interchanges to have occurred.

LANGUAGES IN BRITAIN BEFORE ENGLISH

Celtic Languages

The first culture in England of which we have definite knowledge is the Celtic culture and language. It is assumed that the coming of the Celts to England coincided with the introduction of bronze on the island. There were—and still are—Celtic tongues spoken on the British isles.

- Celtic Languages in Britain are Welsh, Cornish, Scots Gaelic, Manx, and Irish Gaelic. The main groups of Welsh, Scots and Irish Gaelic still exist, as does Manx, and are even promoted in order to preserve the *language community*. Cornish, however, became extinct 200 years ago when the last recorded speaker died. Due to the above mentioned promotion, the rest of the Celtic languages have a better chance of surviving. Other Celtic tongues are also still spoken in Brittany (France) and, also on the verge of becoming extinct, are sponsored as well.

LANGUAGE	AREA	STATUS
Welsh (Cymric)	Wales	still spoken
Cornish	Cornwall	Extinct
Scots Gaelic	Scotland	still spoken
Manx	Isle of Man	still spoken
Irish Gaelic	Ireland	still spoken

Latin

Another language in England was Latin. It was spoken extensively for a period of about four centuries before the coming of English. In 55 BC, Julius Caesar decided to invade Britain. Because of the unexpectedly powerful resistance of the Celts, however, a final conquest could not be accomplished until about 100 years later. Almost all of what is now England was then subjected to Roman rule. Naturally, the military conquest of Britain was followed by the romanization of the province, as was the case in other countries and provinces conquered by the Romans, such as Gaul of present day France. The Roman culture and the Latin language were introduced. Note, however, that the Celts, who then inhabited the whole of the British isles, withstood the Romans in the other parts of the country. Hence, Latin did not spread further north or west of what are roughly the present day English borders.

Latin did not replace the Celtic language in Britain. Its use was confined to members of the upper classes such as landowners and the bureaucracy. Nevertheless, vocabulary for items not known to the Celts prior to romanization infiltrated the language of the, mainly lower class, Celts, to some extent.

OLD ENGLISH

About the year of 449 an event occurred that profoundly affected the course of history in Britain: the invasion of Britain by certain Germanic tribes. These were the *Angles, Saxons, and Jutes* who came from regions of Northern Europe where natural disasters and famine, due to overpopulation, had forced them to leave. Since the Roman Empire was under heavy attack at many of its borders at that time, no legions could be spared to defend the British province.

The emperor in Rome, therefore, left the British population on their own devices. The British inhabitants, bereft of a military force, subsequently failed to defend themselves and what was once Roman Britain became inhabited by the newcomers. The Celtic population was forced to leave and take refuge in other areas of Britain.

The struggle of the Celts against the Anglo-Saxons has been preserved in the myth of the legendary King Arthur who led his people in their resistance.

The names "English" and "England" were then drawn from the name of the predominant tribe of the Angles, who had established their most powerful kingdom in the former Roman province.

Features of Old English

Old English (OE) was spoken from 449 to 1100 AD. Characteristic features of Old English are that the vocabulary is almost purely Germanic. OE is a period of full inflections: in form of *endings* to the noun and pronoun, the adjective and the verb. Since the grammar of such languages depends on the synthesis of words and endings, we call them "synthetic languages".

• *Verbs*. There are certain differences between OE verbs and Modern English (ModE) verbs. Verbs are divided into two classes: regular and irregular verbs. Regular verbs all follow the same inflection pattern, while there are irregularities among the second group. The latter consists of strong, weak, and anomalous verbs. Strong verbs are called so because a change of tense is there indicated within the word itself, by a modification of the verb's root vowel, such as in sing, sang, sung. In weak verbs, like walk, walked, walked, this change is dependent on being indicated by an additional syllable.

Scandinavian influence on Old English

Invasions and conquests were quite common during the first millennium AD in Britain. From 787 on, the Danes raided the English coasts and the hinterland quite frequently. In 850, they started large-scale invasions. In this period, Alfred the Great, king of Wessex, gained recognition due to his long but successful struggle against the Danes. In 878 he defeated them and saved his kingdom, although the invaders still remained in the eastern territories. The Danish rule in these countries was also called Danelaw. To cut a long story short after a lot of battles, defeats and victories, the Danish king Svein became king of England in 1014. The Danish rule lasted until 1042. Their language naturally had some influence on the English tongue.

This influence can be seen mainly with the English vocabulary, for example word-borrowings. In Old English, the sound *sk*, which it had inherited from its Germanic ancestors, had soon been changed to *sh*. The under the Danish rule introduced Scandinavian words, however, retained their *sk* sound until today, helping us to identify the Scandinavian word-borrowings in English. This development also produced a range of word pairs newly introduced Scandinavian words then stood side by side with the already existing altered sh-version, such as *skiff—ship; skirt—shirt*. The words of these word pairs are thus closely related on a semantic level, but serve to designate different aspects or understanding of the items.

Word replacements also occurred. Several of the new foreign words replaced OE ones, as with *take—niman; cast—weorpan; cut—ceorfan.*

In 1066, the Normans invaded England. Through the influence of Norman French, the OE period gradually ended.

Chapter 4

The History of English II: Middle English

THE CHANGE FROM OLD ENGLISH TO MIDDLE ENGLISH

The Middle English (ME) period lasted from about 1100–1500. Major historical events influenced the language change. In 1066, the Duke of Normandy, the famous William, henceforth called "the Conqueror", sailed across the British Channel.

He challenged King Harold of England in the struggle for the English throne. After winning the battle of Hastings where he defeated Harold, William was crowned King of England. A Norman Kingdom was now established.

The Anglo-Saxon period was over. The Norman invasion naturally had a profound effect on England's institutions and its language. The Norman French spoken by the invaders became the language of England's ruling class.

The lower classes, while remaining English-speaking, were influenced nevertheless by the new vocabulary. French became the language of the affairs of government, court, the church, the army, and education where the newly adopted French words often substituted their former English counterparts. The linguistic influence of Norman French continued for as long as the Kings ruled both Normandy and England.

When King John lost Normandy in the years following 1200, the links to the French-speaking community subsided.

English then slowly started to gain more weight as a common tongue within England again. A hundred years later, English was again spoken by representatives of all social classes, this new version of the English language being strikingly different, of course, from the Old English used prior to the Norman invasion.

The English spoken at this turn of events is called Middle English. About ten thousand French words had been taken over by English during the Middle English period, and most of them have remained in the language until the present day. Aside from the already mentioned new vocabulary pertaining to the affairs of government, court, the church, the army, and education, many words relating to food and fashion were introduced as well. In some fields an original English terminology did not exist.

Therefore, many French terms were borrowed. One example is the names of animals and their meat. Whereas the names of the animals remained the same, their meat was renamed according to the Norman custom. This correlated to the sociological structures: the farmers that raised the animals were predominantly English natives and could afford to keep using their own vocabulary while farming those serving the meat at the dining room table to the mainly French upper classes had to conform to the French language.

Animal	meat
Sheep	mutton
Cow	beef
Swine	pork

The English language also has doublets—these are pairs of words that have the same etymology, i.e. the same source, but that differ in meaning because they had been introduced into the English language by two separate languages. The Latin and French influence, for instance, made for many of such word pairs. Latin vocabulary adopted by the Celts directly became a part of English. The same vocabulary was sometimes adopted by the Gauls and introduced to English via Norman French.

Doublets	Meaning
*Adj.*urbanurbaine	(area) having qualities of large settlement (person) having a certain sense for culture
*Noun*curtsycourtesy	female gesture of respect (bending the knees) politeness

As far as grammar is concerned, a *reduction of inflections* began. The grammatical gender disappeared and inflections merged. As the inflections of the Old English disappeared, the word order of middle English became increasingly fixed. This change made for a great loss of strong verbs. At a time when English was the language mainly of the lower classes and largely removed from educational or literary domains and influence, it was natural that many speakers applied the pattern of inflecting weak verbs to verbs which were historically strong. This linguistic principle of adopting the pattern of a less common form to a more familiar one is called *analogy*.

The exclusive use of the pattern SVO (subject - verb – object) emerged in the twelfth century and has remained part of English ever since.

MODERN ENGLISH

The Modern English (ModE) period began in 1500 and lasts until the present day. The complex inflectional system of Old English had been simplified during the ME period. Modern English is therefore called the *period of lost inflections.*

An important phonological change of English vowels took place between 1450 and 1650, when all long vowels changed their qual y to a great extent. This development is called the *Great English Vowel Shift.* For information on phonology,

Each long vowel came to be pronounced with a greater elevation of the tongue and closing of the mouth. Those vowels that could be raised were raised and those that could not be raised became diphtongs. Diphtongs are sounds where two vowels are pronounced after another so closely that they become one acoustic phenomenon, like in German *"Eu*le" or

"Auto". "Raising" here refers to the position of the tongue in the mouth. This movement is commonly illustrated with the help of the following graphic, which shows where the vowels are produced in the mouth.

Some examples can be drawn from the pronunciation of words at the time of Geoffrey Chaucer, one of the most famous authors of ME, and William Shakespeare, whose use of English was already modern.

	Chaucer		Shakespeare
Iˇ	[fIˇf]	five	[fAIv]
eˇ	[meˇd′]	meed	[miˇd]
Eˇ	[klEˇn′]	clean	[kleˇn] (now [kliˇn])
aˇ	[naˇm′]	name	[neˇm]
çˇ	[gçˇt′]	goat	[goˇt]
oˇ	[roˇt′]	root	[ruˇt]
uˇ	[duˇn]	down	[dAun]

Short vowels were not affected by the Great English Vowel Shift. Thus, ME *sak* [sQk] remained ModE *sack* [sQk], *ME fish* remained *ModE fish* [fIS]

This phonological change did not, however, express itself in any alterations of writing conventions. This fact is confusing for many learners of English. The spelling conventions of English vowels had essentially been established by the time of William Caxton, who founded his printing press in 1476. This was some time before the phonological change had progressed very far. Caxton's spelling reflects the pronunciation of the Middle English period and thus does not do justice to Modern English pronunciation.

Chapter 5

Language Acquisition and Disorders

Apart from the general *historical development* of languages, there is another, rather personal development in each of us when we acquire a language. We undergo child language acquisition, development, and maturation. We acquire second, third, fourth or even more languages in school or when we travel abroad. Another feature of personal linguistic developments are language disorders due to malfunctions of certain areas of the brain. In this chapter, we will examine some of the findings of Neurolinguistics. This branch of linguistics investigates the relationship between the brain and language.

CHILD LANGUAGE ACQUISITION

Children have to learn language from scratch, although the capability to speak is inherent in everyone. There are certain milestones and stages of language acquisition during the child's first months and years.

Milestones

- I: 0-8 weeks. Children of this age are only capable of *reflexive crying*. We also call this the production of *vegetative sounds.*
- II: 8-20 weeks. *Cooing* and *laughter* appears in the child's vocal expression.
- III: 20-30 weeks. The child begins with *vocal play*. This includes playing with vowels (V) *and* consonants (C), for example: "AAAOOOOOUUUUIIII".

- IV: 25-50 weeks. The child begins to *babble.* There are two kinds of babbling, a) *reduplicative babbling* CVCV, e.g., "baba", and b) *variegated babbling,* e.g., VCV "adu".
- V:9-18 months. The child starts to produce *melodic utterances.* This means that stress and intonation are added to the sound chains uttered.

After having passed these milestones, children are, in essence, capable of pronouncing words of the natural language.

Stages

From this time on, children start to produce entire words. There are three stages, each designating an increasing capability to use words for communicative purposes:

I *Single words* and *holophrases.* Children may use a word to indicate things or persons, e.g., "boo" (=book), or "mama". Also, a single word is employed to refer to entire contexts. At this stage, "shoe" could mean "Mama has a nice shoe", "Give me my shoe" or even "I want to wear my new red shoes when we go for a walk"!

II The next stage is the usage of *two word phrases.* This stage is also called *telegraphic speech.* It begins around the second birthday, maybe sooner or later, depending on the child. Examples are "Dada gone", "cut it", "in car", "here pear". At this stage, children design so-called *pivot grammars.* This means that the child has a preference for certain words as the pivotal (axis) words, implementing a variety of other words at different points in time to create phrases.

III The child begins to form *longer utterances.* These lack grammatical correctness at first and are perceived as, though meaningful, rather rough assemblies of utterances. Examples are "dirty hand wash it", "glasses on nose", "Daddy car coming", or even "car sleeping bed", which a boy uttered, meaning that the car was now parked in the garage.

There are many phonological and grammatical features of speech development, all of which cannot be listed here. A characteristic of children's early language is the *omission of consonants* at the beginning, ending, or in consonant clusters in words.

Examples: "boo" instead of "book", "at" instead of "cat", or "ticker" instead of "sticker". Children learn grammatical morphemes, commonly referred to as "endings", in a certain order. They often start with the present progressive "-ing", as in "Mama talk*ing*". More complex forms, such as the contractible auxiliary be (as in "Pat's going") are learned at a later point in time.

LANGUAGE DEVELOPMENT AND MATURATION

Parents from different cultures behave differently towards their children as far as linguistic education is concerned. In some areas of the world, people think that *baby talk,* or *Motherese* hems linguistic development.

There are also cultures where parents talk to their children as they would to adults), or where they do not put so much thought into how to teach their children language at all. When taking a closer look, no particular advantages or disadvantages can be found.

Children's language is creative, but rule-governed. These rules comprise the seven *operating principles* of children's language. These principles correspond to the essential communicative needs of a child. One main aspect in all principles is the predominant use of the active voice, the passive voice requiring a more complex understanding of concepts.

- The instrumental principle serves to indicate the personal needs of the child. These are the "I want" phrases.
- The regulatory principle helps to demand action of somebody else: "Do that."
- *"Hello"* is the utterance - among others - which represents the interactional principle. It is very important for establishing contact.

- The personal principle carries the *expressive function*. "Here I come" is a proper substitution for many phrases.
- The heuristic "Tell me why"-principle is very important because once the child is able to form questions, language helps in the general learning process.
- The imaginative principle comes in when the child wants to impart his or her dreams or fantasies. It is also what applies when the child pretends.

Information is also important for children's communication. To tell others about the own experience soon becomes important.

Another major step in language development is taken when the child learns how to write. Again, there are several stages:

I Preparatory. Age approx. 4–6 years.
The child acquires the necessary motorical skills. Also, the principles of spelling are learned.

II Consolidation. Age approx. 7 years
When the child begins to write, its writing reflects its spoken language. This does not only refer to the transcription of phonetic characteristics, but also to word order and sentence structure.

III Differentiation. Age approx. 9 years
Writing now begins to diverge from spoken language; it becomes experimental. This means that the writing of the child does not have to reflect speech. The child learns to use writing freely and sets out to experiment with it.

IV Integration. Age approx. mid-teens

Around this age, children/teens develop their own style. A personal voice appears in the written language and the ability to apply writing to various purposes is acquired.

SECOND LANGUAGE ACQUISITION

Some aspects of second language acquisition are similar to first language acquisition. The learner has already acquired learning techniques and can reflect on how to learn best. However, learning languages depends on the personality, age, intelligence, and active learning strategies of the learner.

The learners of a second language (L2) start out with their own language, which we call *source language*. They are on their way to learn a *target language* (TL). All that lies in-between we call *interlanguage*. All L2 speakers are on some stage of interlanguage. Beginners are closer to their source language (SL), experts of L2 are closer to the target language. And if we don't continue with our studies, our interlanguage competence may even decrease. People who have lived in foreign countries for a long time are often so close to the target language that they hardly differ from native speakers. There are some features of interlanguage which are worthwhile to look at. They play an important role in the learning process. Everybody experiences their effects in language learning.

- Fossilization. At a certain stage the learner ceases to learn new aspects of the TL. Although perhaps capable to express herself in a grammatically correct way, the learner here does not proceed to explore the great reservoir of language any further in order to express herself in a more refined and sophisticated manner.
- Regression. The learner fails to express herself in areas (phraseology, style or vocabulary) that he or she had mastered at an earlier point in time.
- Over generalization. The learner searches for a logical grammar of the TL that would cover every aspect of the language, or seeks to find every aspect of existing grammars confirmed in the living language. In doing so, the learner draws on aspects of the target language already earned and overuses them.
- Over elaboration. The learner wants to apply complex theoretical structures to contexts that may call for simpler expression.
- Interference from L1 (or L3), with phonological interference being the most common example. Syntactic interference and semantic interference are

also possible, e.g., so-called false friends. These are words that exist in the source language as well as in the target language. However, their meaning or use might differ substantially, as in the German "Figur" vs. the French "figure" (="face"), or the English "eventually" vs. the German "eventuell" (="possibly").

- Variable input. This refers to the quality of education in the TL, the variety and extent of exposure to the TL and the communicative value of it to the learner. This is why the design of learning material and contact with many TL native speakers plays a vital role in learning a new language.
- Organic and/or cumulative growth. There can be unstructured, widely dispersed input which is not always predictable. This is structured by the learner in progressive building blocks.

LANGUAGE DISORDERS

The principle language disorders are *aphasia, anomia, dyslexia,* and *dysgraphia*. Usually, language disorders are caused by injuries or malfunctions of the brain. Neurologists were able to locate those areas of the brain that play a central role in language production and comprehension by examining patients whose brains had suffered damages in certain areas.

Aphasia

This is a disorder in the ability to process or produce spoken language. Two scientists, Broca and Wernicke, were able to locate two areas of the brain responsible for these activities.

- Broca's area. In 1864 the French surgeon Broca was able to locate a small part of the brain, somewhat behind our left temple. This area is responsible for the organization of language production. If it is damaged, the patient usually knows what (s)he wants to say but can't organize the syntax. More nouns than verbs are used. There is hesitant speech and poor articulation. Comprehension and processing are usually not impaired.

- Wernicke's area. Carl Wernicke identified another type of aphasia in 1874. He located a part of the brain behind the left ear where he found comprehension of language to take place. Speech production and syntax are generally possible with Wernicke's patients. However, comprehension and, also to some extent, production is impaired, and patients show the tendency to retrieve only general nouns and nonsense words from their mental lexicon and to lose specific lexis, or vocabulary. They do not seem to be aware of their problem and thus do not react to treatment easily.

Both Broca's and Wernicke's areas are located in the left half of the brain. The executive centers, however, are located in the right hemisphere. A separation of the two halves of the brain effects the capability of converting linguistic information into action, or vice versa. Apart from the types of aphasia identified by Broca and Wernicke, there are also other kinds of aphasia.

- *Jargon*. In "neologistic jargon aphasia", patients can only produce new approximations of content words (nouns), they will never hit the exact word. In general, messages are hard to understand and often completely incomprehensible or not decodable by listeners, although the speakers have good syntax.
- *Conduction*. Patients understand what is being said to them, however, they are unable to repeat single words and make other errors when speaking. However, they are aware of their errors. In this kind of aphasia, it is neither Broca's nor Wernicke's area that is damaged, but the connection between them.
- In *transcortical aphasia,* there is a weakness in comprehension. The best preserved feature is the ability to repeat heard phrases. Therefore, the processing of language is impaired, but the patient is able to hear and pronounce the acoustic chain.

- *Global aphasia* has the worst effects on the patient. All language abilities are seriously impaired in this case. Both Wernicke's and Broca's areas are damaged.

Anomia

Anomia is the loss of access to certain parts of the lexis. Anomia patients are unable to remember the names of things, people, or places. There is often a confusion between semantically related words. Undoubtedly, you will have experienced this phenomenon yourself! We are all prone to it at times. It usually increases with age, although pure anomia is a much more acute state and is not related to aging.

Dyslexia

This is a disorder of reading where the patient is not capable to recognize the correct word order. Patients also tend to misplace syllables. There is also an *overgeneralization* of the relation between printed words and their sound value. For example, a patient may transport the pronunciation of "cave" =/keIv/ to "have" = */heIv/ instead of/hQv/.

Dysgraphia

Dysgraphia is a disorder of writing, mainly spelling. Patients are not able to find the correct graphemes when putting their speech into writing. Also, they are not able to select the correct order of graphemes from a choice of possible representations.

ERRORS

Errors in linguistic production are not a malfunction caused by disease. They occur frequently and are part of the communication process. Here are examples of the usual types of errors made:

- *Anticipation.* Sounds appear in words before their intended pronunciation: take my bike → bake my bike. This error reveals that further utterances were already planned while speaking.
- In *preservation* errors, the opposite is the case. Sounds

are "kept in mind" and reappear in the wrong place: pulled a tantrum → *p*ulled a *p*antrum

- *Reversals (Spoonerisms)* are errors where sounds are mixed up within words or phrases: harpsichord → *c*arpsi*h*ord
- Blends occur when two words are combined and parts of both appear in the new
- Word substitution gives us insight into the mental lexicon of the speaker. These words are usually linked semantically. Give me the orange.→ Give me the *apple.*
- *Errors on a higher level* occur when the structural rules of language above the level of pronunciation influence production. In the below example, the past tense of "dated" is overused. The speaker "conjugates" the following noun according to the grammatical rules of "shrink-shrank-shrunk": Rosa always dated shrinks → Rosa always dat*ed* shr*a*nks.
- Phonological errors are the mixing up of voiced and unvoiced sounds: Terry and Julia → *D*erry and *Ch*ulia.
- *Force of habit* accounts for the wrong application of an element that had been used before in similar contexts. For example, in a television broadcast by BBC, the reporter first spoke about studios at Oxford university. When he then changed the topic to a student who had disappeared from the same town he said: "The discovery of the missing Oxford studio" instead of "The discovery of a missing Oxford student."

Chapter 6

Communication

There is more to communication than just one person speaking and another one listening. Human communication processes are quite complex. We differentiate verbal and nonverbal, oral and written, formal and informal, and intentional and unintentional communication. In addition, there is human-animal communication and human-computer communication.

A famous statement says that we are not able *to not* communicate. In this chapter, we will concentrate on verbal communication between humans in either spoken or written form.

Verbal communication involves the use of linguistic symbols that mean something to those who take part in the process. These symbols are spoken words in oral communication and their realization as alphabetical units in written communication.

Oral communication refers to messages that are transmitted "out loud" from one person to another. We all participate in this process every day, for example, as speakers or listeners when talking, watching TV, or answering the phone. The most prominent feature of oral communication is that it is not permanent unless it is recorded.

Written communication is primarily verbal but involves also other elements due to the variations in writing. In contrast to oral communication, it is not transitory, but permanent. Thus, written messages enable us to keep exact records of language and communication.

Living in a purely oral culture would limit our capacity

of cultural development enormously.

The communication process involves certain elements. Let us have a look at these elements by examining some *communication models.*

SAUSSURE'S MODEL OF THE SPEECH CIRCUIT

On the one hand, communication is linear in that two persons, A and B, communicate in a way that a message is conveyed from one to the other: On the other hand, the participants in the communication process are both simultaneously active.

Person B does not only listen, she or he may answer or at least show some reaction. On the basis of this understanding, *Saussure* devised a circular communication model, i.e. the model of the speech circuit.

It shows the mechanisms of a dialogue: Acoustic signals are sent from a speaker A to a receiver B, who then, in turn, becomes the sender, sending information to A, who becomes the receiver.

Saussure outlined two processes within this framework. The first one is phonation. Here the sender formulates mental signs in the mind and then gives acoustic shape to them. The second one, audition, is the opposite process of the receiver transforming the acoustic message into mental signs.

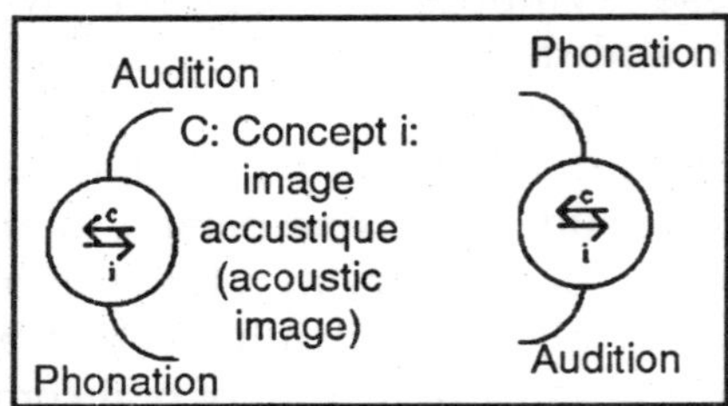

Part of the Saussurean model of the speech circuit consists of his model of the *linguistic sign.*

You now know its most important feature, namely the division into acoustic shape, or *acoustic image,* and the idea related to the image, the mental *concept.*

Concept and acoustic image are transported in communication.

SHANNON'S AND MOLES' COMMUNICATION MODELS

In 1949, the American engineer Shannon developed a model which explains what basically happens in communication:

The input, or intended message, is sent by a sender via a channel. The message received becomes the output. Input and output may differ substantially as a channel is usually exposed to circumstances that may alter its intended quality of transmission. For instance, the channel of a telephone communication line is usually impaired with noise, which in turn affects the outcome, i.e. output, of the message.

Moles appended Shannon's model in 1963, adding a crucial element, the code. The sender and receiver have to have at least a fundamental set of codes in common, in order for them to communicate successfully.

For example, two speakers from different countries who do not speak each other's language can only rely on internationally known words, thus making the sought for communication hardly possible. But even speakers of the same language often have problems of the same sort if their 'personal codes' differ greatly.

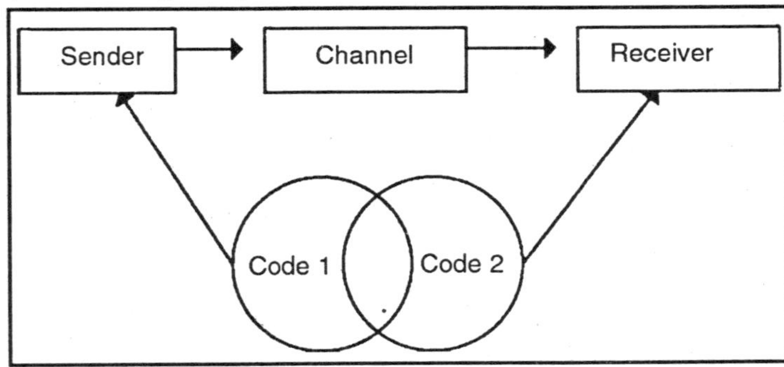

Elements of the Communication Process

Here are the various components of the communication process in detail.

- *Input:* The sender has an *intention* to communicate

with another person. This intention makes up the *content* of the message.

- *Sender:* The sender *encodes* the message. Thus he gives expression to the content.
- *Channel:* The message is sent via a channel, which can be made of a variety of materials. In acoustic communication it consists of air, in written communication of paper or other writing materials.
- Noise: The channel is subjected to various sources of noise. One example is telephone communication, where numerous secondary sounds are audible. Even a solid channel such as paper can be crushed or stained. Such phenomena are also noise in the communicative sense.
- Receiver: The *receiver decodes* the incoming message, or expression. He "translates" it and thus receives the *Output*. This is the *content* decoded by the receiver.
- Code: In the process, the relevance of a *code* becomes obvious: The codes of the sender and receiver must have at least a certain set in common in order to make communication work.

Bühler's Organon Model

Plato was the first to discuss an instrumentalist definition of language. According to this definition, language primarily serves the purpose of communication.

It is a linguistic tool. From this instrumental approach, Karl Bühler devised a model which described the communicative *functions*.

In his words, language is an "*organum* for one person's communicating with another about things" "Organum is Greek for tool.

The three main functions of language Bühler distinguishes in his model are *representation, expression,* and *appeal.*

Which function applies to which communicative action depends on which relations of the linguistic sign are predominant in a communicative situation.

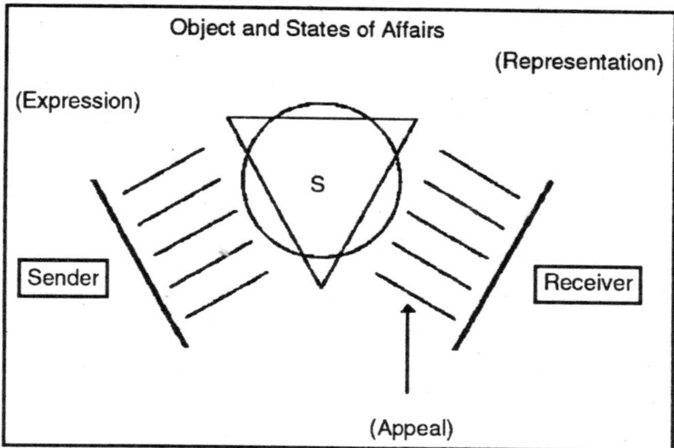

How does this model work?

Bühler's model describes the communication between a sender and a receiver *by including* a third party, the objects or states of affairs. A communicative function is then attributed to each act of communication, depending on which of the three parties involved was focused on most heavily.

When the focus is on the sender, we speak of the *expressive function* of communication. When the focus is on the objects, the function is *representative*. The third function refers to communication where the focus is on the receiver. This function is called *appeal*.

The circle symbolizes the phenomenon of the sound, that is the actual word spoken. The triangle symbolizes the linguistic sign and shares common space with the circle in some areas, while extending beyond it in other areas. This overlapping portrays the two key features of the relationship between the sign and its physical realization.

Abstractive relevance. Where the circle overlaps the triangle, the phenomenon sound contains more acoustic information than the sign does. We are, however, capable of filtering out the relevant information without being hindered by all the additional stuff, e.g. the "ahs" and "ehms" of casual conversation.

Apperceptive enlargement. The triangle also covers space beyond the circle. This means that part of the message may be lost, due to either misspellings or omissions on the part of the sender, or because the channel is subjected to noise. In this case, we are still able to fill in the gaps to create a meaningful message. Somehow we gather what got lost. This is what we call *apperceptive enlargement*.

JAKOBSON'S MODEL OF COMMUNICATIVE FUNCTIONS

Jakobson extended Bühler's system of communicative functions. His model reminds us of those lined out at the *beginning of this chapter* containing all the components of Moles', except for one, namely context. Jakobson stated that a common code is not sufficient for the communicative process. A context is necessary from which the object of communication is drawn. This context resembles Bühler's object correlate. Jakobson allocates a communicative function to each of the components.

The *emotive* function focuses on the addresser and resembles Bühler's expressive function. The addresser's own attitude towards the content of the message is emphasized. Examples are emphatic speech or interjections.

The *conative* function is allocated to the addressee. Bühler called it the appelative function, so it is possible to find both terms in the literature. It is directed towards the addressee. One example is the vocative.

The *referential* function refers to the context. Here we, again, have the function emphasizing that communication is always dealing with something contextual, what Bühler called representative.

The *phatic* function helps to establish contact and refers to the channel of communication. Some of these utterances only serve to maintain contact between two speakers.

The *metalinguistic* function deals with the code itself. This is the function of language about language. This whole reader is an example of *metalanguage*. We use it to examine the code. The metalinguistic function is also predominant in questions like "Sorry, what did you say?" where the code is misunderstood and needs correction or clarification.

The *poetic* function is allocated to the message. Messages

convey more than just the content. They always contain a creative 'touch' of our own. These additions have no purpose other than to make the message "nicer". Rhetorical figures, pitch or loudness are some aspects of the poetic function.

Naturally, several functions may be active simultaneously in utterances. To find out which function predominates requires analysis.

Chapter 7

Phonetics

Phonetics is a branch of linguistics that studies the material aspects of speech sounds. What is meant by "material aspect" ? And what other features exist which characterize sounds? Well, material aspects of sounds are those aspects that make for the physical production, transportation and comprehension of the sound. Another aspect of a sound is its function within a language. The function of sounds is, however, examined by another linguistic discipline, namely *phonology*. Please take note of the fact though that this represents the European (including the English) categorization of these linguistic disciplines and that Americans follow a different convention. Americans use the term "phonology" to refer to our understanding of both phonetics *and* phonology. They refer to what we call 'phonetics' also as 'phonetics', but refer to what Europeans call 'phonology' as 'phonemics'. So if you ever come across the American terminology, do not be confused. In any way, in this textbook we will stick to the European terms.

The modern alphabet does not suffice to transcribe all sounds on a one-to-one basis. There are many instances though, when we need an internationally comprehensible code for the detailed transcription of sounds, such as in linguistic research, as well as in foreign language teaching. A special *alphabet* devised by the International Phonetic Association (IPA) is then used. Phonetic characters refer to the actual utterance of a sound. In phonetic writing, the symbols for these sounds are put within brackets, such as: [T].

Back to phonetics. We stated above that there are three

different physical aspects of a sound. These are the articulatory aspect of the speaker, the acoustic aspect of the channel, and the auditory aspect of the hearer.

- Articulatory phonetics researches where and how sounds are originated and thus carries out physiological studies of the respiratory tract, trying to locate precisely at which location and in which manner a sound is produced.
- Acoustic phonetics examines the length, frequency and pitch of sounds. Special instruments are required to measure and analyze the sounds while they travel via the channel.
- Auditory phonetics studies what happens inside the ear and brain when sounds are finally received. It also interested in our ability to identify and differentiate sounds.

ARTICULATORY PHONETICS - CONSONANTS

In this textbook, we will concentrate on articulatory phonetics, which also happens to be what modern linguistics has traditionally focused on. Our notion of the typical, classical linguist, zealously studying speech sounds, such as the famous Dr. Higgins from George Bernard Shaw's Pygmalion, is derived from this stage in the discipline.

Any speech sound is caused by a stream of air that, originating in our vocal apparatus, escapes our mouth or nose. The various sounds all differ according to the voicing, location and manner of their production. A minor change of any of these three factors may alter a sound significantly. For example, if a stream of air leaves the vocal tract unhindered, the result is a vowel. If the stream of air is obstructed in any way the result is a consonant. Although the procedure is very complex, it is possible to determine the exact voicing, location and manner of articulation of all sounds of a language.

Voicing

Try to utter two long consonants, first [z], then [s], continually: "zzzzzzzzsssssssssszzzzzzz". Hold your fingertip to your larynx (Adam's apple) and try to notice what happens. You will feel a vibration. This is caused by a stream of air that is being pressed through a narrow aperture, called *glottis*, between the vocal cords. It is the pressure of the air on the walls of the glottis that causes the vibration of the cords. We are able to produce two different sets of sounds, which are otherwise identical: voiced and voiceless sounds, by this small change of the glottis. There are many consonants which are differentiated in this way, like [f]—[v], [t]— [d], or [g]—[k].

Manner of Articulation

Plosives and Continuants

Another fundamental distinction of consonants is made between so-called *plosives* and *continuants*. Plosives are consonants that are brought about by an explosive release of air from the mouth, e.g. [t]. They are also called *stops*, or *oral stops*. If the air is released through the nose, we call the resulting consonant is a *nasal* plosive, as in [m] or [n], which is also called nasal stop since the mouth is kept closed for the most part.

If the air continues to be released after the articulation of the consonant, the sound is a *continuant*. If we let out air continuously through a space behind the upper teeth, the so-called *alveolar ridge.*, we produce a type of continuant sound called *fricative*, e.g., [f]. *Affricates* are produced by a plosive and a fricative continuant following immediately thereafter, as in [tS], e.g., in the word "chair". Fricatives and affricates with a hissing sound, as [z] in "zip", or [Z] in "measure" are also called *sibilants*. Oral stops, i.e. nonnasal plosives, and fricative and affricative continuants all have in common that the air is *not* let out through the nose; consonants produced in this way are called obstruents. If air is released also through the nose, these consonants are called *sonorants*. The sounds [l] and [r] are called *liquids*.

Aspiration

A further manner of articulating a sound is by either

aspirating or not aspirating the sound. Try to pronounce these: [pit]—[spit].

You will notice that while saying the word 'pit', a stream of air evades your mouth, whereas when saying 'spit', your glottis starts to vibrate immediately after the pronunciation of [sp]. Hence, we may call the [p] aspirated when saying 'pit, while it is unaspirated when saying 'spit'. This distinction results from the glottis remaining open after certain occasions of a sound, namely in the case of aspirated ones.

PLACE OF ARTICULATION

Consonants are distinguished also according to the location of their production, that is, after the various organs of the vocal tract.

- Labials are consonants that are articulated by use of the lips. Some of these are created by bringing the lips together, like [m]. These are called *bilabials*. Other consonants are brought about by bringing the bottom lip to the upper teeth. These are called *labiodentals,* e.g., [f].
- Alveolars. These are articulated by raising the tip of the tongue to the *alveolar ridge,* like [d].
- Velars. If you raise the back of your tongue to the soft *velum,* velars are produced. An example is [g].
- Interdentals are the sounds at the beginning of "thin" and "then", in IPA: [9] and [6]. In order to articulate these, you have to press the tongue between the teeth. Again you can se that the difference is voicing.
- Palatals (or Alveopalatals) as in the middle of the word "measure" are produced by the contact of the front part of the tongue with the hard palate just behind the alveolar ridge.

With the help of this detailed information we can now refer to every consonant by its location and manner of articulation; [f], for example, is a voiceless, labiodental fricative.

ARTICULATORY PHONETICS — VOWELS

In contrast to consonants, where voice, manner and place

of articulation serve as descriptive categories, vowels are differentiated by their position of the tongue and the lips.

These categories are indicative of the different ways in which the two sounds are produced while consonants are produced with the help of many organs, vowels depend only on the position of the tongue and the lips.

The positioning the tongue and the lips allow for a great amount of variation, enabling us to voice many more vowels than the familiar five vowels a, e, i, o, u. English has more than a dozen different vowels. Also, in English we find several diphtongs.

Vowels can be produced by raising the tongue high, keeping it in the middle, or low in the mouth; also, the tongue can be moved to the front, center or back. The lips can be rounded or nonrounded. If you try to articulate while moving your lips and your tongue around, you will notice how manifold the resulting vowel-like sounds are.

This chart is a rough sketch of the mouth. It is similar to a coordinate system, with the positions high, middle, and low representing one axis, and the positions front, central, and back the other axis. The only position not used in English for the pronunciation of vowels is the high central point.

ENGLISH SOUNDS — AN OVERVIEW

In the following, you will find a general characterization of English sounds. With this table at hand, all sounds can be easily identified according to their place and manner of articulation.

Here is a summary of the characteristics:

- Oral stops, fricatives, and affricates are consonants referred to as obstruents:

The stream of air cannot escape through the nose and where it passes through the mouth, it is *obstructed*.

- All other consonants are sonorants.
- Glottals are sounds produced by the air stream

moving along the glottis. The glottal stop is produced by a complete closure of the glottis. You may test this by saying "ah-ah-ah."

- Another feature of vowels is whether they are *rounded* or *unrounded*. This refers to the position of the lips.
- English front vowels are always unrounded. German [y] is an example of rounded front vowels.
- English central vowels are always unrounded.
- English back vowels are always rounded.

		Sounds								
		Consonants								Vowels
		Place of Articulation								See 7.2
	Manner of Articulation	Bilabial	Labio-dental	Inter-dental	Alveolar	Palato alveolar	Palatal	Velar	Glottal	
Stops/Plosives	Glottal Stop								ʔ	
Stops/Plosives	Oral Stops (Plosives) voiceless / voiced	p b			t d			k g		
Stops/Plosives	Nasals/ Nasal stops	m			n			ŋ		
Continuants	Fricatives voiceless / voiced		f v	θ ð	s z	ʃ ʒ		x (exceptional)		
Continuants	Affricates voiceless / voiced					tʃ dʒ				
Continuants – Approximants	Liquids vcd central / vcd lateral				r l					
Continuants – Approximants	Glides voiceless / vcd central	w					j		h	

Chapter 8

Phonology

Phonology deals with the *function* of sounds within a language. Let us have a close look at these functions. Every language has a precisely defined set of sounds. This set consists of the so-called *distinctive* sounds. The system of the speech sounds and their usage is defined as *duality of patterning*: with a given set of components, we may construct an unlimited number of new arrangements of the components. In other words: Our language provides us with a limited set of sounds, but we can arrange these to ever new utterances.

PHONEMES AND ALLOPHONES

By calling a sound distinctive, we refer to its capability of changing the meaning of a word. Naturally, single sounds cannot carry any meaning. "B" or "P", for example, are meaningless utterances. But when several distinct sounds are assembled to a word, each of them suddenly contribute to a meaning. And by exchanging individual distinct sounds, we may change this meaning. We call these sounds *phonemes*, the smallest distinctive elements of a language. They are easy to discern.

Compare two words which differ only by one sound, e.g., "pin" and "bin". By replacing the beginning consonants, the meaning of the word changes. We call such pairs *minimal pairs.* The test we just performed to locate the phonemes is called *Commutation Test.* The phonemes thereby discerned are then put within dashes, such as/p/,/b/, for phonological transcription. These are, of course, ideal units of the sound system of a language. They should not be confused with the sounds of actual utterances examined by phonetics. Phonetics tries to differentiate among the sounds with the highest possible degree of accuracy. It does so without regard for the influence a sound may have on the *meaning* of an utterance. These phonetic units are put in brackets, as you can see in the chapter on *phonetics.*

Not all sounds of a language are necessarily distinctive sounds. Compare the English and American pronunciations of "dance": [dQns] versus [dA¢ns]. Although there are different sounds in the pair, the meaning does not change. Thus, [A¢] and [Q] are not phonemes in this case. We call this phenomenon *free variation.* The two sounds can be referred to as *allophones.* These sounds are merely variations in pronunciation of the same phoneme and do not change the meaning of the word. Free variation can be found in various dialects of the same language. In this case, the different pronunciations of words throughout a country do not change the meaning of those words.

Another example of sounds which are not phonemes are those which occur in *complementary distribution.* This means that where one sound of the pair occurs, the other does not. An example for complementary distribution are the aspirated and unaspirated allophones of/p/. The initial consonant as in "pill" is aspirated. The consonant after/s/ in "sprint" is unaspirated. The respective transcriptions would be [pHil] and [sprInt], where [H] indicates aspiration. Aspirated [pH], as you can see in this example, occurs only at the beginning of words. [pH] and [p] are only allophones of the same phoneme/p/.

DISTINCTIVE FEATURES

From our studies of phonetics, we know how to describe the features of sounds. The same techniques apply for the description of phonemes. In the pair "vault " and " fault ", for example, the difference lies in the voicing of the first phonemes:/v/ versus/f/, the first representing a voiced consonant [+voiced], the second an unvoiced consonant [-voiced]. Voicing is of great importance in the English sound system. Therefore we call it a *distinctive feature.* Other distinctive features are [±nasal] (for consonants only)or [±consonantal], etc.

REDUNDANT FEATURES

Some features of sounds may be redundant in a language. This means that these sounds have a specific feature, but do not constitute minimal pairs. An example for such a redundant feature is [±nasal] of vowels in English. You have already seen that phonetics treats consonants as nasal or nonnasal only. Still, vowels can be positive nasal [+nasal] or negative nasal [-nasal]. This does not make them into phonemes; they are merely allophones of the same vowel. In the English language the redundant feature of nasality is found to abide to a general rule: Vowels that are [+nasal] are always followed by consonant that are also [+nasal]. Likewise, 'Consonants that are [+nasal] are always preceded by vowels that are also [+nasal]. For example, the vowel in "band" is [+nasal], while in "bar", it is [-nasal]. Still, nasality *is* a distinctive feature in English consonants. In languages other than English, nasality of vowels may well not be a redundant feature. The general rule stated above says that nasality in English vowels is *predictable,* because you can tell if a vowel is nasal or not by looking at the consonant following it.

RULES OF PHONOLOGY

The sequences of phonemes are determined by certain laws that are peculiar to that particular language. The English language, for example, does not allow consonants such as/b/ or/g/ to be followed by a consonant similar to it. The phoneme sequence */bgliz/, to give another example, is not permitted in English due to the consonant cluster/bg/ at the beginning. The following rules have been found to apply to the assembly of phoneme sequences in the English language.

Assimilation Rules

The rule stated above concerning the nasalization of vowels preceding [+nasal] consonants is an *assimilation rule.* The vowel segment is assimilated to the consonant segment by copying the [±nasal] feature of the latter to the former. You can observe this phenomenon in your own language. There are many instances in which we try to ease articulation and the easiest way of doing this is to simplify articulation by assimilating sounds. The assimilation rule also reflects a phenomenon called *coarticulation*. According to this principle, features of phonemes spread in anticipation of sounds or perseveration of articulatory processes.

Feature Addition Rules

Sometimes, features are added to phonemes when they occur in a specific *phonetic context*. We have already looked at aspirated and unaspirated occurrences of stops like/p/. At the beginnings of words as in pill,/p/ is aspirated. The feature of aspiration is hence added because/p/ is a sound at the beginning of a word. In other phonetic contexts, the feature of aspiration is not added.

Segment-deletion and Addition Rules

Phonological rules of a language may result in the addition or deletion of segments from a phoneme sequence. A good example for this rule is French, where wordfinal consonants are *deleted* when a consonant follows. But they are maintained when the following word starts with a vowel or a glide:

Before a consonant:	petit tableau	[p'ti tablo]
Before a vowel:	petit ami	[p'tit ami]

Movement (metathesis) Rules

In some languages, and in some English dialects, phonemes are rearranged. Consider the example "ask". In some English dialects, it is pronounced [Qks]. Historically, "ask" derived from OE "aksian". A metathesis rule changed it in most English dialects to the form commonly known today, whereas in others, the old form is pertained.

Chapter 9

Morphology

Whereas phonology studies the *smallest distinctive* elements of a language, morphology is the study of the *smallest meaning units* of a language. This smallest meaning unit is also called a *morpheme.* The overriding rule is that a morpheme must be able to stand alone, i.e. to yield meaning independently of its general context. Let's start out by taking a closer look at the term 'smallest meaning unit' and how it may be understood.

- We are inclined to think that a 'word' fits the definition of 'smallest meaning unit'. How ever, not all words are single meaning units. Some words are 'nonsense words' and lack any meaning whatsoever. These are invented words mostly, for example "brillig", or "chorps". Then there are words that are composed of more than one meaning unit.

Examples of words which consist of more than one meaning unit are: blueñberry, autoñbus, henceñforth

Although a word may be a smallest meaning unit, such as 'blue', it does not necessarily have to be one, as in 'blueberry'

- Neither can syllables be regarded as the smallest meaning units. They are, in the first place, phonological units. They consist of a nucleus, which is a vowel, a diphthong, or a vowel-like consonant, and one or several satellites. A satellite is always a consonant.

(satellites) +	nucleus	+ (satellites)
(C1, C2,...) +	V	+ (C1, C2,...)

Words may consist of several syllables, but not all of them are necessarily meaning units. *Example*: Masñsañ = chuñsetts, poñlice, moñther.

Thus, while a syllable may be a smallest meaning unit, such as the syllable 'end' in the word 'endless', it does not necessarily have to be one.

As we can see, a morpheme cannot necessarily be confined to a particular form of a word or a syllable. The study of morphology seeks to, in the first place, determine the precise form (Greek- morph) that an elemental meaning takes. However, it does, as we will see later, remain within the abstract domain, in cases where form either varies or where form is simply nonexistent.

Morphemes are also referred to as the *minimal linguistic signs*; you may also come across the term *moneme,* which is the French term for morpheme.

The above may have given you an understanding of why linguists have been engaged in endless debates over the definition of the word "word". The term remains ambiguous, and we should try as best to avoid it. After all, linguistic terminology is available to describe linguistic units in higher detail.

TYPES OF MORPHEMES

We can discern different types of morphemes when analyzing a text corpus. The process of sorting out which morpheme is which is called *distributional analysis*.

Grammatical Classification

Grammatically speaking, there are two classes of morphemes:

- Free morphemes: these may occur on their own, they can be used freely according to the rules of sentence structure, for example "boy, tree, church, go, leave, love."
- Bound morphemes: These are an exception to the rule that a morpheme must be able to stand alone; they have no meaning of their own, but add substantial

meaning to other morphemes to which they are attached. They are used for various purposes, such as inflection. Example: "-ing, -er" in "work*ing*, work*er*.", where "work" is a free morpheme accompanied by various bound morphemes, namely suffixes.

Morphological Classification

Morphological classification will help you to understand exceptions and different occurrences of morphemes.

- *Homophonous* morphemes *sound* the same, although their morphological function and visual realization may be different, for example the "in" in "inn", and the "in" in "incongruous".
- *Discontinuous* morphemes. A morpheme of this type does not appear in one continuous string in a word, but is split up into fragments. For example, the morpheme "ge- and -t" in the German word "ge-reis-t". Still, both parts belong together.
- A *portmanteau* morpheme is the result of a fusion of two other morphemes. For example, the French "au" is a fusion of the former morphemes "à" and "le".
- *Unique* or *residual* morphemes. These are a further exception to the rule that a morpheme must be able to stand alone. Representing bound morphemes, unique or residual morphemes are, by themselves, meaningless and gain meaning only in combination with other morphemes. Examples for this kind of morpheme are the "cran" in "cranberry", or the "mit" in "transmit", "commit", and so on.

Zero morphemes. As already mentioned above, there do exist meaningful grammatical features that are not materialized, neither in writing nor in sound waves, in a consistent manner. The plural of a noun, for instance, is not always formed by adding a bound morpheme 's' to the word. Some words are not changed at all when meaning the plural. We usually simply understand which case the speaker meant from the context of the conversation. One such example is the word 'sheep', designating singular as well as plural sheep. The zero morpheme 'plural' would, in this case, designate the abstract concept of the plurality. It then *means* the plural sheep as opposed to the singular sheep.

Morph, Morpheme, and Allomorph

Note that any language has a register of morphemes, the physical realizations of which are called *morphs*. While morphemes remain ideal abstract units, the corresponding morphs may show some variation. In the case of the plural morpheme, various realizations are possible. These variations sound and look differently:

/z/ in "dogs, beds";
/s/ in "cats";
/iz/ in "garages"

All three morphs are different representations of the same morpheme of plurality. Several morphs that belong to the same morpheme are also called *allomorphs*: variants of one morpheme.

In morphological transcription, morphs are commonly put in-between braces. The plural morph in "cats" thus becomes {cat}+{s} in morphological transcription.

MORPHOLOGY AND WORD-FORMATION

We have already seen that the term *word* is highly ambiguous. Now we come to consider it anew. Commonly, various grammatical forms of linguistic units such as "sing", "sang", "sung" are referred to as various *words*. In all three words of our example, however, we are confronted with various forms of the same unit, namely "sing". We will use a more specific term for these "pure" linguistic units than *word*. We thus refer to the more abstract units, regardless of their representation as phonological or orthographic units in various inflectional forms, not as words, but *lexemes*; in linguistic transcription they are distinguished by capitals. Hence the word "cut" can offer three forms of the lexeme CUT: present, past and participle. The sum of the lexemes of a language is called the *lexicon*.

The lexicon of a language is not fixed. New entries may occur, or old ones might become extinct. New entries are called *neologisms,* if they are created from existing resources of the language. New entries can also be *borrowed* from other languages. As for the process in the former case, we are able to create new words by applying the *morphological rules* of our language. Morphological rules apply to both *inflection* and *word formation.*

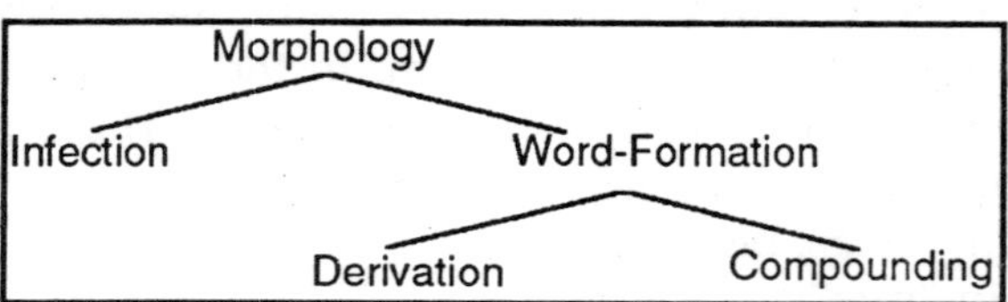

Inflection

There are two kinds of inflection: The *declension* of nouns, adjectives, and pronouns, and the *conjugation* of verbs.

There is a set of morphological rules which we apply in order to form the correct tenses or cases. We combine free morphemes with bound morphemes, the latter marking tense, gender, number, case, and so forth. Bound morphemes like {to}, which appears as a marker of the infinitive, are also used in order to form correct sentences. These *markers* help to create sentences that are correct according to the syntactic rules of a language. We see here that *morphology* and *syntax* cannot be regarded as entirely different disciplines.

Word Formation

Derivation

There are morphemes in English that allow us to change words. These are *derivational morphemes*: new words are *derived* in the process.

Derivational morphemes are *affixes.* If affixes are added to the front of a word, we speak of *prefixes* like in-, a-. If they are attached to the end of the word, they are called *suffixes,* such as -able, -ish. Derivational morphemes may or may not cause a change of the grammatical class of the word. In any event, the following morphological rules apply to most cases cover the main changes brought about by affixes. We speak of word formation as the *productive* feature of a language. By changing one element, new classes of words can be produced.

Noun to Adjective	**Verb to Noun**	**Adjectiv e to**	**Noun to Verb**	**No Change in Class**
{boy}+{ish}	{acquitt}+{al}	{exact}+{l	{moral}+{ize}	{a}+{moral}
{virtu}+{ous}	{clear}+{ance}	{quiet}+{l	{vaccin}+{ate	{mono}+{theis
{Eliza-	{confer}+{ence		{brand}+{ish}	{ex}+{wife}
{alcohol}+{ic}	{predict}+{ion			{sub}+{minim

Compounding

We may also create new words by combining two free morphemes. The product of such a process is called a *compound*. While German is notorious for compounding a multitude of units (e.g., Weihna chtsbaumschmuckvertrieb sorganisation-shandbuchverkäufer), compounds in English usually don't exceed two units. In a compound, the two morphemes always serve two different purposes.

The initial morpheme is also called the *head* of the compound, the following is the *body*. The head of the compound always determines the body semantically, e.g., {black} + {bird}→ a *black* bird, whereas the body usually determines the grammatical class of the whole compound. There are various possible combinations of English compounds:

	-ADJECTIVE	-NOUN	-VERB
ADJECTIVE-	{bitter}+{sweet}	{poor}+{house}	{high}+{born}
NOUN-	{head}+{strong}	{rain}+{bow}	{spoon}+{feed}
VERB-	{carry}+{all}	{pick}+{pocket}	{sleep}+{walk}

Other Processes of word-Formation

Apart from the above mentioned morphological

processes, there are also other ways of creating new words:

- *Invention*: Xerox, Exxon.
- *Acronymy*: NATO, Unicef.
- *Reduplication*: zigzag, chitchat.
- *Blending*: smog, brunch.
- *Clipping*: bus, auto, flu.

WORD CLASSES AND SENTENCE FUNCTIONS

Traditional grammars often begin with a classification of *word classes*. There are the following eight classes (including typical examples):

- *Nouns* (communicator, starship, captain)
- *Pronouns* (I, you, he, which)
- *Adjectives* (fast, deep, many)
- *Verbs* (see, retire, laugh)
- *Prepositions* (on, in, at)
- *Conjunctions* (and, but, because)
- *Adverbs* (much, deservedly, partly)
- *Interjections* (alas, oh)
- *Articles* (the, a)
- *Numerals* (one, two, three)

Some difficulties remain, such as with adverbs: one cannot, for example, exchange the adverbs "very" and "quickly" freely in a sentence:

*he ran very *versus* he ran quickly

To avoid this problem, the subcategory of the *intensifiers* is used to distinguish adverbs such as 'very', from the common adverbs.

The classing of words gives us overall categorical information about those words. Note that words from the same class can take on different functions depending upon their use in a sentence. Nouns, for example, may appear as subjects or objects in sentences. This additional specification of the function of words within the context of a sentence, such as subject, object, etc., is called *functional* information.

Chapter 10

Syntax

We have studied the phonological and morphological structures of the English language. But to know a language and to speak it correctly also involves being able to articulate complete sentences. The study of the syntax of a language is the study of its *sentence structure* as well as the linguistic knowledge necessary to form sentences.

WHAT IS A SENTENCE?

At first sight, this may seem like a trivial question to you. If you take into consideration though that there is a branch of linguistics that has been devoting its energy solely to the analysis of sentences, the question may be worthy of scrutiny. Let's take a look at some definitions of sentences first. Then we will go into models of grammars in detail.

Aristotelian Definition

Aristotelian logic claims that a sentence is an utterance consisting of *subject* and *predicate*. These terms have been rephrased *theme* and *rheme* by the communicational sciences. Here, theme means the part of the sentence that is already known and that is to be specified. Rheme then means the specifying part, the new information revealed on the theme. However, subject-predicate and theme-rheme do not always correspond. Consider the sentence "I went to London by train last weekend." If this sentence answers the question "Where did you go by train?", 'London' is the rheme. But, if it answers the question "How did you go to London last weekend?", 'by train' is the new information and, therefore, the rheme.

Logical Definition

A logical definition claims that a sentence is the expression of one single, complete thought. However, complex sentences may consist of several thoughts which are interwoven. Thus, this definition does not apply to all sentences. One example of a complex thought structure are subordinate sentences.

Structuralist Definition (Bloomfield)

Following the American structuralist *Bloomfield,* a sentence is "an independent linguistic form, not included by virtue of any grammatical construction in any larger linguistic form." A sentence is independent of any other linguistic form because it can stand alone, other than a single lexeme, which represents no independent syntactic unit. According to this definition, subordinate clauses are not sentences of their own because the depend on the main clause. In the following, we will see how structuralist analysis deals with sentence structure where subordinate clauses appear.

Grammaticality and Acceptability

Sentences can also be categorized under the aspects of *grammaticality* and *acceptability*. Sentences of a language can be grammatically correct or not. In the latter case, we call them *ungrammatical sentences*. This term may sound contradictory, since a sentence is, per definition, grammatically correct and complete. Sentences can, nevertheless, lack correct grammaticality, e.g.: *Susan put the knife.

Ungrammatical sentences appear in everyday language. When you observe your own language, you should find plenty of them.

Also, sentences may be grammatically correct, but still make no sense at all. In this case, they lack acceptability. Examples from English and German are:

Colorless green ideas sleep furiously.

Nachts ist es kälter als draußen.

Acceptability hence means that the meaning content of the sentence must be clear, understandable or acceptable to the reader.

SENTENCE TYPES

There are various types of sentences.

- *Simple sentences* consist of one clause only. These clauses contain only one verb:
  "Mary went to town."
- *Coordinate sentences* (also: *compound sentences*) consist of two or more clauses joined by words like "and", "or", "but", etc. These words are called *conjunctions*. The clauses in coordinate sentences hold equal status, i.e. they could each stand alone as simple sentences:

"The captain gave an order but the crew hesitated to confirm."

- *Complex sentences* consist of two or more clauses. Here, one clause serves as the grammatical part of another. We call these *embedded clauses*. Embedded clauses do not have a status equal to a simple sentence. In other words, they cannot stand alone and depend on the sentences which contain them.

"Peter said Jane became ill yesterday."

Most times embedded clauses are introduced by special words such as "whether", "that", "if", etc. These are called *subordinators*:

"Peter said that Jane became ill yesterday."

Complex sentences may also differ in form from simple sentences because the word order or grammatical form of words is altered:

"The captain said the starship took up speed immediately.", *but*

"The captain wanted the starship to take up speed immediately."

SENTENCE STRUCTURE

What are the constituents of a sentence? We have seen that morphemes are packed together to form strings of morphemes. These are called sentences. Nevertheless, not every single morpheme in a sentence may have independent status. Several morphemes may belong together more closely than others do.

Bearing this in mind, we must look for units larger than

the morpheme if we want to know what actually makes up a sentence. This discovery procedure is again called *distributional analysis*. The method of distributional analysis is called *segmentation*. Consider the following example:

"Aggressive Romulans relentlessly attack unguarded starships." We will now analyze the sentence for its constituents.

Segmentation

Reduction by Omission

Which of the elements may be omitted without damaging the essential structure of the sentence?

Aggressive Romulans relentlessly attack unguarded starships

Romulans attack starships

Romulans attack

A loss of the original meaning may occur in this reduction process that is concerned only with the grammaticality of the sentence.

Reduction by Substitution

Which of the elements may be substituted by shorter ones? Again, a change of the meaning content may be possible.

Aggressive Romulans relentlessly attack unguarded starships

Aliens attack Starfleet

They attack

Possible substitutions are pronouns, equivalent phrases or *synonyms*.

Expansion and Reduction

Another method of distributional segmentation is the expansion and reduction of phrases within the sentence. By doing so, we can find out what information is essential and what information is not essential for forming the sentence.

Naturally, the phrase at the peak of the expansion contains many elements which can be deleted without changing the grammaticality of the sentence. Let us examine a phrase from the sentence:

Two experienced aggressive Romulans seized control of the starship.

Expansion	Romulans
	aggressive Romulans experienced
	aggressive Romulans two
	experienced aggressive Romulans
	Reduction

IMMEDIATE CONSTITUENTS

We have now analyzed the sentence and learned that it can be segmented into several levels of *constituents*. The broadest category of a constituent is the one that is discerned 'immediately', at the beginning of the analysis; for this reason this type of constituent is called the *immediate constituent*, short 'IC'. Let's have a look at the sentence: "Poor John ran away."

Our first step in analyzing the sentence would be to distinguish "poor John" and "ran away"; therefore these two elements are the immediate constituents of the sentence.

If we were to proceed with our analysis, we could discern the immediate constituents of "poor John", which are "poor" and "John". The immediate constituents of "ran away" would be "ran" and "away."

Noun Phrase and Verb Phrase

Immediate constituents of a simple sentence are thus the

- *Noun-phrase* ("poor John") and the
- *Verb-phrase* ("ran away")

These immediate constituents can then, as mentioned above, be analyzed for their own respective constituents.

As we will see below, the structures of these noun- and verb-phrases can be very complex.

The determination of the immediate constituents of all levels of a sentence is called IC-analysis.

Modes of Representation

The results of distributional analysis can be presented in various forms. These representations then serve as tools for the *disambiguation* of sentences. For example, in the sentence "Old men and women dance.", the adjective may be understood to refer to both "men" and "women", or "men" only. The acronyms in the examples mean: NP = noun-phrase, VP = verb-phrase, N = noun, A = adjective, V = verb, Adv = Adverb.

Labeled Bracketing

Bracketing is one way of representing the results of distributional analysis. Different bracket types are here reserved for particular structure levels of a sentence. Braces {}, for example, contain whole sentences. To remind of its function, the brace is additionally labeled after the opening with an "s". Parentheses () indicate noun- or verb-phrases, and brackets [] indicate nouns, verbs, adjectives, or adverbs.

$\{_{S}(_{NP}[_{A}\text{poor}]+[_{N}\text{John}])+(_{VP}[_{V}\text{ran}]+[_{Adv}\text{away}])\}$

This method of representation is agreeable in that it adheres to the actual sentence format.

It has the drawback, however, that it is rather laborious to present and to grasp visually. Even in our short example, the elements are hard to distinguish.

Block Diagram

In this way of representing the constituents, the broadest structure appears at the bottom of the diagram, with each row further up showing a more segmented level. Each row thus shows the immediate constituents of its lower row.

Poor	John	ran	away
Poor	John	ran	away
Poor	John	ran	away
Poor	John	ran	away

Tree Diagrams

Tree diagrams have proven to be the most convenient way

of representing an IC-analysis. In the diagram, so-called *nodes*, where the NP, VP, etc. are situated, are connected by *links*, which serve for connection similar to the branches of a tree.

At the top of the diagram, the "s" represents the sentence. The immediate constituents of the sentence are the NP and VP.

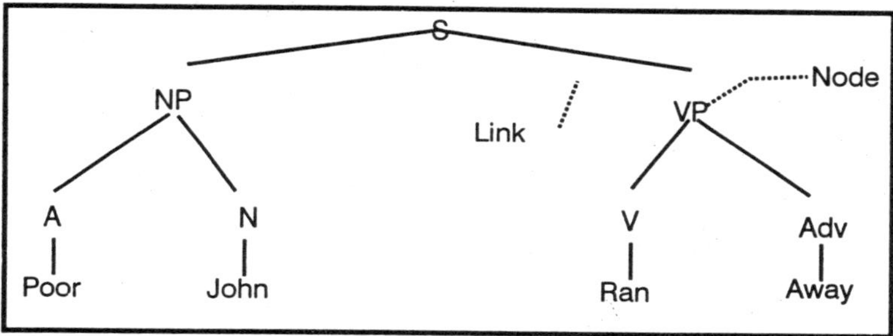

Phrase Structure Grammar

Another type of analysis of sentences, phrase-structure analysis, aims to sort out the *rewrite rules* or *phrase-structure rules* (*PS-rules*) of a sentence.

A sentence is here analyzed for its constituents, or phrase-structure. From there on, alternatives are sought that are capable of substituting these phrase-structures, hence 'rewrite rules'.

As you can see, the system allows for *alternatives*, with one element having the possibility of being rephrased in various ways. These alternatives are due, in part, to the structure of the *transitive* and *intransitive* verbs. Transitive verbs take a direct object. Thus, transitive verbs always appear with two noun-phrases. These are called the *arguments* of the verb:

"The dog frightened the man."

Intransitive verbs do not take objects:

"The dog barked."

Some verbs can be used transitively and intransitively:

"George won."

"George won the race."

The variability of rewriting is thus important for the creativity of a language.

Recursivity Rules

Recursivity is a property all languages share. We can always add another sentence to a sentence to get an even longer sentence. Also, we could extend phrases infinitely. In the rewrite rules given above, you find the recursivity rule VP → V + S. Why is this recursive? Well, a sentence consists of a NP and a VP. If the VP again contains a sentence, such as a subordinate clause, another VP must appear within that subordinate clause:

VP → V + S;
S → NP + VP;
VP →V + S;
S → NP + VP; etc.

Other recursivity rules are:

NP → NP + NP
VP → VP + VP

Problems with IC-Analysis

In some cases, there remain ambiguities with IC-analysis, as in:

"World War I was started by Austria." and
"World War I was started by 1914."

There are two different meanings behind these sentences, but an IC-Analysis of both sentences will yield the same structure. Thus, we are forced to rely on our "feeling" or "linguistic knowledge" if such sentences occur. Furthermore, there are *discontinuous constituents*, as in:

"Al turned the light off."

Here, constituents appear separated from each other, although they do belong together. Unfortunately, this is difficult to show with the IC-analysis. Obviously, there seems to be a level *beyond* the actual sentence on which such structures appear more clearly. We will investigate this in the chapter on *transformational generative grammar*.

TRANSFORMATIONAL GENERATIVE GRAMMAR (TGG)

The American linguist Noam Chomsky revolutionized the

theory of syntax by formulating this completely new approach. Chomsky defined a language as an *infinite set* of *grammatical sentences*. According to him, a grammar is a *finite* set of rules *generating* the grammatical sentences. The grammar must be *explicit* and *projective*. It describes the *competence* of an ideal native speaker and ignores *performance*, the actual utterances.

This last point, in particular, caused criticism: "Chomskyans" tend to acknowledge only those examples of a language that fit into their TGG, disregarding everyday language. This "idealism" thus neglects many non-grammatical phenomena of the language.

THE COMPONENTS OF TGG

- *Phrase structure rules*. You already know them. They make up the framework for the underlying, basic structure of a language. Chomsky labels the phrase structure rules the *base component* of the grammar.
- *Deep structure* (also: underlying structure). This component is generated by the phrase structure rules. The deep structure is what lies "behind" the actual sentence. Two sentences which *mean* the same may have the same deep structure, but two sentences which mean something completely different may also show the same deep structure. Due to this stress on meaning, the deep structure makes up the *semantic component* of the model.
- *Transformational rules*. These serve to transform the "raw" construction of the deep structure into the surface structure.

One transformational rule is:

If you want to construct a question in English, you have to either change the word order, or add an auxiliary verb.

Examples:

I can help. → Question: Can I help?

I go to town. → Question: Do I go to town?

Another transformational rule applies to forming the imperative: Leave away the subject.

Example: You go to town. → Imperative: Go to town!

- The result of the transformation is called the surface structure of the sentence. Nevertheless, this is still not the actual utterance. Remember that TGG does not deal with the performance of speakers. Thus, the surface structure is what is in our minds just before we say it. The examples above show two samples of surface structure.
- The surface structure is then expressed, i.e. pronounced, according to the phonological rules of that language.

Summary of TGG

The following diagram gives an overview of the transformational processes:

PHRASE-STRUCTURE RULES

↓

Deep Structure

↓

TRANSFORMATIONAL RULES

↓

Surface Structure

↓

PHONOLOGICAL RULES

Spoken Sentence

In this model, sentences are *generated* by *transformations*. Hence the name TGG.

Transformational Rules

TGG is a very complex subject matter. Let's take a look at the basic transformation rules:

- Deletion. A simple deletion rule deletes "that" when it precedes a NP at the beginning of a "that-clause"

Example: I believe that he went to town. → I believe he went to town.

- Movement. Prepositions that "belong" to verbs are moved to the end of sentences in certain cases. Example: They called up the police. → They called the police up.
- Addition. In negative sentences, "do" is added. The element "not" does not occur on its own.
- We say They do not like worksheets. but not *They not like worksheets.

Chapter 11

Semiotics

What is semiotics? Newcomers in the field of languages often wonder what field this discipline deals with. Well, we have an answer at hand that sounds both simple and puzzling:

Semiotics is the *science of signs*.

And so you might ask 'But what is a sign'? When people talk about others "making" or "giving signs", they usually refer to gestures. Then there are "signs" which help to guide and regulate traffic. Wherever we go "signs" appear, such as words, books, architecture, signs in people's behavior, etc. There are even events that are regarded as "signs".

As you can see from this brief survey, the term "sign" is used quite casually. Of course, semiotics is not the science of how to perform gestures, or of ordinances or municipal regulations for traffic signs. In terms of semiotics, signs always serve a *communicative purpose*. Furthermore, signs are always part of a *system* of signs. The system of human gestures or the system of traffic signs and their *meaning* could thus indeed be subject to semiotic inquiry.

Generally, signs consist of a *sign vehicle* and some *meaning* connected with it. So gestures or traffic signs are interesting because of their *meaning content*. We shall see later on what this means in detail.

Semiotics investigates a wide range of fields, starting from *zoosemiotics* and *cultural semiotics* up to *aesthetics* and *computer semiotics*, to name only a few. Semiotic theory can, in fact, be applied to almost any field since most processes in nature and culture rely on communication, and with that, rely on signs that serve that communicative purpose.

In this chapter we will concentrate on the linguistic sign and semiotic *models of the sign*. And of those there are quite a few. They differ mainly in one characteristic: Most models of the sign are either *dyadic* or *triadic* models. This means that they show either two or three sides, or apices. The most prominent example for the dyadic, or two-sided sign, is the one developed by Ferdinand de Saussure. The three-sided, or triadic model of the sign, was created by Charles Sanders Peirce and influenced semiotic theorists of the 20 century more so than any other model.

SAUSSURE

Ferdinand de Saussure, the founder of modern semiotics, designed a dyadic or *bilateral* sign model. According to him, the sign is two-sided. Unfortunately Saussure did not live to see his theory spread. His insights received their due recognition posthumously, when his students published his theories that they had written down in their scripts. Luckily, several versions of these scripts exist. This enabled the publishers to give a very detailed survey of Saussure's theories.

The Two-sided Sign

Saussure's idea of the sign is based upon a notion of *duality*. The word "dual" implies the number of two. Hence, Saussure's sign shows two sides. In order to understand the more complex construct of Saussure's, consider a trivial example: When you look at a thing, e.g., a tree, you instantly know the word that designates the thing. Words and things are connected in our minds. The same goes for words you hear without seeing the respective things. So when somebody tells you: "There's a tree in my father's garden", you know what "tree" means in this context, even without ever having seen that tree.

This explanation, however, does not entirely meet Saussure's terminology. From his point of view, language is an entirely psychological entity. Therefore, "things" in the real world do not play any role in the model. Saussure so to speak focuses on what goes on in our heads. So, neither the physical aspects of things nor those of sounds are considered. The two aspects of the linguistic sign Saussure identified are therefore *mental* aspects: the *ideas* or *concepts* of things and the *mental images* of sounds, both of which are stored in our memory.

Concept and Sound Image

Concept and sound image, Saussure contended, cannot be separated. He compared them with the two sides of a piece of paper: Just as one cannot cut the front side of a piece of paper without cutting the back side as well, our mind is structured such that the concept automatically evokes the sound image and, vice versa, that the sound image automatically evokes the concept. Therefore, concept and sound image belong together and form a unity.

The following figures illustrate the idea of the two-sided sign: The figure on the left shows the relationship between the terms *concept* and *image acoustique*. These two sides of the sign are brought together by an ellipse encompassing them. The figure on the right demonstrates this using an example.

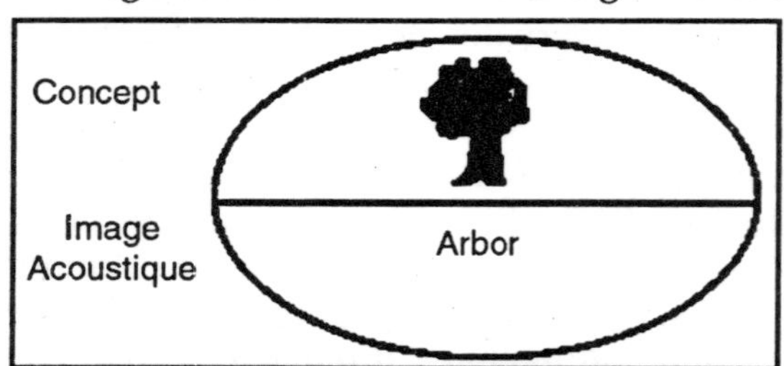

Later, Saussure coined the term *signified* for concept, and the term *signifier* for sound image (the original French terms are *signifié-concept, signifiant-image acoustique*). These terms are interchangeable. The concept, or signified then, as mentioned above, is the correlate of the sound-image, or signifier. Saussure claims here that these mental concepts always abide to the ideal and prototypical features that the signifier ideally was to refer to. For instance, when we hear "arbor", or "tree", we do not think of a particular tree, such as a birch tree, or the old oak tree in our backyard, but of an abstract concept that entails the ideal, prototypical features of "tree", for example the trunk, branches, leaves, tallness, etc. The sound chain, i.e. the actual utterance, may have brought about this concept, however, it is the "impression" of this sound chain in our minds that is of interest to Saussure. It is this impression that he refers to with his term 'sound image' and he regards it, as mentioned above, to be completely cut off from the physical world.

The relation between the concept and the sound image, furthermore, is an *arbitrary* one. There is no natural, inherent connection between the two. Instead, we associate concepts with sound images and vice versa following *conventions*. (The concept of arbitrariness is discussed in the introduction of this reader.)

A sign, with its signifier and signified, has to be, finally, acknowledged by a social group, or language community in order to be regarded as a sign. That is to say, a random utterance of one individual, although he or she may want it to signify something, may not have gained sufficient acknowledgment to be regarded as a sign. This is because Saussure regarded semiotics to be a social science. According to him, signs are *collective entities*.

Meaning as Opposition

According to Saussure, language is a structure. This is why his work and that of his followers has been called structuralism. Within this structure, meaning comes into being through opposition. We have already seen that, for Saussure, meaning is not connected with physical objects, since he claimed that nothing existed outside the semiological system of signifiers and signifieds.

In other words: without some *structure* superimposed to it, nothing gains meaning. This applies not only to the physical world, but also the realm of thought. Thought would be thus, without the structure of language, "amorphous", "uncharted", "vague". This important notion manifests Saussure's theory of linguistics, and semiotics, as a science concerned not with *substance*, but *form*. Do not be confused by this terminology! People use the term "substance" in everyday language in order to designate, say, a chemical substance. But Saussure's term "substance" by no means refers to physical shape. It is rather "that which needs to be structured". For example, the substance of thought depends on the structure of language, or form, to gain meaning.

Meaning takes form, comes into being, within this structured system only. And this meaning, according to Saussure, holds exclusively; in other words, a sign designates a concept that *no other sign* designates. or example, the sign "table" designates something exclusively. There is no other sign which means "table".

Hence, when we hear the word "table", we can easily make out what it means. Saussure says that the sign stands in opposition to all others. In other words: A sign designates a concept as opposed to all others which *do not* designate the same concept. All signs form a semiotic network in which the oppositions between all signs give meaning to the individual ones. Naturally, this is valid for *individual* systems of signs only. The counterargument that correlate signs from other languages do exist, such as "Tisch" meaning the same as "table", does not hold.

PEIRCE

Charles Sanders Peirce was a contemporary of Saussure, unfortunately however, neither of them had contact with or knowledge of the work of the other. While Saussure's model has been recognized as important for linguistics in general and semantics in particular, Peirce is considered one of the most important figures in the history of semiotics. Some scholars regard him to be the founder of the modern theory of signs.

There are some profound differences between Saussure's and Peirce's views of the sign. Saus-sure two-sided model of the sign claimed to regard language only (Remember 'the world outside' was not a part of language for Saussure.). Peirce, in contrast, saw that 'world outside' to be a part of the system of language and incorporated it into his *triadic* model of the sign. Saussure's two-sided model is, furthermore, static in that it offers an explanation of how a sign is structured and an analysis of its state. Peirce's model is dynamic in that it does not regard the sign as a set entity and in that it takes the overall production process of signs, *semiosis,* more so into consideration.

This *semiosis* is, furthermore, a *pragmatic* procedure: In this procedure everybody is seen to have his or her own view of the world and by using signs to express this individual view, is seen to contribute to an endless generation of new signs. It is easy to see why this makes for a much more dynamic understanding of language as people's individual views of the world can not be ascertained in a consistent, static manner. This is the main, foremost difference between Saussure's and Pierce's approaches to language.

It is important to keep in mind that Peirce's model cannot be regarded merely as an extention of Saussure's model. It is based on different notions of the sign altogether and thus needs to be approached in its own terms.

The Triadic Sign

Peirce's triadic model sees the sign as a phenomenon of *thirdness,* with the various aspects of a sign relating to each other as best represented with the triangle.

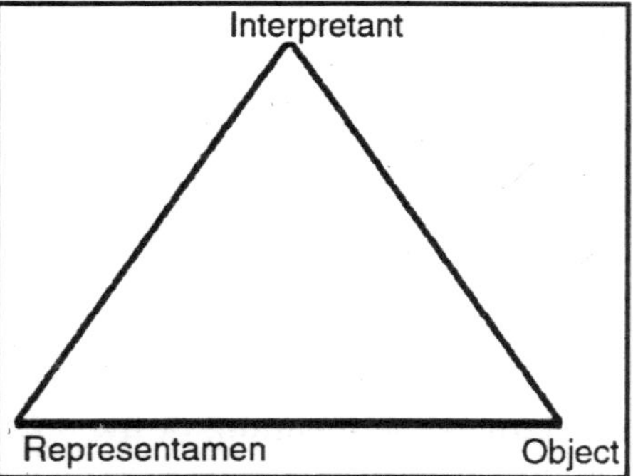

The Representamen

This part of the sign model is what we already know from Saussure who introduces it by another name, namely the sign vehicle, the signifier, *expression* respectively. From this you can see that semiotic theory, though it evolved differently, drew on the same ideas and concepts quite often. The representamen is the first correlate of the sign. Still, Peirce sometimes mixed up his own terms and said the representamen was the sign in the whole. In most cases, however, Peirce makes quite clear that the sign is the whole, and the representamen is only part of it.

The Object

We have seen that the representamen is the sign vehicle. Thus it refers to something which it itself is not. In other words:

"Table" is only a chain of sounds. The thing it refers to is nothing acoustic, but a body. Any real or ideal unit we can refer to can be described as an *object* in the Peircean sense. Peirce names two classes of objects:

- Immediate object: We speak of an immediate object when a sign can spontaneously be associated with some specific object. "Hunger", for example, assumingly evokes the idea of the desire to eat.
- mediate or dynamic object: How we experience objects is a highly individual process that takes place independently in each of us. The main, or direct, correlation of the sign as to some object can, moreover, change over time. Somebody who starved, will, for example, entertain a different notion of 'hunger' from then on. This is referred to as semantic language change. The mediate or dynamic objects are, in this sense, possible variations of the association of the immediate object.

The Interpretant

The interpretant is the meaning of the sign as created in the mind of the interpreter. Peirce also said that this was the "effect" of the sign. This effect can be measured by everyday experience. Everything we learn day by day changes our view of the world. Thus, we may *interpret* signs differently today, if our knowledge of them or experience with them has changed since yesterday. For example, linguistics will mean something else to you at the end of this class than it did at the beginning. The *interpretant* is thus the meaning as created on the basis of our sum of experience. This is a part of the overall process of creating signs, *semiosis,* to which we will get right now.

Unlimited Semiosis

The process of creating signs is called *semiosis*. The representamen stands for something: the object. Also, there is a person to whom the representamen is a representation. In the mind of this person, the interpreter, the interpretant is thus created.

Peirce speaks of a process that could go on indefinitely, of an endless succession of signs. In it one thought leads to another and every interpretant can in the course be the representamen of another sign. As such, the search for a first or last sign in this process, a coherent whole with a beginning and ending, ceases to be the predominant aim. Peircian semiotics, instead, focuses on the process itself.

Firstness, Secondness, Thirdness

According to Peirce, a sign can stand in relation to that which it stands for in three different ways. These potential relationships are what he calls a trichotomy of firstness, secondness, and thirdness. Peirce then elaborated this trichotomy, leading to a very complex sign theory. In this course we will start out by understanding this trichotomy in regard to the correlate *object*.

- Icon. Icons are signs that are similar to that which is denoted. One of the best examples are photographs, where the picture resembles the object to a great extent. Icons stand in relation of *firstness* to the object.
- Index. The index does not resemble the object itself as the icon does, though it does depict a physical context having to do with that object. Smoke, for example, does not resemble fire, but it does refer to fire nevertheless. The relation between indices and objects is secondness.
- Symbol. Peirce regards symbols as arbitrary and

conventional signs. Symbols refer to their objects "by virtue of law". All linguistic signs, i.e. words, are therefore symbols. (Note that many linguists have different understandings of the term "symbol"; thus, when reading linguistic texts, make sure that you are familiar with that linguist's notion of "symbol".) Thus, in order to use symbols (in the Peircian sense of the term) effectively, you simply have to know, i.e. learn, their meaning. This type of relation is what Peirce called a relation of thirdness.

Chapter 12

Semantics

Actually, this chapter ought to bear the name "linguistic semantics", since semantic theories have been developed by many schools of thought. However, philologists concerning themselves with semantics regard it as the *meaning structure* of human language.

We have already come across the term *meaning* in the chapter on semiotics. We saw that the words of a language carry meaning. In this chapter, we will take a look at the semantic relations that exist between the words of a language and the meaning these words designate (semantics comes from Greek "semantikos", *belonging to the sign*. Also, we will take a look at the two main linguistic phenomena that modern linguists concerns itself with, namely *metaphor* and *deixis*.

THE MEANING OF "MEANING"

Scholars have been busy thinking about the concept of meaning since the beginning of philosophy. When we try to explain the meaning of a word, say 'woman', we find that we quite naturally take recourse to other words, such as 'human', 'female', and so on. But what is "human", we could go on to ask. What is "female"? What does "what", "is", "define" mean? What is the meaning of "meaning"?

At some point, we will undoubtedly fail to produce new words in order to explain others. This means that finally we arrive at a point where we must accept that some basic words are left undefined. Nevertheless, they are understood by all speakers of a language. These basic words are called the *primitive semantic elements*.

We've seen that language always refers to objects of one kind or another, either physical (e.g., things) or mental (e.g., ideas or feelings). When talking about meaning, however, language itself becomes the object of investigation. Thus, it is *language about language,* describing, for example, the units, characteristics, or sounds of a language. We call this language about language the *metalanguage.* When we discussed the functions of language as defined in the communication model by Roman Jakobson, we mentioned this term for the first time. We use metalanguage whenever we discuss linguistic theory in any of its aspects. In the following, you will see again how important it is to be able to move to the metalinguistic level. Otherwise, we would not be able to discuss semantics at all!

WORD MEANING AND SENTENCE MEANING

When we look at a language, we find that there are different kinds of meaning behind different kinds of words.

- *Content words.* These are principally nouns, verbs, adjectives, and adverbs. All of these refer to concrete objects, actions, or abstract concepts, feelings, etc. In other words: there is always some immediate *content* which can be associated with the word.
- *Function words.* These are prepositions or articles. There is no immediate content ascribed to these words. They help to construct meaning in larger linguistic units, in other words: they have a *function.*

As you have seen now, meaning has to do with words. Words serve to build sentences. How do we know the meaning of the sentence? Is it merely the sum of the meanings of its words? Of course not. Consider this example:

The hunter bit the lion. — The lion bit the hunter.

In both sentences, the same words occur. However, the meaning of each sentence is quite different from the other. Sentence meaning, hence, depends not only on the words, but also on word order, pronunciation, etc. Trying to determine what a sentence means and why it means what it means, is what is referred to in semantics as looking for the *semantic role.* This is, in essence, nothing other than a basic process of asking '*who* did *what* to *whom*, with *whom*, or for *whom*'. Features such as word order, pronunciation and stress help us to define the semantic role.

LEXICAL SEMANTICS

We have already discussed the term *lexeme*. In principle, all words in the *lexicon* of a language are lexemes (see *Morphology*). Examining the meaning of words in the lexicon then is *lexical semantics*.

Semantic Features

When we use a word, we know its meaning (or at least we ought to). This means, we know many things about the word in question. In the above example we mentioned "woman." Well, these aspects are also called *semantic features* or *semantic properties*. We can list the features of all words. They help to differentiate between words that sound or look the same, such as "bachelor". Can you think of any more semantic features for this word?

bachelor	*bachelor*	*bachelor*
+animated	+animated	+animated
+human	+human	-human
+male	...	+male

The + and - signs indicate whether a lexeme is specified by a certain feature or not. Sometimes, features do not apply to lexemes, as in our example: while the bachelor on the left hand represents an unmarried young man, who naturally is male, that feature does not apply to the meaning in the middle: Here we have the person holding the university degree (both male and female).On the right, we finally have the animal bachelor: a young male seal.

Denotation versus Connotation

There are two aspects to the meaning of a word. We also say that there is a "core" meaning to every word, as well as some additional meaning. The "core" meaning is the meaning of a word in its literal sense. We call this the *denotative meaning*.

The additional meaning is what we add according to our feelings about the term. This is the *connotative meaning*.

A good example is the disease called cancer. The denotation of "cancer" is the mere disease that can be described by growing tumors, malfunctioning organs, etc. The connotation of cancer is all the emotional additions, as "cruel", "frightening", "hard to heal", etc.

While the denotation of a lexeme is subject to language change in the broad sense, the connotation may change according to the taste *en vogue*. A few decades ago, "fur coat" had a connotation of value and high social status. Nowadays, "fur coat" evinces a connotation of "animal murder", "cruelty", "ignorance", and so on. In short, the wearer of such a coat might find that people judge her (or him) differently.

Lexical Fields

There are always words in a language that seem to belong together more so than others.

Consider the following words:

hammer, tongs, screwdriver, cutter, saw

All of these have something in common: they are tools. These words with "something" in common belong to the same *lexical field*. Other lexical fields contain emotions, vehicles, furniture, and so on.

Markedness

We do not use all lexemes equally often: we use them with different *frequency*. Consider the example of the following color terms:

blue, red, yellow, green

indigo, saffron, royal blue, aquamarine

The first set of color terms seems more familiar. Both sets have a different status; we say that the "more familiar" set is *less marked*. Less marked forms are easier to learn and are used more frequently.

Another example is the use of male and female forms. Female forms are more marked than male ones in languages such as German and French.

The Most Relevant Semantic Relations between Lexemes

Some semantic relations between lexemes determine their semantic locus within the lexicon of a language. Others simply govern the possibilities of substitution and differentiation of lexemes.

Hyponymy

Consider again the example of hammer, tongs, screwdriver, cutter, saw.

All of these belong to the lexical field "tools". In this case, "tool" is a semantically higher term, in that it stands for a group of items. All of the terms (hammer,...) are *hyponyms* of the broader term. "Hypo" is Greek for "below". Thus all tools are hyponyms of "tool". The term "tool" is, consequently, the *hypernym* for all tools ("hyper" = Greek "above").

Synonymy

Two words are synonymous if they "mean the same thing." We all know words which serve the same purpose. An example from German is "Geldbörse – Portemonnaie – Geldbeutel." An English example is "film – movie – motion picture."

True synonyms are hard to find in a language. Most synonyms originate from local differences. For example, in Austria people refer to a street as "Gasse", whereas for the rest of the German-speaking community the same object is referred to as "Straße."

Antonymy

Apart from equality in meaning, as with synonyms, there is also the opposite. Opposition in meaning is known as *antonymy*. Large-small, wide-narrow, white-black, fat-slim are some examples for antonyms. All classes of words can have antonyms.

Verbs: go-stand
Nouns: male-female
adjectives: good-bad

Asymmetry of the Lexeme

As an ideal, the linguistic sign shows *one* meaning connected with *one* expression. However, there are some exceptions to this ideal.

Homonymy.

Two lexemes that *look* or *sound* the same may *mean* something different. Hence, there are two types of homonymy, according to visual or acoustic equality.

- *Homophony.* These lexemes sound the same, such as "whether-weather" and "meet-meat".
- *Homography.* These lexemes look the same, as "read", meaning as well/ri:d/ as/red/ in the past tense.
- There are even homophones which are at the same time homographs, as "ear-ear." This pair designates as well the auditive organ ("Ohr") as the fruit of corn ("Ähre").

Polysemy

We say that a word is polysemic when it looks the same and has more than one meaning. This term, although it is closely related to, and has overlappings with, homography, is used to exclusively refer to words of a common *etymology.* The different meanings here usually constitute a specific stage in the etymology of the word, and/or the altering meaning is brought about by a metaphor.

Example: ride (to ride by car or to ride a horse), or the German word "Stufe" (a step of a staircase or a level in school).

METAPHOR

The issue of metaphors is central to the debate over 'meaning'. Traditionally metaphors have been regarded as a type of extension of, or analogy to, the literal sense of linguistic signs. Most commonly they are extensions of visual, physical objects or experiences onto the abstract or emotional domains of thinking. For example, the metaphorical use of the word 'branch', as in the sense of 'branches of sciences', is derived from a meaning originally denoting a physical object. The debate carried out over 'metaphors' is thus largely a philosophical one that questions our traditional dialectic between the body and the soul. In trying to overcome this dialectic, or in trying to understand it, some argue that everything is a metaphor, while others question exactly how it is that the meaning of a sign can be extended with a metaphor.

We can also say that people use and also create new metaphors much more often than one might think. Most of the metaphors we use are so conventionalized that we are not aware of using them as metaphors. For example, if you *see the point*, you should understand that this is a metaphor, since one cannot "see" an utterance.

As we see, there is some "literal" meaning in the linguistic signs. However, signs may be used to create new meaning. Metaphors work on the principle that something in the original meaning is *similar* to the new one.

DEIXIS

Deixis comes from Greek, meaning "to point." Indeed we frequently point at things, people, and events in our language. We need function words, e.g., prepositions and pronouns, to construct deictic utterances. We use deixis to articulate the orientation of ourselves or things to some points of reference. There are three forms of deixis:

- *Personal deixis*. This form of deixis refers to the utterances which refer to ourselves or the persons involved in the discussion or the general context. Personal pronouns are used to denotate persons.

I think this is right.

Did you hand in the worksheet as you are required to?

Personal deixis may also point at persons mentioned earlier in the text:

Beverly was quite upset yesterday. I hope she is in a better mood touay (she = Beverly)

- *Spatial deixis*. We use this to mark the position of the speaker:

I've been living in Kassel for several years.

But also relative positions can be referred to: Here there be dragons!

- *Temporal deixis*. Finally, we use temporal deixis to mark our place in time.

You will be attending classes for several years from now.

As you can see, function words suddenly become relevant in the formulation of deictic utterances. They constitute meaning in the context.

Chapter 13

Pragmatics

We have investigated two of the main issues of language so far. The first was *syntax,* which deals with the relations among the various signs in a sequence of speech. The second was *semantics,* which deals with the linguistic sign and the meaning behind it, that is, the relation between language and objects. There is, however, a third issue to the linguistic sign. What this issue is easy to guess when considering the following example:

Speaker A (looks about a big square she's standing on: "Oh, I just *love* Trafalgar Square!"

Speaker B (responding): "But this is the Place de la Concorde!"

What's wrong with speaker A's utterance? Well, it's correct both semantically and syntactically. It makes sense and it is acceptable, apart from one aspect: It does not fit into the context.

Here we see that there must be a relation between the sign and its *user* in a certain context. Obviously, sentences can be correct both semantically and syntactically and still be contextually wrong.

According tc the American philosopher Charles William Morris, this third relation of the sign is called the *pragmatic* dimension of the sign. Morris was a follower of Peirce, which accounts to why he adopted the model of the sign and its three dimensions:

This chapter deals with pragmatics. We will take a look at *information structure* and *speech acts,* investigating why we say what in which context.

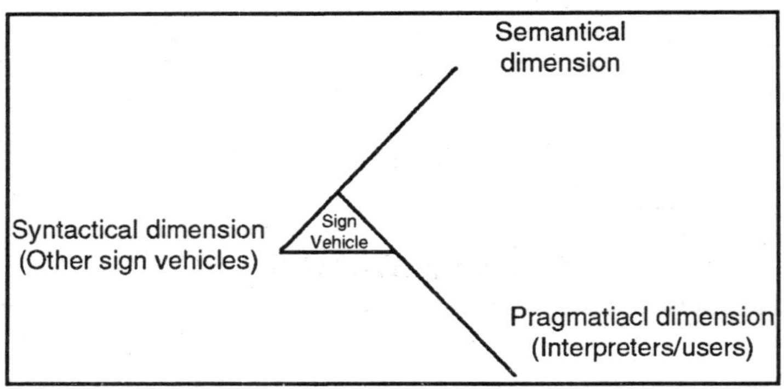

INFORMATION STRUCTURE

As we have seen in the example above, information must be organized according to the given context. We may "understand" people all right in a conversation. Still, if information occurs that does not fit the context, we are puzzled:

Jack: "Hi, Helen. Nice to see you. Are you coming to my party tonight?" Helen: "Well... I don't know yet." Jack: "O come on, it's my birthday!" Helen: "My father owns a red sports car." Jack: "What the hell are you talking about??"

"Contextually correct" does not only mean that information can be correct or not, but also that the surface structure of a sentence is generated from the deep structure due to some regulative force in the language. In a birthday card, for example, you do not expect the sentence:

"On this day, which is the 24 anniversary of the day of your birth, these words shall mean to you that the undersigned wishes to transmit her best wishes, namely congratulations."

You will rather find something like:

"Happy birthday and best wishes. Yours, Elvira."

Obviously, there are alternatives of saying the same thing. We are "told" how to structure information in a sentence by several categories.

Categories of Information Structure

- Given and new information. In every conversation

there are phrases that are taken to be commonly known. These receive less stress and are expressed less elaborately than those representing new information. For example:

"Yesterday my mother went to this new mall, the one in Queen's road, you know, where the old cinema burnt down last year."

"Yesterday" and "my" are obviously known elements in this sentence. "New mall" is new information. It requires further explanation.

- *Topic:* The topic is the core of attention in a sentence, as the underlined word in:

"I know it was you who took away my sandwich!"

It is not always that easy to say where the topic is in a sentence. In:

"O damn it!" the topic is definitely outside the spoken language, e.g., a mischief or bad luck. The word "it" is obviously too vague to represent the topic in a sufficient manner.

- *Contrast:* Where nouns or noun phrases occur in opposition to each other, we find contrast. Examples are:

"It was not Tom but Jerry who made me laugh more."

"Only Kathleen was able to pass the test."

In the second example, contrast occurs between "Kathleen" and all other members of a given group.

- *Definiteness:* Noun phrases are marked as *definite* when it can be assumed that the listener

is able to identify them without difficulty.

"Where's the pub?" (definite) is appropriate in a small village where one single pub exists, whereas "Where is a pub?" or "Are there pubs around here?" (indefinite) would fit the situation of a larger neighborhood or city.

- *Referentiality:* Noun phrases are referential if they refer to a *particular* entity. In the sentence "This is the book I bought at Dillon's", for example, the noun phrase "book" is referential as it is defined more precisely by the subordinate clause. The noun phrase "it" in the sentence "It's fun to study linguistics", on the other hand, is nonreferential as it remains vague. Nonreferential phrases are thus used whenever some noun is required that cannot be derived from the general content of the phrase. In European languages, for example, nouns are required for the construction of any sentence. Due to this, phrases like "It's raining" exist. Try to think about whatever is actually raining: is it the weather? The cloud? Is it the rain itself? God? The answer is no. The word "it" serves a purpose in itself because we require a noun phrase, something that "does rain" similar to "I run", "Joe swims", "Eva sleeps".

PRAGMATIC CATEGORIES AND SYNTAX

As we have seen before in the chapter on syntax, the same deep structure of sentences can be transformed into different surface structures.

In this chapter, you will see when pragmatic categories apply to trigger certain transformations.

- *Fronting:* Moving phrases to the front of a sentence serves to indicate givenness or contrast.
  Givenness: "Latin lessons I cannot stand."

The speaker in this sentence presumes that the listener already knows that he/she can't stand something. Therefore that part of the sentence is a given, something already known. Placing the noun phrase to the front then serves to distinguish the new and the given information of the sentence from each other.

Contrast: "I really don't like Tim. Harvey I find nice."

In this example, contrast is expressed through fronting. The unusual position of "Harvey" serves to emphasize the like/dislike opposition

- *Left-dislocation:* This is syntactically and formally similar to fronting; a noun is moved from its usual place to the left, i.e. front of the sentence in order to indicate givenness or contrast. The difference here is that the noun remains in the form of a pronoun in its original place as well. It is frequently used to reintroduce given information.

"Linguistics, I'd just die for it."

- *Clefting and pseudoclefting:* Consider the following sentence:

"Spock met Kirk in the transporter room."

Cleft sentences are of the form: "It + BE + that..."

"It was Kirk that Spock met in the transporter room."

Pseudocleft sentences are of the form: "WH-word (usually 'what') + ... + BE"

"What Spock met in the transporter room was Kirk."

Both constructions serve to facilitate the information process for the listener. Because the given information is distinguished from the new, the listener can focus more readily on the new information. Between the two constructions, though, it is cleft sentence structure that has more force in achieving this effect.

In pseudocleft sentences the new information is, though marked, not presented in one block at the front.

The listener thus, after receiving the "what" element of the new information, has to contribute somewhat more concentration to the given information in the middle before resuming with the latter part of the new information at the end of the sentence.

- *Sentence stress:* In most languages, noun phrases that represent new information receive more stress. But stress can also serve the purpose of marking opposition. Stress refers to intonation. In fronting and left-dislocation, stress is added to strengthen the emphasis on the acoustic level.
- *Passive:* Usually, the active voice is preferred in English. Sentences as: "A good time was had by all" sound ridiculous. This is because we prefer to name the agent in a sentence as the active part. Still, the two possible kinds of passive sentences in English fulfill important functions:

Agent passive constructions are used when the subject of the sentence is of predominant interest, yet when a noun other than the subject of the sentence takes the active role in shaping the state of that subject.

"The Klingons were driven back by the *Enterprise*"

Agentless passives are used when the agent is either known or irrelevant and thus unimportant in the sentence:

"The Klingons were driven back."

SPEECH ACTS

In the 1960's, Two linguists, Austin and Searle, made up a theory on how language serves to perform action. Austin's famous book is hence called: *How to do things with words*.

When we communicate, we do not only intend to send some information to a receiver. In fact, we are always *acting* in one way or another when we talk.

This does not mean that we perform some sort of play with our bodies, but that we are imparting something beyond the mere surface structure of the utterance. Just consider your own everyday communication: You do not merely 'seek and provide information', instead you declare, pronounce, give orders, commiserate, approve, etc. Speech acts can be quite diversified.

Types of speech acts

- *Representatives*: these represent states of affairs, such as assertions, statements, claims, hypotheses, descriptions, and suggestions. They are commonly regarded as being either true or false.
- *Commissives*: these commit the speaker to something, such as promises, pledges, threats, and vows.
- *Directives* intend to make the hearer carry out some action: commands, requests, challenges, invitations, entreaties, and dares.
- *Declarations* bring about the state of affairs: blessings, firings, baptisms, arrests, marrying, declaring a mistrial.
- *Expressives:* these indicate the speaker's attitude, such as greetings, apologies, congratulations, condolences, and thanksgivings.

- *Verdictives* make assessments or judgements: ranking, assessing, appraising, condoning.

Locution, Illocution, Perlocution

A speech act has three aspects to it. Note that we are here not interested in the denotative meaning, but rather in the connotative meaning, i.e. what is actually inferred, brought about, and effected by the speech act.

- *Locution.* This is the acoustic utterance that can also be transcribed into phonetic transcription. It is also called the *utterance act.* We referred to this earlier as the acoustic chain.
- *Illocution.* Whenever you say something, you have an *intention* to say something. There may be one or more intentions behind the utterance. We say that there are one or more *illo-cutionary acts* in the speech act.
- *Perlocution.* This is the effect of the speech act on the hearer. There are two aspects of the *perlocutionary act.* First, there is the effect that the sender wants to evoke in the listener, and second, the effect that is finally achieved. An example is an order from someone without authority: The effect that the sender wanted to evoke was obedience; what was finally achieved, however, was disobedience.

But how is it that we know what illocutionary force is behind a speech act, i.e., how do we know that somebody asking "Are you free tonight?" is not merely expecting a "yes/no"– answer, but wants to line up a date with us.

We infer the illocutionary act of a statement from its *context.* This means that we presume, for one, that a speaker always has some intention for wanting any information. The context here 'boy-girl-evening-free time' allows the listener to deduce 'He wants to spend his time with me.'. If the context were such that both the speaker and the listener have part-time jobs at McDonalds, the illocutionary act could well be very different, namely "Could you take my shift tonight ? (so that I could go on a date with someone else?)".

Whether a context counts as a valid context of a speech

act usually rests on a number of *conditions* that, together, render that context. There are also always a number of conditions that have to be fulfilled so that a speech act can be interpreted as intended. "I now pronounce you husband and wife", for example, is valid only if the speaker is entitled to wed couples, the two are willing and legally qualified to marry, all persons are present in an appropriate environment, such as a church, or a court, and so on.

Most of these conditions are a matter of *convention*. In other words, whether a priest has the authority to marry couples, rests on our Christian convention of entitling such people with this authority. A promise is valid only if the convention of truthfulness is acknowledged by the promising person.

As such, a directive, such as the invitation, is subject to interpretation according to different conventions of that specific condition. For instance, the invitation "Call me whenever you want" has become, by convention, to function also as a way of expressing a general willingness to help a person. The offer itself is thus usually not expected to be taken up at 4:30 in the morning. The pledge "I'll pay you back as soon as I get the money." on the other hand, is usually taken literally, i.e. our conventions for dealing with money matters are usually literal.

The Cooperative Principle

As you can well imagine, sorting out the different conventions that govern speech acts can be very complex. There are, however, four maxims that can be regarded as general principles in all speech acts.

- Maxim of quantity. If you are asked something, you are expected to give neither too little nor too much information. If you don't abide by this maxim, you will usually be regarded as uncooperative. If your answer doesn't convey all of the information asked for, the listener has incomplete data, whereas too much information distracts the listener.
- Maxim of relevance. Imagine asking somebody: "What time is it?" and getting the answer: "I've been

to Switzerland three times." This answer clearly lacks all relevance in the given context.

- Maxim of manner. This refers to the *importance* of details within the *chronological order* they are presented. "First comes first" is a principle that is violated in the following examples; the phrases that violate the maxim of manner are marked.

"For the station, you turn left at the next crossing. Then you walk for half a mile. Down the street is a subway. Use it to cross the street. Turn left again. *The subway's walls are painted yellow*. From that point, you'll be able to see the station."

"Germany is located in the center of Europe. You'll find Hessen in the center of Germany. Kassel is a city in the north of Hessen. There's a university in Kassel. *Hessen is also famous for Frankfurt*. At Kassel university, there's a language department."

- Maxim of quality. This maxim refers to the truth or falseness of a statement. If a speech act lacks this principle, it is a lie. Successful communication rests on the assumption that the other is telling the truth, i.e. earnest about her/his statements. Hence this maxim is the most important. It doesn't really matter if other maxims are violated, as long as the quality of the speech act is assured. Note that the maxim of quality refers to the conscientiousness of the speaker, in other words, it is secondary if she/he is mistaken or not. A statement such as "I think Marx was right" is qualified if the person really does think Marx was right; the question then of whether Marx really was right or not is another subject matter.

There are cases, as you may know from your own experience, where even these cooperative principle can be legitimately violated.

Some lies are necessary due to cultural conventions.

You would not reject a birthday present given to you by your best friend, saying it was *Kitsch,* even if you did think it was Kitsch.

This leads us a step further, to the *indirect speech act*.

Indirect Speech Acts

In these speech acts one or more maxim is violated, however, since both participants of the speech act recognize the violation the speech act as a whole is seen to follow cooperative principles. The example given above belongs to this type as, although the listener may not overtly recognize the violation, he/she would potentially tolerate the violation. As such speech acts that violate these maxims are seen to follow these principles indirectly. The following applies to the indirect speech act:

- At least one maxim of the speech act is violated.
- The literal meaning of the locution differs from the illocutionary force conveyed by it.
- Hearer and speaker recognize due to the context, that 2 (through 1) is the case and, both assuming that they both acknowledge this vice versa, view their communication as cooperative and proceed their conversation.
- The indirect speech act has thus been identified and the intended meaning of the locution has been constructed by the interlocutors with the help of their knowledge of the context.

In the following, you will find some examples:

- Jeff: "Am I late?"

John: "The boss went crazy."

Jeff: "All right, I'll go straight to his office and apologize."

Here John seems to ignore Jeff's question and thereby violates the maxim of relevance. John's remark on the angry boss and, following that, John's reply to that, confirms that both John and Jeff have identified the illocutionary act, i.e. they both know that what is of interest is the consequences of Jeff being late, not the denotative meaning of his being late. As such John's speech act is an indirect speech act; i.e. as a whole it is cooperative.

- Mary: "Are you finished with your work sheet?"

Charley: "Is Rome in Spain?"

The answer seems to have nothing to do with the question; again the maxim of relevance is violated. Both participants, however, rely on *shared knowledge*. The basis of the indirect speech act here is that two questions are being compared.

The natural answer as to the question whether Rome was in Spain is "no".

This answer then is being transferred to the first question. Recognition of this procedure in both parties then allows the indirect speech act to be cooperative

- Sometimes maxims are violated due to *politeness*. If you ask somebody "Can you shut the window?" you are actually saying: "This is a polite request. Please shut the window." You are not really interested in the person's capability of performing the act.
- *Metaphors* are also indirect speech events. Consider the utterance

"Jane is a block of ice."

This violates the maxim of quality, since Jane most definitely does not consist of frozen water. However, literal meaning is not intended here. Listeners quite naturally attribute their associations of coldness to Jane and so arrive at the intended meaning.

Chapter 14

Text Linguistics

TEXT LINGUISTICS

So far, we have dealt with the term "text" quite freely. You may or may not have realized, however, that the use of this term is not quite that simple. None of the branches of linguistics we are looking at in this course regards the complete entity of *texts* as their primary subject matter in the way text linguistics does. Instead, they focus rather on, e.g., the nature and function of morphemes and words within texts on a very abstract level. Sentences are examined with syntax, and word as well as sentence meaning are discerned by semantics. Although all of these domains deal with parts of texts, namely sounds, words and sentences, they fail to generate a broader understanding of the substantial and unique import of texts as such.

This we can only understand when observing how texts are *produced, presented,* and *received*. Whereas our inquiry so far was geared towards the *structure* of language, we are now going to ask: 'In what way do processes in text production, that is: *decision* and *selection* and their impact on *communicative interaction* generate structure?' This approach to linguistics, that is of regarding complete texts as entities of inquiry, is still fairly young, having come into being only in the 1970's. It is also referred to as text linguistics. However, the origin of this regard for texts goes way back to Ancient Greece and Rome, where philosophers founded the science of *rhetoric*. This science cultivates speech and examines the complete text for its applicability for an oral presentation and its overall effect and persuasive potential. As a discipline rhetoric received high esteem and was acknowledged as one of the main branches of science. This cultivation for spoken speech continued on even up to the Middle Ages, where the church implemented it for its aims. As a science of texts, rhetoric shares many concerns with text linguistics. Some assumptions are:

- The accessing and arranging of ideas is open to *systematic control.*
- The transition from idea to expression can be *consciously trained.*
- Among the various texts which express a given configuration of ideas, some are of a higher *quality* than others.
- Texts can be evaluated in terms of their *effects* on the audience.
- Texts are vehicles of *purposeful interaction."*

You may remember some of these notions from our chapter on pragmatics, however, while the emphasis then was on the use of language, it is now the whole text which is of interest.

THE PRINCIPLES OF TEXTUALITY

What constitutes a text? Usually, we do not think about how we produce or understand speech, i.e. the texts for speech. Still, there are basic principles that structure texts and it is, for example, thanks to our intuitive compliance to these principles that we still know what a discussion is all about even after ten minutes of talking. Also, you do not have to return to the first pages of a book whenever you start reading the next chapter, because you know that the text *proceeds.* You can even refer to other texts written in other books or taken from other media, such as newspapers. These constructive elements of texts are known as *textuality.* They help us in recognizing where texts start, where they end and how to perceive a text as an entity.

Cohesion

Texts are regarded as *stable systems* the stability of which is upheld by a *continuity of occurrences.* This means that elements re-occur throughout the text system and can thus be interrelated. Our short term memory does not lend itself for storing information on a larger scale. The *continuity of occurrences* thus serves to refresh this short term memory, creating a basis for a long term memory to function. Whereas cohesion within a sentence is constituted by syntax, it is this factor of the continuity of occurrences that makes for cohesion within a text. As you can already guess, cohesion is established by means of syntax. The way sentences are constructed help in establishing cohesion. The following features belong to the re-occurrences that make for the cohesion of texts:

Recurrence

The direct repetition of elements is called *recurrence*. It can fulfill many functions. However, whenever applied, the phenomenon of recurrence must be derived from a comprehensible motivation. The phrase "I met Sally and I met Sally.", for instance, seems awkward as there is just no reason for repeating the same element.

- One function recurrence fulfills is, as mentioned above, the enhancement of memory.
- In the recurrence of the following example, emphasis is the primary function.

"The other day, I met *Sally*. I mean, you know *Sally*. This *Sally* Atkins from the linguistics department. She's a nice person, good old *Sally*."

- Recurrence can also be used as a means to *repudiate* the assumptions of the other, as in the following example:

"I guess you love *snow, ice,* and the whole of *wintertime*!" — "Good grief! I certainly don't like *snow*, nor *ice*, and definitely not *wintertime*!"

- In poetic texts, recurrence is often used to emphasize the emotional peak of poems, as in the famous recurring last line of almost every stanza in Edgar Allan Poe's "Raven":

"Quoth the raven: nevermore."

In this example, the recurrence also helps to establish a

strong connection among the various stanzas. The reader may expect the same line to occur again.

Junction

Events and situations are combined in texts. This action is called *junction*. *Junctive expressions* are commonly known as *conjunctions*.

- *Conjunctions* link things of the same status: "and".
- *Disjunctions* link elements of an alternative status: "or".
- *Contrajunctions* link elements of the same status which are incompatible: "but".
- *Subordinators* link things where the status of one depends on the other: "because", "since"

Coherence

Whereas cohesion is the syntactical means of keeping a text together, there is also the meaning which interweaves the whole of a text. This meaning principle is called the *coherence* of a text.

Coherence can happen only under the condition of a set of prerequisites. For one, speakers must have a common *knowledge base* that they draw from. Secondly, there must be a *context* which is important in respect to the meaning (as we have seen in the chapter on pragmatics, the meaning of phrases depends on the intention and situation. Concepts in texts may hence change their meaning regardless of their sememe.)

Coherence, that is meaning, in texts, is in subsequence to these prerequisites determined by the so-called *control centers*, also called *primary concepts*, which are the pivots of the meaning structure of a text.

Control centers are:

- *Objects*: these have a stable identity, their core meaning does not change substantially. Persons, abstract concepts or things of any kind that are mentioned in a text play the role of objects.
- *Situations*: are configurations of objects in the present state of affairs.

- *Events*: these are occurrences which change a situation.
- *Actions*: events intentionally brought about by an *agent*. An agent is not necessarily a person or living being. Any item can gain the status of an agent. In the sentence "The wave rolled up the beach", 'wave' is the agent, performing the action of rolling.

There is a far more elaborate set of *secondary concepts*, which range from the *agent* to the *value* of an entity, but we will not go into this in detail.

Consider the example:

"The big red bus approached the stop. Its roaring exhaust frightened the small children and old ladies. A conductor was at hand to provide the group with tickets. The sun shone at the scene."

The dominating control center of the first part is clearly an object: "the big red bus". There is also an action, namely its approaching the bus stop. The next sentence just adds more information to the first, being attached directly to the primary concept by the cohesive means of *pro-forms* ("its"). As you can see, the object control center happens to be the subject of the sentence as well. It is grammatically the most important part of the sentence.

But the second part of the text is not so obviously coherent with the first part. What needs to be done to combine the two parts is called *interference*. By interfering, we fill gaps in the textual world with our knowledge from the real world. What makes us understand that the 'conductor' and 'tickets' can somehow be related to a bus exhaust, small children and old ladies is our common world knowledge. The 'conductor' is associated with the bus because this is where he works, the other persons are probably commuters. The 'scene' must be the setting of the bus standing at the stop with a group of people waiting to get in, etc.

Interferences are carried out intuitively by means of imaginative associations. However, empirical tests have shown that a slight degree of intuitive association takes place in all types of language processing. As thus it takes place not only when having to fill the gaps of explicitly textual worlds with real, experienced worlds.

Intentionality and Acceptability

You can also read the Speech Act Theory. We will thus only rehearse the basic principles here:

Cohesion and coherence are the most important principles of textuality. However, there are texts which are neither fully cohesive nor coherent. Hence, we must take the *attitude* of the language users toward the text into consideration. What is their *intention*? Presumably there is some planning involved in order to put the intention into words. Speakers may fail to clad their intention into a pattern both cohesive and coherent:

"You know, I – where am I? Ah, yes, last night I visited Dan, and he – but you do know Dan, don't you?"

We all know such inconsistent sentences from our everyday experience. They derive from the change of intention during the utterance. The change may be caused by an internal reflection or by some external event, such as a frowning listener. Nevertheless, when listening and talking we follow a *cooperative principle,* which, in turn, places the text into an *acceptable* framework, even if their surface structure neglects cohesion and coherence.

Informativity

Informativity refers to whether the contents of a text is new or whether it was expected by the receiver. We differentiate here with the following features:

- *Probability*. Is the utterance probable? A sentence like: "I like Chinese food" is quite probable as far as *statistical probability* of correct sentences is concerned. But a sentence such as "All you foul dishes of the degenerate West, you cannot compete to my favorites from the East!" is much too unique to be statistically probable. Another aspect is *contextual probability*. When talking about food, for instance, a sentence like "And the new BMW is really nice to look at." is grossly out of context and as thus improbable.

- *Orders of informativity*. If the predictability of intention, cohesion, and coherence is high, we speak of *first-order informativity*. An example is the "stop" traffic sign, the content and structure of which is very unambiguous and conventionalized. First-order occurrences are also called *defaults*: they are used very often, such as certain phrases. But in order to make texts more interesting, informativity of second or third order must appear. Usually, texts consist more or less of second-order occurrences. These are *upgraded* or *downgraded* in order to produce either more predictable or more interesting bits of text. In a short story or novel, the author will rather use downgraded, unpredictable text. This will keep the reader focused on the book.
- *Text types*. The rate of informativity differs in the many various text types, such as literary, poetic, and scientific texts. Naturally, in poetry, the number of third-order occurrences is much higher than in scientific texts.

Situationality

Texts must be relevant to the current situation in which they appear. We distinguish between the following:

- *Situation monitoring* is being performed if the primary function of a text is to describe a given situation as best as possible.
- *Situation management* means that a text is designed to fit into a situation as best as possible.

Although texts have to be relevant to the situation in which they appear, the situation does not have to be a real situation, i.e. it can be fictional.

For example, in drama the audience is drawn into a situation generated on the stage. Thus, when Hamlet says "All's not well...", his monologue naturally does not mean that the audience is in Denmark, the setting of the play. In short, literary texts have the prerogative to present alternative situations in which they fit quite well.

Intertextuality

No text is really independent, i.e. all texts relate to others in one way or another. The expressions *textual field* or the *text universe* have been created by scholars to refer to this textual network.

The principle of intertextuality is that the structure (i.e. those principles listed above) of texts is determined largely by texts that have been received by authors or readers prior to that. Citations or a reuse of texts is one of the more obvious ways in which this principle applies. But intertextuality can also be detected in more subtler forms and occurs between various text types as well.

In the narrower sense of texts within the framework of text linguistics, we speak of intertextuality as the phenomenon of interference between various texts in a conversation. Situation management and monitoring depend heavily on other texts which have been uttered in the conversation. A receiver does not remain uninfluenced by these uttered texts and interrelates them with his own textual production.

Chapter 15

Sociolinguistics

If you study language as it is spoken by humans in everyday life, including the variations from area to area in a country or within different levels of society, you are dealing with *sociolinguistics* - the study of language in society. The discipline is still quite young, having been founded only in the late 1960's, but it now belongs to one of the established branches of linguistic study. In the Anglo-Saxon countries, sociolinguistics receives high esteem, especially in England, where the study of *dialects* and variations in the *stratified society* are a never-ending subject of research.

VARIATION IN LANGUAGE

It is quite obvious that different people use different languages. This is a given fact which you can experience when you travel from one country to another. Also, there are variations within one single *language community.*

There are various definitions of what a language community is. In general, we call a group of people using a common variant of a language a language community. For example, all people speaking a certain dialect of English are one speech community. However, speech communities can be discerned on other levels of society. There are male and female speech communities among the speakers of English. These differ due to the contrast of language use in men and women. On a social as well as a regional scale, such differentiations gain in weight. If you travel to Bavaria, people speak a kind of German which sounds quite different from the one spoken in Hamburg. A professor uses a different language than a janitor does. It then happens sometimes that values are attributed to these variations. People are considered to speak a "good" or "bad" English. The language of the teenage generation is sometimes valued as "declining". Sometimes, exotic languages spoken in foreign parts of the world are labeled "inferior" by people who are convinced that European languages should be regarded as the topmost standard. All these opinions are of no value to sociolinguistics. Rather, we try to classify various variants of languages by neutral features. Here are some of these basic features by which language variations can be classified.

- *Standardization*: Is the language variation recognized/ understood/spoken by a majority of speakers of one language community?
- *Vitality*: Is the language variation still developing or has it become static/unchangeable?
- *Historicity:* Does the language variation have a literate historical background? Note that this aspect does *not* mean the historical development of a variation.
- *Autonomy*: Is the variation an autonomous state of a language, i.e., can it be studied on its own or is the language variety a daughter language? In the latter case, it is dependent on the mother language which must be studied as well.
- *Reduction*: Is the variation a reduced form of a standard language, i.e., is its spectrum of features a part adopted from another variation that has a larger spectrum?
- *Mixture*: Is the variation a mixture of several languages?
- *'De facto' norms*: Is there a system of rules that govern the variation? These rules have to be acknowledged by all users. It must be recognizable whether these rules are violated.

The following chart gives examples for variations of English. These variations are from all over the world and cover many centuries. This aspect of language variation, language change in the course of history, we have discussed when we talked about the history of the English language. At this point it is important to keep in mind that language change should not be equated with the decay of a language, a notion which seems to be shared even more so by common, everyday people than by scholars. Language variations from all times and from all areas prove to have highly elaborated structures. Furthermore, if language was decaying over the times, we would have arrived at a devastated state already. The attribute numbers in the following chart refer to the attributes listed above.

ATTRIBUTES 1	2	3	4	5	6	7	LANGUAGE TYPE	EXAMPLE
+	+	+	+	±	–	+	Standard	Standard English
+	–	+	+	–		+	Classical	Classical Bible English
–	+	–	+	–	–	+	Vernacular	'Black English'
–	+	–	–	–	–	+	Dialect	Cockney
–	+	–	–	+	+	+	Creole	Krio
–	–	–	–	+	+	+	Pidgin	Neomelanesian
+	–	–	+	+	–	+	Artificial	'Basic English'
–	–	–	±	–	+	?	Xized Y	'Indian English'
–	–	–	–	+	+	–	Interlanguage	'Learner A's English'
–	–	–	–	+	±	–	Foreigner Talk	'B's simplified English'

Key to symbols: + possession of attribute – lack of attribute ± either + or – insufficient evidence

Regional Variation in Language

When we refer to language variations within an area

occupied by a language community, we speak of *dialects*. They have not evolved on their own accord, however, contrary to popular opinion, they can influence or even give rise to a standard language. The Romance languages are an example for this development. Originally, the languages French, Spanish, and Italian were very much alike. They were all variations of Latin and a citizen of the late Roman period would have regarded them as dialects of the same Latin. Today, the Romance languages are much more distinct. We can still see that they are closely related to each other, but they are definitely not dialects. We find *national variations* here.

The many peoples that inhabit Germany, for example, the Frisians, Saxons, Bavarians, and many more each constitute a distinct group of people. But unlike the different language groups of the Romance languages, the varieties of German spoken from the north to the south of Germany are only *regional variations* of the same language. The variations remain regional, because the German peoples have maintained close ties with one another throughout history. In many areas it is the geography that allows a speech community to either merge or diverge. The vast mountain ridge of the Pyrenees dividing France and Spain, for example, separated the speech communities so that their linguistic development diverged.

As you can see, languages distinguish themselves from one another or they may merge. Presently, the dialects of the German tongue are merging, for example. Some of its rare dialects have even become extinct.

Dialect vs. Accent

These are two terms which should not be confused. While a dialect is a distinct variation of a language bound to geographical regions or a social stratification, the accent of a speaker is a blend of his linguistic background with his effort to pronounce the standard language or a distinct dialect of a completely different language group. The accent a person may show hence only occurs when he or she uses a language variety or a language different from their own. A person can speak French with an English accent, or Standard English with a West

Midland accent. The variety of English the person is used to at her or his home is then the dialect, e.g. "Black Country English" of the West Midlands.

Varieties of English

There are variations in the English within any one English speaking country just as there are variations between the English of different English speaking countries. You are already aware of the different pronunciation of the/A:/ (British),/Q/ (American) respectively, as in "dance". There are, however, many more differences. One of these is the vocabulary. There are different words used in both countries for the same things:

American	British
Elevator	Lift
Flashlight	Torch
Can	Tin
Truck	Lorry
TV	Telly

The various dialects within the countries are dependent on geographical regions. In order to locate them with more precision on a map, the usage of words or expressions is documented and evaluated throughout the country. These statistics then allow for marking the boundaries that separate the regional dialects. These boundaries are called *isoglosses*.

Three dialects of North America, for example, North Midland, South Midland, and Southern can be identified by the variation of the standard word "bastard". In the North, such a person is called a "come-by-chance", in the Midlands an "old-field colt", and in the South a "woods colt".

Sodial Variation in Language

A language variation may well reveal social rank. This applies to language variations of the whole country on a *macro level* as well as to regions on a *micro level*. In the 1950's, a linguist named Bernstein examined social differences in language. He could trace two profoundly different *codes*, namely the elaborated and the restricted code.

Elaborated vs. Restricted Code

- The restricted code is used by a certain social group only. Speakers of the restricted code wish to establish and maintain close contact with the group. They do not use it when in contact with representatives of other social groups.
- Elaborated code is less personal and more formal. It applies to situations where the speaker cannot rely on the immediate sympathy or understanding of the group. In the following, you find differences in more detail.

Restricted code	**Elaborated code**
• Consists of short, grammatically simple	• Accurate grammatical order and syntax sentences
• Simple and repetitive use of conjunctions	• Logical modifications & stress are mediated through range of conjunctions and relative clauses
• Infrequent use of impersonal pronouns	• Rigid and limited use of adverbs • Frequent use of "one" ("one") as subject
• Discriminative selection from a range of adverbs and adjectives	• Statements formulated as implicit questions which set up sympathetic circularity
• Frequent use of short commands temporal and spatial contiguity	• Frequent use of prepositions indicating logical relations and
• A statement of fact is often used as both a reason and conclusion	• Individual selection from a group of idiomatic phrases will frequently be found

Objections

Consider the following example:

- "The blokes what was crossing the road got knocked down by a car."
- "The gentlemen were crossing the road and a car knocked them down instantly."

Although the first sentence is not standard, it is, according to the above features, more elaborated than the second one in certain respects. There is a subordinate clause in the sentence while the second sentence consists of two main clauses.

The use of subordinate clauses is held to be more elaborate.

Still, the lexis, that is, word choice of the second sentence is located on a higher level. Elaborated code and restricted code seem to blur in our example. This phenomenon leads to the conclusions that

- Everyone uses a restricted code,
- There is not an exact correlation between restricted-non-standard and elaborated-standard codes.
- However, the restricted code does not lend itself for logical, theoretical purposes, or for expressing a temporal succession of events.

We find that it is due not only to the existence of different social classes, but also to diverging circumstances of people as individuals, that these different codes have come to develop. Middle class people, for instance, are confronted more often with theoretical topics, which is why they use the elaborated code more frequently than working class people do. On the strictly individual level, a person never forced to deal with more complex ideas may not use metalanguage, while others may seek complexity on their own accord.

Code Switching

Humans are known to be flexible. They easily adopt the habits of their surroundings in order to fit into the respective social group. This is why we are able to *switch codes*. Watch yourself closely: you will find yourself using elaborated and restricted sentence structures according to the situation: family, university, friends, etc. Each group seems to prescribe a certain code.

Ethnic Variation in Language

Variation in language among ethnic groups is somewhat similar to the one among social classes. Whether or not a person identifies him-/herself in the first place with his/her ethnic origin or with his/her social class may depend on many factors. One factor has to do with whether this ethnic group is a minority in that society - a person who belongs to an ethnic group that is a minority of that society is likely to identify him- or herself more with his ethnic group than with a social class. In any event -

- Ethnic groups may speak a language which is different from that of the dominating society
- If ethnic groups speak the same language, it has a series of linguistic variables

Examples are the Italian and Jewish groups in New York City. Most of these immigrants who arrived in New York in the 19th century never quite learned to speak English. Their children grew up with the English language as it was spoken in schools and in everyday life, however, their ethnic background left its marks on their English. It is for this reason that in the New York accents of both groups, some characteristics appear that cannot be found anywhere, by no member of any social class in the United States. One example is the *high onglide of mid vowels* in the words "dog" and "coffee":/dog/ and/kofI/ became/dUog/ and/kUofI/. This *high onglide* is considered very poor language by other American speakers of English.

The most outstanding example for ethnic variation in the English language is *Black English Vernacular* BEV. It has been cultivated to the extent that this same dialect is spoken by Blacks throughout the United States.

Obviously it is also the racial conflicts that continue on up to the present that have led this ethnic minority to distinguish themselves from white, main-stream America by language. One feature of *Black English Vernacular* is that verbal skills are valued very highly. What we know as *rap,* only recently made known to a wider public through pop music, has long been a means of poetic expression among blacks. Some street poets are able to do spontaneous rap rhymes of several hours' length.

Lingua Franca, Pidgins and Creoles

These are special cases of variation which come to exist where people speaking various languages meet and need to communicate.

- 'Lingua franca' refers to any variation that evolves out of the need to facilitate communication among people whose mother tongues are different. The variation does not necessarily have to be the mother tongue of any one of the participants and does not have to be fully developed. One example is "air speak", a variation of English spoken by pilots and flight personnel. The term lingua franca most probably derived from the name given to the simplified French dialect spoken by the crusaders in the Middle Ages: lingua franca, language of the Francs. This variety was widely used around the Mediterranean.
- 'Pidgin' is a variation deriving from the need of speakers of differing mother tongues to communicate within a restricted context, such as trade. In contrast to a Lingua Franca, a pidgin Language derives by mixing various features of two or more languages. In most cases, the native languages of the people living in European colonies were mixed with the colonists' languages. A pidgin is a language variety invented by the speakers. Therefore, there is no native speaker of a pidgin language; i.e. no speaker born into this language as their mother tongue. Various Pidgin languages arose from the contact of whites with native people in the Americas and Africa as well as Asia. Among the qualities that all Pidgins have in common is that they evince a rather restricted

vocabulary and lack tense markers. Their grammar is therefore elaborated to a minimal extent. Examples from Neo-Melanesian or Tok Pisin are:

"mi go" = "I go", but also "I went", "I will go", etc.
"mi lukim yu" = "I see/will see you", etc.
"gras bilong het" = "hair"

- 'Creole', etymologically derived from the native tribe of the *Criollio,* refers to a Pidgin variation that has become established and conventionalized to the extent that it can be called a language. For instance, if two people of different language communities marry, they will create a Pidgin variation. This, in turn, becomes the mother tongue of their children who elaborate this Pidgin with more grammatical features, such as case markers and an expansion of vocabulary. The language variety can then be called a *Creole language.*

This phenomenon occurs on a wide scale wherever two cultures mix, as has happened during colonization. In the second and third generations, Creole languages tend to merge more and more with the dominating parent language. In former colonies, this is the respective European tongue. The Creole then merges into the so-called *Post-Creole Continuum.* At the end of the process, only traces of the original Pidgin or Creole languages remain. The language spoken then resembles the standard, usually a European language. In some countries, native languages are also official languages, but Creoles are mostly doomed to become extinct.

Variation in Language and Sex

In most languages of the world, men and women do not speak identically. In English, some words are used more often by females than by males and vice versa. Some of the "female" words are, for instance, "lovely, darling, cute". Linguistic tests have also shown that boys prefer the/In/ to the/IN/ in words like "testing, riding, hiking", while the opposite is valid for girls. In speaking, males tend to speak a variety that is diverging from the standard while women's language tends to converge with the standard. This may even lead to over corrections by female speakers. Hence our gender does seem to influence our way of speaking. The English as well as the German language is, furthermore, very male-dominated as masculine titles and pronouns are applied when references to a general public or an unknown addressee are made.

An example is 'chairman', while it could just as well be a woman.

The branch of *feminist linguistics* has thus evolved to explore these matters in more detail and to strip language of its discriminatory features.

Some results are the he/she statements which you find throughout this paper or the famous capital "I" in German words, like "Student Innen". Other novelties are "chairperson" instead of "chairman". Policemen became police officers, etc.

REGISTER AND STYLE

Style

Stylistics is a science which explores all the formal characteristics of language. *Style* then is a selection of a set of linguistic features from all the possibilities in the language.

It includes, for example, word choice and grammar. We have a 'feel' of what has 'no style', or what it 'out of style', yet when trying to pinpoint just what it is that makes a text, speech, or anything for that matter, stylish, we may be at a loss for words.

Stylistics tries to explore this matter.

Style is something which is of importance to the speakers of a language. There is "good style" and "bad style", "high" as well as "low" style, etc.

These qualifications are commonly made by examining to what extent the possibilities of, say, grammar have been exploited by a speaker.

A speaker performing incomplete sentences will not be regarded to have "good" style. An individual may use one particular style all his life, but there is also something called *style shifting*.

This is in some aspects similar to code switching. People can adapt their style to any context. Some aspects of style can be the use of tenses (more past or more present), frequency of foreign words, amount of vocabulary.

Register

Linguists try to also observe and register the different *occupational varieties* or *role relatives* of language.

They are differentiated according to a various criteria and are then comprise a compendium of 'registers'.

Some of the aspects that are observed in a register are:

- Job relativity. Is written language used frequently? Is it broadcast spoken language?
- Length of sentences. Are there many subordinate clauses involved? What is the average amount of words per sentence?
- Specific vocabulary. Does the speaker use a certain amount of foreign words? Does he/she use a basic vocabulary or are there specialist words in the texts?
- Archaic language. Can we find old-fashioned pronunciation, word choice, etc. in the language variety?
- Appearance in writing, such as capital letters, etc. This is interesting for registers of the print media, such as newspapers, books, reports, written laws.
- Rules to save time. Are there acronyms? Military English, for example, is full of those. Abbreviations and elliptic sentences are further examples.
- Thematic ordering (first things first, etc.). Is there a thematic structure in the register? Again, newspaper articles are a good example. The yellow press will first name the amount of a disaster's victims, their age, family relations, etc. while a conservative magazine will most probably inform the readers about the cause, time, place, etc.

By examining speech varieties, we can easily discern registers.

Some registers in English are:

- Children's programs. No subordinate clauses, simple sentences, slow voice, simple lexis.
- Scientific texts. Many adjectives, technical terms, long sentences, argumentation lines, present tense, special graphic presentation.
- Language at court (legal language). Formal language, ancient words, repetition of certain structures, formal, slow language.
- Letter writing. Colloquial expressions, emotional, handwriting, syntax approximates thought structure.

Chapter 16

Cognitive Linguistic and Unified Style Sheet for Linguistics

Language, in general, has always been an intricate matter for research. In the course of development of the linguistics as a field of studies particularly dedicated to the task of exploring the language faculty and its features a lot of breakthrough discoveries have been made. With respect to the particular point of research, there are several subcategories of linguistics that are the direct result of the interactive research on a particular phenomenon.

The cognitive linguistics is, doubtlessly, one of the few such linguistic branches, that is composed of the research fields of sciences such as: psychology, anthropology, philosophy and computer science. However, cognitive linguistics does not focus on particular features of language or particular parts of the grammar, but attempts to discover its interplay with perception of the world, that is, the reality that surrounds the human beings. In its characterisation of the language as part of the cognitive system and not an independent feature, the cognitive linguistics is in opposition to the generative linguistics and the Chomskyan postulation that language faculty is inborn.

Moreover, Chomsky claims that language is "modular", that is, it exists individually from the other cognitive faculties. The main aim of the cognitive linguistics is to discover the laws of structure of natural language categorisation as well as the intricate connection between language and thought. Terry Regier defines its function in the following manner: "In the domain of semantics in particular, cognitive linguistics seeks to ground meaning not directly in the world, but in mental and perceptual representations of the world". As the methodology and historical development of this field of studies are quite extensive, this paper will rather focus on the analysis of the main division of classical, also known as Aristotelian and modern theory.

In the analysis of these two juxtaposed theories the pioneer work of the linguist William Labov and the psychologist Elisabeth Rosch would be taken into consideration. An emphasis would be put on Eleanor Rosch's findings with respect to the extent of her contribution to the new ways of understanding categorisation of entities and clarification of certain aspects. Furthermore, some critical approaches of her findings would be regarded.

Cognitive linguistics is, above all, concerned with the phenomenon of categorisation and the ways in which humans categorise the entities in the real world. The process of selecting and combining certain entities into groups is a process of perceiving the real world and by organising the impressions in groups, a clear overview of the experiences is established.

Furthermore, this concept of categorisation allows room for classification of new entities that may occur in a language in the course of time and thus, understanding them without any additional coaching.

Even the field of study, that is analyzed in this paper, is a part of a particular categorisation. Although this process of perception of the real world has been accepted by many philosophers and other scientists involved with its analysis, the conception of the way in which the categories of entities are created is not always identical.

Ray Jackendoff discusses the essence of categorization for the cognitive linguistics: An essential (perhaps the essential) aspect of cognition is the ability to categorize: to judge that a particular thing is or is not an instance of a particular category.[...]

The ability to categorize is what makes it possible to use previous experience to guide the interpretation of new experience, for without categorization, memory is virtually useless. Thus, an account of the organism's capacity for categorization is not just a matter of the semantics of predicative sentences; it is central to all of cognitive psychology.

Numerous studies have been conducted on the topic of the elements that constitute the term of categorisation. Jackendoff states further in his book Consciousness and the Computational Mind what is understood under primary distinction within the frames of categorisation: The primary distinction that must appear in conceptual structure in order to be able to encode categorization is between the individual things (tokens) being categorized and the categories (types) to which the tokens do or do not belong.

UNIFIED STYLE SHEET FOR LINGUISTICS

These guidelines grew out of discussions among a group of editors of linguistics journals during 2005-2006 and were approved on January 7, 2007. They are intended as a "default, but with discretion to use common sense", to quote David Denison on the matter. Our principles, as elaborated primarily by Stan Dubinsky, are:

- Superfluous font-styles should be omitted. Do not use small caps for author/editor names, since they do not help to distinguish these from any other bits of information in the citation. In contrast, italics are worthwhile for distinguishing volume (book, journal, dissertation) titles [+ital] from article and chapter titles [-ital].
- Superfluous punctuation should be left out. Once italic is adopted to distinguish volumes from articles/ chapters (as above), then single or double quotations around article titles are superfluous and only add visual clutter.
- Differing capitalization styles should be used to make category distinctions.

Use capitalization of all lexical words for journal titles and capitalize only the first word (plus proper names and the first word after a colon) for book/dissertation titles and article/ chapter titles.

This is a useful diagnostic for discriminating between titles that are recurring and those that are not.

The journal style for capitalization should also be applied to the title of book series.

Thus, the citation of a *SNLLT* volume would be punctuated: *Objects and other subjects: Grammatical functions, functional categories, and configurationality* (Studies in Natural Language and Linguistic Theory 52).

- All author/editor first names should be spelled out. Not doing so only serves to make the citation less informative. Without full first names, the 20th century index for *Language* alone would conflate five different people as 'J. Smith', four as 'J. Harris', three each under 'A. Cohen' and 'P. Lee', two each under 'R. Kent', 'J. Anderson', 'H. Klein' and 'J. Klein'.
- The ampersand is useful. Use ampersand to distinguish higher and lower order conjuncts, i.e. [W & X] and [Y & Z], as in Culicover & Wilkins and Koster & May. It is relatively easy to see that reference is made here to two pairs of authors here (cf. Culicover and Wilkins and Koster and May).
- Name repetitions are good. While using a line ____ may save a little space, or a few characters, it also makes each such citation referentially dependent on an antecedent, and the effort of calculating such antecedents is more than what it saved typographically. Each citation should be internally complete.
- Four digit year plus period only. Extra parentheses are visual clutter and superfluous.
- Commas and periods and other punctuation. Separate citation components with periods (e.g., Author. Year. Title.) and subcomponents with commas (e.g., Author1,Author 2 & Author 3). Please note the ampersand (&), rather than the word "and" before the name of the last author, and no comma

before the "&". The use of the colon between title and subtitle and between place and publisher is traditional, but we do not use it between journal volume number and page numbers.

- Parentheses around ed. makes sense. Commas and periods should be used exclusively to separate citation components (e.g., "Author. Year."), or subcomponents (e.g. "author1, author2 & author3). Since "ed." is neither a component nor a subcomponent, but a modifier of a component, it should not be separated from the name by a comma: surname, first name = author surname, first name (ed.). = editor (NOT surname, first name, ed.) surname, first name & first name surname (eds.) = editors
- For conference proceedings, working papers, etc. For conference proceedings published with an ISSN, treat the proceedings as a journal: Include both the full conference name and any commonly used acronym for the conference (*BLS, WCCFL,* etc.) in the journal title position. For proceedings not published with an ISSN, treat the proceedings as any other book, using the full title as listed on the front cover or title page. If the title (and subtitle if there is one) only includes an acronym for the conference name, expand the acronym in square brackets or parentheses following the acronym. If the title does not include an acronym which is commonly used for the conference name, include the acronym in square brackets or parentheses following the conference name. The advantage of including the acronym after the society title is that it makes the entry much more identifiable in a list of references.
- Use "edn." as an abbreviation for "edition", thus "2nd edn.". This avoids ambiguity and confusion with "ed." (editor).
- Names with "von", "van", "de", etc. If the "van" (or the "de" or other patronymic) is lower case and

separated from the rest by a space (e.g. Elly van Gelderen), then alphabetize by the first upper-case element:

The addition of "see ..." in comprehensive indices and lists might be helpful for clarification:

van Gelderen, Elly.

- Names with "Jr.", "IV.", etc. Following library practice, list elements such as "Jr." as a sub element after names, separated by a comma. Smith, Sean, Jr.
- Use "In" to designate chapters in collections. This makes the book's format maximally similar to the standard citation format. This, in turn, would be time-saving when the author or the editor notice that more than one article is cited from a given collection and hence that that book's details should be set out as a separate entry in the references (and the full details deleted from the articles' entries). author. year. chapter title. In editor name (ed.), collection title, pagenumbers. publisher.
- Journal volume numbers. We favor: volume number (volume issue). starting page- ending page. Note the space between volume number/issue and page numbers. Special formatting (e.g., bold for volume number) is superfluous. Issue numbers are a parenthetical modifier (cf. "ed." above) of the volume number. While it is not necessary information for identifying the article, it is extremely useful information.
- Dissertations/theses. These conform to the already-widespread Place: Publisher format and fit readily into the rest of the standard: Cambridge, MA: MIT dissertation.

Instead of archaic state abbreviations, use the official two-letter postal abbreviations. Note that national and other traditions vary in exactly what is labeled 'thesis' versus 'dissertation' and in distinguishing 'PhD' from 'doctoral' dissertations. Cambridge, MA: MIT dissertation. Chapel Hill: UNC MA thesis.

- Online materials. The basic information here — author, date, title — remains the same, and the URL where the resource was found takes the place of publisher or journal. We urge authors to include the date the material was accessed, in parentheses! after the URL, since new versions often replace old ones. For a .pdf file, this would be the date of downloading, but for a resource like an online dictionary consulted repeatedly, a range of dates may be needed.

Chapter 17

Stress, Information and Language Typology

Stress theory covers word stress and phrasal stress. The former can differ from language to language. Whether the latter can also differ from language to language is still an open question. This article reviews several theories of phrasal stress and points out their shortcomings. Then a new theory is proposed, which is called the 'Information-Stress Principle', according to which phrasal stress is determined by information load: words with more information should be stressed and words with less information need not. The information load of a word can be determined by the speaker and his/her environment; it can also be determined by information theory, syntactic structure, and the context. The new theory is simpler that previous ones, without their shortcomings, and offers a simpler view of language typology.

INTRODUCTION

Every language has stress. In some languages, stress can distinguish word meanings, as shown in

- In some languages, stress is not used to distinguish word meanings, but it still occurs, such as in contrastive stress, exemplified in (2). For clarity we use underline to indicate stressed syllables.
- Stress used to distinguish word meanings (English)
  Noun: *content*
  Verb: *content*
- Contrastive stress (Shanghai Chinese)

wo bu xing Wang, wo xing Huang I not named Wang, I named Huang 'My name is not Wang, but Huang.'

A stressed syllable is usually longer, with a full rime (no reduction), and often a certain pitch contour, or wider pitch range. However, in tone languages (such as Chinese and Japanese), since pitch is used to contrast word meanings, native judgment for stress is often unclear.

Most stress theories often focus on word stress. Less discussion is given to stress above the word level. In this study we focus on the latter, which we shall refer to as phrasal stress, which covers both compound stress and phrasal stress.

THEORIES OF PHRASAL STRESS

In this section we review main theories of phrasal stress in the past 40 years.

Chomsky and Halle: Two Phrasal Stress Rules

Chomsky and Halle discuss English and propose two rules, which are the Compound Stress Rule and the Nuclear Stress Rule, rephrased in (3) and (4), where A and B are the immediate constituents of a compound or phrase, and underline indicates words that receive stress from the rules.

- Compound Stress Rule:

In a compound [A B], if B is a compound, then B gets stress, otherwise A gets stressed. Examples:

[A B] *black-board*
[A [B C]] *stone black-board*
[[A B] C] *black-board store*

- Nuclear Stress Rule:

In [A B], B gets stress.
Examples:
[A B] *many people*
[A [B C]] *many old people* [[A B] C] *many people arrived*

Chomsky and Halle did not discuss stress in other languages, nor did they explain why compounds and phrases have different stress rules. For them, therefore, it is possible that in some languages compounds and phrases both have left-headed stress (i.e. stress on the left), or both have right-headed stress (i.e. stress on the right), or compounds have right-headed stress and phrases have left-headed stress.

Halle and Vergnaud: Stress Parameters

Chomsky proposes that differences among languages can be attributed to different settings of a few parameters. Following this idea, Halle and Vergnaud propose that stress differences in different languages can be attributed to a set of stress parameters. .

Stress parameters:

[+/-bounded] whether the length of a foot is limited

[left/right] whether stress in a foot is on the left or on the right

For example, we can translate the rule in (4) as the parameter settings in (6).

Nuclear Stress Rule:

[-bounded, right] unlimited foot length, stress on the right

It can be seen that the parameter settings of Halle and Vergnaud do not depend on syntax. For example, when choosing stress parameters for compounds, some languages can choose left-headed stress, and some can choose right-headed stress.

Therefore, in principle some languages can have stress patterns that are opposite to those in English: compounds are right-headed (instead of left-headed), and phrases are left-headed (instead of right-headed). However, the focus of Halle and Vergnaud is still word stress. Although they assume that phrasal stress can differ in different languages, no examples are given.

Non-head Stress

Duanmu propose that the two phrasal stress rules can be combined into one, shown in (7), where underline indicates a constituent that receives stress.

- Non-head Stress:

In a syntactic structure [A B], one is the head and the other the non-head. Phrasal stress is assigned to the non-head.

Examples: [X YP]

[YP X]
[ZP [X YP]]

In most cases, the Non-head Stress rule gives similar results as the two rules of Chomsky and Halle.

• Illustration of the Non-head Stress rule

Compounds:
[A B] *black-board*
[A [B C]] *stone black-board* (not [A [B C]])
[[A B] C] *black-board store*

Phrases:
[P NP] *in school*
[V NP] *watch movies*
[AP (F) NP] *pretty (F) woman* (not [AP N])

For compounds, there is a slight difference for the structure [A [B C]], where the result of Duanmu seems to agree with native intuition better. In phrases, the structure [AP (F) NP] follows the analysis of current syntactic theory, where the syntactic head is not the noun, as traditionally assumed, but a functional element F (similar to the *de* in Chinese).

Cumulative Stress

Cinque proposes that phrasal stress us directly related to the depth of syntactic structure. Stress starts from the deepest syntactic units (the innermost brackets) and accumulates along the way.

The proposal of Cinque is very similar to the Non-head Stress rule of Duanmu, because in a syntactic structure, the syntactic non-head always has a deeper structure than the syntactic head. The syntactic non-head has a deeper structure because it is phrasal in nature and can expand. In contrast, the syntactic head is a word (or a morpheme), which cannot expand.

Phrasal Stress can Differ in Different Languages

According to Duanmu and Cinque, phrasal stress can be derived from syntax, and it works the same way for all languages. Ladd offers a different view. He believes that 'accentuation ... is a matter of the grammar of specific languages rather than of universal principles'. Ladd does not discuss in which ways phrasal stress can differ from language to language, but offers some hypothetical examples.

- Hypothetical examples of variation in phrasal stress (uppercase indicates stress)

Language A	Language B
This is book RED	*This is BOOK red I bought car*
NEW	*I bought CAR new He has nose*
BIG He has NOSE big	

Even if two languages have exactly the same syntax (in terms of word order), they can still differ in phrasal stress. Ladd also offers some other examples, to be discussed later.

Focus Stress

Phrasal stress can be derived from syntax. However, unlike previous people, who treat normal stress and focus separately, normal stress and focus can be treated in the same way.

It can be shown by answers to question sentences. A focus can be large or small, ranging from one word.

- Focus (new information, indicated by underline)
  - Question: Who watched a movie?
    Answer: John watched a movie.
  - Question: What's the news today?
    Answer: John bought a book.

The focus of the answer is *John*. The focus of the answer is the entire sentence. The two answers have the same syntax, but the main stress falls on different words.

When the focus is the entire sentence, the stress rule of Zubizarreta and Vergnaud, which is similar to those of Duanmu and Cinque.

- Assign main prominence to the first selectional dependent.

Example: [XP X], [X XP], [XP [XP X]]

Or: Assign main prominence to the category that is lowest in the asymmetric command ordering.

Example: [XP X], [X XP]

The 'selected dependent' and 'c-commanded category' are similar to the syntactic non-head of Duanmu, and the 'lowest category' is similar to the deepest constituent of Cinque. *Book* is the lowest category, which is also the location of main stress. Therefore, the prediction of stress assignment is correct.

When the focus is smaller than the entire sentence, how is stress assigned? Zubizarreta and Vergnaud propose a de-accent rule, rephrased in .

- The de-accent rule:

Anaphoric material is de-accented.

Watched a movie is the anaphoric material, which is de-accented. In the tree representation in (13), the de-accented part is shown in parentheses.

- Representation of de-accenting

John (watched a movie)

The original stress inside the parentheses will be ignored. As a result, only *John* is visible, and therefore it carries main stress.

PROBLEMS WITH CURRENT THEORIES

There are some common problems in the theories just reviewed. First, why should some constituents (such as the syntactic non-head) have more stress than others? No answer is offered.

Second, why should there be more stress on the focus? There is no explicit answer either.

Third, it has been noted that frequent words often have less stress than infrequent words.

- Frequent: *information* [Z] *astronomy* [ ]

Infrequent: *importation* [oZ] *gastronomy* [æ]

The word pair *information* and *importation* are similar in structure, yet there is stress reduction in the former but not in the latter.

Similarly, *astronomy* and *gastronomy* are also similar in structure, yet there is stress reduction in the former but not in the latter. Why should frequent word have less stress than infrequent ones? There is no explicit explanation in stress theories either.

THE INFORMATION-STRESS PRINCIPLE

We propose a new theory of phrasal stress, which we call the Information-Stress Principle. It offers a uniformed explanation of the problems just mentioned. Let us consider contrastive stress first, where underline indicates words under contrast.

- Contrastive stress:
  - *My name is Huang, not Wang.*
  - *John didn't buy a movie; he borrowed one.*

Contrastive stress falls on *Huang* and *Wang*. In the next line contrastive stress falls on *buy* and *borrowed*. Words under contrast are spoken with greater prominence and are intuitively quite clear to native speakers. One would assume that all languages have contrastive stress, and that all contrastive stress works the same way, namely, words under contrast have more stress than other words. In particular, we do not expect any language that uses an opposite version of contrastive stress (anti-contrastive stress), where underline indicates stressed words.

- Anti-contrastive stress (hypothetical case)

My name is Huang, not Wang.

Words under contrast have more information of interest, and more stress should be given to words that carry more information. Although this principle seems quite simple, it can explain a lot of problems.

- The Information-Stress Principle:

Words with more information are spoken with more stress.

The words under contrast (and hence with more information) are spoken with more stress, which satisfies the Information-Stress Principle. The words under contrast are not spoken with more stress, which violates the Information-Stress Principle. Next we consider how information load is determined. According to Information Theory, the information load of a sign depends on the probability of its occurrence.

- Information load:
  - The more likely a word is found, the less

information load it has.

- The more possible words there are for a given syntactic position, the less probability each word has, and the more information load it has for that position.

The definition of information load in effect says that the more unexpected something is, the more information it provides. This concept is intuitively natural.

a. The Chinese table tennis team won the championship.

b. The Chinese soccer team won the championship!

c. A patient woke up after seven years in a coma!!!

Let us take a closer look at how information load is calculated. Consider the English sentence in (20), where we focus on the information load of the last two words.

• (He has)	a car.
Word category:	article noun
Number of choices:	2 thousands
Probability per word:	high low
Information load:	low high

A singular noun in English can only take one of two articles (either *a* or *the*), but there are thousands of nouns. Therefore, in the article position, the probability of each article is very high, and its information load is very low. In the noun position, on the other hand, the probability for each noun is very low, and so its information load is very high.

Each Chinese noun has a designated classifier when it occurs with a numeral. There are only a dozen or two common classifiers. In the classifier position, therefore, the number of choices is low, but in the noun position the number of choices is very high. Consequently, the probability of a classifier is high and its information load is low, whereas the probability of a noun is low and its information load is high.

Chao and Yuan have discussed the relation between the number of word choices and their information load. Ladd has discussed the relation between information and stress, although he only focused on compounds. We shall return to Ladd's discussion below.

Before we end this section, let us consider one more question: why should a word with more information be spoken with more stress? There are two possible answers. The first was suggested to me by LU Bingfu and YUAN Yulin independently, according to which the Information-Stress Principle reflects an intentional and functional behavior: the speaker puts more stress on words with more information in order to express ideas more clearly, so that the listener can understand the meaning better.

This explanation in turn can be related to the Cooperative Principle of conversation of Grice. However, while the explanation seems quite plausible, there are some questions. First, it is a hypothesis, and there is no evidence for it; indeed, it is hard to collect relevant evidence for it. Second, apart from contrastive stress and focus, Chinese speakers generally lack intuitive judgment on where phrasal stress is; the same can be said about English speakers, too.

Therefore, it is hard to assume that speakers are consciously manipulating phrasal stress to improve communication. Third, when one is speaking to no audience (e.g. to one self), as it happens sometimes, there is no issue of the Cooperative Principle, yet the stress pattern still follows the Information-Stress Principle. Finally, the Cooperative Principle does not explain how information load is defined, and therefore, it offers no mechanism to assign stress properly. We still need to supplement it with Information Theory, and the application of Information Theory to word categories and syntactic structures.

The second explanation of the Information-Stress Principle is that it reflects a natural and subconscious behavior: when one thinks of words with more information, the relevant neurons are more excited, which in turn leads to greater stress in the articulation. This is similar to laughter: when one is happy, laughing is first of all an instinct, instead of the desire to let others know that you are happy. Similarly, the basic reason we close our eyes when we sleep is first of all an instinctive or natural behavior, instead of wanting to tell others that we are tired.

USING THE INFORMATION-STRESS PRINCIPLE TO EXPLAIN STRESS EFFECTS

In this section we illustrate how the Information-Stress Principle can account for various kinds of stress effects.

The Non-head Stress

We begin with the Non-head Stress rule, because many other effects can be derived from it. According to the Non-head Stress rule, any syntactic unit has a head and a non-head, represented as [X XP] or [XP X], where X is the syntactic head and XP the syntactic non-head. But why should XP have more stress? The answer lies in the Information-Stress Principle.

- The Information-Stress Principle and Non-head Stress

	X (head)	**XP (non-head)**
Level	word	phrase
Choices	limited	unlimited
Probability high	low	
Information low	high	
Stress	low	high

The syntactic head is a unit at the word (or morpheme) level, which cannot be expanded. Regardless of how many choices there are, the number is limited. In contrast, the syntactic head is a unit at the phrase level, which can be expanded freely, and its number of choices is in principle unlimited. Therefore, the syntactic head has a high probability of occurrence and a low information load. In contrast, the syntactic non-head has a low probability of occurrence and a high information load. Therefore, the syntactic non-head has more stress.

THE COMPOUND STRESS RULE

Chomsky and Halle propose that in a compound the first word has more stress. In the present analysis, this is because the first word is the syntactic non-head, which should have stress. As just discussed, the Non-head Stress is itself derivable from the Information-Stress Principle.

THE NUCLEAR STRESS RULE)

Chomsky and Halle propose that in phrases the second constituent has more stress. In the present analysis, this is because in English the second constituent is the syntactic non-head. Example is:

- *buy cars*
  in school

According to Non-head Stress (which derives from the Information-Stress Principle), the syntactic non-head should be stressed. Therefore, stress goes to the right in such phrases.

In some cases, Non-head Stress offers a simpler analysis than the Nuclear Stress Rule. Examples:

- Nuclear Stress: *Mary saw a rabbit*
  Non-head Stress: *Mary saw a rabbit*

The Nuclear Stress Rule assigns stress to *rabbit* only. In contrast, Non-head Stress assigns stress to both *Mary* and *rabbit,* because they are both syntactic non-heads. Specifically, *a rabbit* is a determiner phrase, where the head is *a* and the non-head is *rabbit*. The verb *saw* is the head of the verb phrase. The sentence is either a tense phrase or an inflection phrase, where the head is either a tense or inflection element, and the subject *Mary* is a non-head.

Mary indeed has stress, as Non-head Stress predicts. In order to obtain the same result, the Nuclear Stress Rule must be supplemented with another rule, which is called the Stress Equalization Convention. Its function is to add stress to words that do not lie at the right end of a phrase. In this regard, the Non-head Stress analysis is simpler, because it obtains the result directly, without the Stress Equalization Convention.

THE CUMULATIVE STRESS OF CINQUE (1993)

In the cumulative stress analysis, the deeper a syntactic unit is, the more stress it has. We have discussed earlier that cumulative stress is the same as non-head stress. The reason is that a syntactic non-head can expand, and therefore it can go deeper. In contrast, a syntactic head cannot expand and so it cannot go deeper. As a result, syntactic non-heads are generally deeper than syntactic heads.

THE FOCUS STRESS OF ZUBIZARRETA AND VERGNAUD (2000)

There are two parts in the stress theory of Zubizarreta and Vergnaud (2000). When the entire sentence is the focus, the stress assignment is similar to that of Non-head Stress. When the focus is smaller than the entire sentence, we first exclude the non-focus part, and then apply stress assignment to the remainder, which is again similar to the analysis of Non-head Stress. The question to explain then is: Why should we exclude the non-focus part from stress assignment?

By definition, the non-focus part is what has just been mentioned, or what is already known. According to the Information-Stress Principle, this part has no new information, or low information load. Therefore, it is not have given stress.

STRESS DIFFERENCES AMONG COMPOUNDS

As discussed earlier, according to the Compound Stress Rule of Chomsky and Halle (1968), the first word of a compound should be stressed. However, there are some exceptions in English, as shown below, where underline indicates main stress.

Madison Street Madison Avenue Madison Road Madison Drive

All expressions are street names. However, when the second word is *Street*, main stress is on the first word, but when the second word is *Avenue, Road,* or *Drive,* main stress is on the right. Such differences are hard to explain from a purely syntactic point of view.

Ladd proposes that compound stress should not be derived from syntax, but from semantics, or information load. When a word does not have much information, it should not be stressed, but when a word has a lot of information, it should be stressed. Among English street names, *street* is the most common and the most expected, and therefore it has the least information load.

In contrast, *avenue, road,* and *drive* are less common street names, and therefore they carry more information and should be stressed.

Ladd's conclusion is that English has just one stress rule, which is to assign stress to the right, including compounds. Compound stress is switched to the left only when the word on the right is a common one and has little information, such as *street* for street names.

Ladd's proposal is consistent with the Information-Stress Principle and can be adopted. However, we do not need to follow his conclusion that the default compound stress is on the right. Instead, we can keep the traditional idea that compound stress is on the left, unless the word on the right has high information load, in which case stress is switched to the right. In other words, English still has one stress rule, which is Non-head Stress.

Although both Ladd and the present analysis assume the Information-Stress Principle, and both assume one stress rule, Ladd's analysis is more complicated. First, his right-headed stress is an extra assumption, because it cannot be derived from the Information-Stress Principle.

In contrast, Non-head Stress is directly derivable from the Information-Stress Principle. Second, most English compounds, including newly created ones, have left-headed stress, such as *oatmeal, shoe store, pancake,* etc. If the default stress rule is right-headed, it is hard to explain such compounds. Ladd is aware of such cases and proposes that short compounds can be treated as simple nouns, and they have initial stress because most nouns do. But Ladd's proposal cannot explain why other short nominal expressions, such as *red car, old man, new book,* etc., rarely have initial stress. In other words, why are they not treated as nouns? The answer, obviously, is that compounds are different from phrases, and it is not just a matter of length. In Ladd's analysis, therefore, compounds and phrases follow different rules. In the present analysis, they follow the same stress rule.

STRESS DIFFERENCES AMONG WORD CATEGORIES

Different word categories often have different stress. For example, pronouns are often unstressed. In addition, grammatical words, such as prepositions, articles, and classifiers, are usually unstressed. On the other hand, content words, such as nouns and verbs, usually have stress. Moreover, nouns are more likely to have stress than verbs. Let us see how such effects can be explained by the Information-Stress Principle.

Pronouns pose a problem for several stress theories, including the Non-Head Stress rule of Duanmu, and the cumulative stress rule of Cinque (1993). Pronouns often occur either as the subject or as the object, which is a syntactic non-head and should have stress. Yet pronouns are usually unstressed.

The Information-Stress Principle can explain the apparently exceptional property of pronouns. The referent of a pronoun is often already obvious to the participants of a conversation. Therefore, it has low information load and does not get stress.

The lack of stress in grammatical words (prepositions, classifiers, articles, etc.) is due to two reasons. First, in current syntactic theory, grammatical words are syntactic heads, and according to Non-head Stress, they do not receive stress. The second reason is that there are far fewer function words than content words. For example, English has about ten prepositions, but thousands of nouns. Therefore, in a preposition position, the probability of each word is high and the information load is low. In contrast, in a noun position the probability of each word is low and the information load is high. Therefore, prepositions usually have less stress than nouns.

Both nouns and verbs are content words, but they also have a stress difference, which has been noted before, but without satisfactory explanation. In the present analysis, there are two reasons for their difference. First, verbs usually occur as the head of a verb phrase, and according to Non-head Stress, they do not receive phrasal stress. In contrast, nouns often occur as the subject or the object, which is a syntactic non-head, which is assigned stress by the Non-head Stress rule. The second reason is that there are more nouns than verbs in

English. In particular, in the CELEX English lexicon , there are 4,909 noun morphemes but just 1,628 verb morphemes. Thus, the probability of occurrence of an average verb is three times that of a noun, and its information load is one third of that of the latter. That could explain why verbs usually have less stress than nouns.

EMPHASIS AND CONTRAST

Any word in a sentence can be spoken with stress in order to express special emphasis. An example is shown in (25), where underline indicates emphasis.

She bought two new books.
She bought two new books.
She bought two new books.
She bought two new books.
She bought two new books.
She bought two new books.

Such emphasis may imply a contrastive meaning. For example, the second sentence could imply that *she bought a book, not him.*

According to Non-head Stress or cumulative stress , phrasal stress is determined by syntax. To explain emphasis, additional assumptions must be made.

However, if stress is determined by the Information-Stress Principle, then no additional assumption is necessary: the word under emphasis or contrast has more information of interest, and therefore it has more stress.

VARIABILITY IN PHRASAL STRESS

In an influential article, Bolinger makes the point that phrasal stress is unpredictable, unless 'you are a mind reader'. Whereas word stress is usually stable, phrasal stress is often variable.

Such variability is expected by the Information-Stress Principle.

Word stress is usually unrelated to meaning. In contrast, phrasal stress is based on meaning or information load. In addition, the information load of a word is not fixed but dependent on not only syntax but also the context and the knowledge of the participants of a conversation. Naturally, it can be variable.

FREQUENCY EFFECT

We discussed earlier that frequent words are more likely to undergo stress reduction than infrequent words. Some examples are given below, which show that frequent words undergo vowel reduction because of stress reduction, while infrequent words do not.

Frequent: *information* [æ] *astronomy* [æ]

Infrequent: *importation* [æ] *gastronomy* [æ]

Previous stress theories offer no explanation for such effects.

Under the Information-Stress Principle, an explanation is available.

Frequent words have a higher probability of occurrence and a lower information load. In contrast, infrequent words have a lower probability of occurrence and a higher information load. Therefore, infrequent words are more likely to be stressed.

The frequency of a word can vary from speaker to speaker. For example, Fidelholtz points out that *trombone* is a frequent word for trombonists, who tend to reduce the first vowel to [Y]. For non-musicians, *trombone* is an infrequent word, and the first syllable has a full vowel with secondary stress. Similarly, *Toronto* is a frequent word for people who live in that city, and the word is pronounced as [trTnto], dropping the first vowel. For other people *Toronto* is an infrequent word and the pronunciation is [tYrTnto], where the first vowel is kept.

SUMMARY

The Information-Stress Principle has broad applications. From it we can derive compound stress, Non-head Stress, and other versions of phrasal stress. In addition, the Information-Stress Principle can explain other stress effects which previous stress theories cannot account for.

STRESS AND LANGUAGE TYPOLOGY

Linguistic theories must address two questions. One is the common properties among languages. The other is special properties of individual languages. A popular approach is to adopt the principles-and-parameters approach of Chomsky), according to which variation across languages can be accounted for in terms of a set of parameters.

For concreteness, let us consider how parameters account for language variation in two areas: syllable structure and foot structure.

Blevins proposes a set of parameters to account for variation in the size of the maximal syllable in different languages. The main parameters are shown below, along with their settings for English.

- Syllable parameters

Parameter	English setting
Can the onset have two sounds?	yes
Can a diphthong fill the nucleus?	yes
In the coda allowed?	yes
Can the coda have two sounds?	yes
Can an extra C occur word initially?	yes
Can an extra C occur word finally?	yes

To account for possible and impossible onset clusters and coda clusters, additional parameters can be proposed, which we omit.

Parameters for foot structure have also been proposed

- Foot parameters:
  a. Structure
- Length: At most one syllable/two syllables/three syllables/unlimited ii. Weight-sensitivity: a heavy syllable can/cannot be unstressed
- Head: the head (stress) is on the left/right of a foot
- Head property: a stressed syllable must/need not be heavy
- Direction of foot construction: from left to right/right to left
- Iteration: foot construction is/is not iterative

- Edges: skip the first sound/syllable/foot/word at the left/right of a foot/word/phrase

The parameter approach to language typology is wide spread. In Optimality Theory (Prince and Smolensky 1993), parameter settings are replaced by constraint rankings, but the perspective essentially remains the same: languages fall into different types, which can be predicted by different parameter settings or different constraint rankings.

If the Information-Stress Principle is correct, there is at least one area where there is no language typology, which is phrasal stress. Therefore, linguistic theory may turn out to be simpler than previously conceived.

PHRASAL STRESS DIFFER IN DIFFERENT LANGUAGES

If the information-Stress Principle is universal, one would expect phrasal stress to work the same way in all languages. To many people this claim would seem too strong. In particular, there are languages are thought to have no stress. In addition, for languages that have stress, it is often thought that each can choose its own phrasal stress rules, different from those in others.

In some languages, such as English, it is possible to obtain a reasonable amount of agreement on phrasal stress. In other languages, such as Chinese, Japanese, Korean, and Thai, native judgment on stress is harder to obtain. Naturally, there is a lack of studies on stress in the second group of languages and many linguists thought they have no stress. For example, in a typological study of stress, However, we have argued elsewhere that both Standard Chinese and Shanghai Chinese have stress , and that the lack of native judgment on stress in some languages is due to the fact that the pitch contour has been used for other purposes, in particular lexical tones or pitch accents. We shall also discuss a specific case in Japanese.

Let us now consider to what extent phrasal stress can vary across stress languages. Ladd argues that phrasal stress is not determined by universal principles; instead, each language can choose its own phrasal stress rules. As a result, in similar syntactic structures, the location of stress can differ from language to language. Let us consider some examples that Ladd offers.

First, consider Russian and English. In some Russian question, main stress falls on the verb, not the object. Two examples are shown below, where uppercase indicates main stress.

- Russian questions: main stress on the verb
  - Ona SPIT? 'she SLEEPS?'
  - Ona KUPILA knigu? 'she BOUGHT book?'

English questions: main stress on the verb or the object

- *Did she SLEEP?*
- *Did she buy a BOOK?*

The examples seem to show that Russian and English have different phrasal stress rules. However, in these examples the languages do not have the same syntax. For example, in English the auxiliary verb is fronted, whereas in the Russian sentence there is no fronting of an auxiliary verb. It can be shown that, if the syntax is different, main stress can be different, even if the meaning remains similar. Consider the following examples:.

- *You saw WHAT?*

  What did you SEE?

The two sentences have similar meanings but differ in syntax. They also differ in main stress, in that it is on the object in one case and on the verb in the other case. Therefore, we should not compare sentences that have different syntax.

Ladd's second set of examples compares Rumanian and English. In Rumanian, the main stress of each clause falls on the same word. In contrast, in the corresponding English sentence, the main stress falls on different words in each clause.

- Rumainian:

[...o sa vedem] ce AVETI, si ce nu AVETI [...we'll see] what YOU.HAVE and what no YOU.HAVE

English:

[...*we'll see*] *what you HAVE, and what you DON'T have.*

In the sentences, Rumanian and English indeed differ in what main stress falls. On the other hand, the tv'o sentences do not have the exactly same syntax. Therefore, we do not expect them to have the same stress pattern.

Ladd's third set of examples concerns English itself. Sentences that seem to have similar syntax can differ in main stress:

- Main stress on the subject: non-action
  - *My UMBRELLA broke.*
  - *The SUN came out.*
  - *His MOTHER died.*
- Man stress on the object: action
  - *My brothers are WRESTLING.*
  - *Jesus WEPT.*
  - *The professor SWORE.*

However, as Ladd points out, the two groups of sentences differ in the property of the verb.

- English appearance verbs

Out comes the sun.
There dies the tax bill.

- Chinese appearance verbs
  - huai-le yi-ba san
    broke an umbrella
    'An umbrella broke'
  - chu taiyang le
    appear sun ASPECT
    'the sun appeared'
  - hen zao sile ma
    very early dies mother
    '(his) mother died very early'

Action verbs cannot occur before their subjects. Therefore, the two sets of verbs may have different syntax after all, and they do not constitute evidence for the claim that phrasal stress is independent of syntax.

STRESS IN JAPANESE

In Japanese every word has a specific pitch contour. In addition, to predict the pitch contour correctly, we only need to mark one specific location in the word, which is the last H-toned mora, after which the pitch would be L. This mark is called the accent . Phonetic studies also show that the accented syllable has greater prominence . It is reasonable to assume then that the accented syllable is a stressed syllable, although its phonetic realization is not entirely the same as that of a stressed English syllable.

However, Japanese poses at least two problems for the Information-Stress Principle. First, about 50% of the words in Japanese have no accent , in the sense that the pitch remains H through the end of the word, even when suffixes are added. The lack of stress in so many words poses a problem for the Information-Stress Principle, according to which we expect at least all content words, such as nouns and verbs, to have stress. Also, in a verb phrase, the syntactic head is the verb, and we expect it to have less stress than the object (the syntactic non-head). However, if the verb has an accent and the object noun does not, we get an unexpected stress pattern: the verb has stress but the object noun does not, contradicting the prediction of Non-head Stress.

A second problem is that in a compound noun, the first word (the syntactic non-head) is unaccented, whereas the second word (the syntactic head) is accented. This again contradicts the prediction of the Information-Stress Principle, according to which the first word should have more stress. An example is shown below, where the accented vowel is followed by an apostrophe.

- Compound stress in Japanese (traditional analysis)

[+A]-[-A] [-A]-[+A]
a'Npo-jooyaku -> aNpo-jo'oyaku
'security treaty'
[+A]-[+A] [-A]-[+A]
sha'kai-shu'gi > shakai-shu'gi 'society principle (socialist)'
[-A]-[-A] [-A]-[+A]
kyooiku-seesaku > kyooiku-se'esaku 'education-policy'

In the first compound, 'security' has an accent ([+A]), which is lost in the output ([-A]), and 'treaty' has no accent but gains one in the output. In the second compound, both words have an original accent, but the first word loses it in the output. In the third compound, neither word has an original accent, but the second word gains one the output. In other words, regardless of the original accents, a compound word must have an accent on the second part and no accent on the first part, in contradiction to the prediction of Non-head Stress.

Every Japanese word has at least one accent, and some have two. The first accent, if present, is invariably on the first syllable. The location of the second accent, which is the same as the traditional accent, is variable and must be lexically specified.

In the new analysis, every word has an accent. In addition, it is possible to claim that compound stress is assigned to the left. Finally, there is an explanation why the compound stress is A-B: if a compound is treated as a word, it should have a word stress pattern, and the largest word stress pattern is A-B.

CONCLUSIONS

Although word stress can differ from language to language, stress above the word level (phrasal stress) seems to be similar across languages. Every language has phrasal stress, and every language follows the same principle for phrasal stress, which is the Information-Stress Principle. According to the principle, words with high information load should be stressed and words with low information load need not. The principle can explain a range of stress effects, including regular phrasal stress, contrastive stress, the relation between stress and syntax, and the relation between stress and word frequency.

Chapter 18

Mathematical Linguistics

MATHEMATICAL LINGUISTICS is the study of mathematical structures and methods that are of importance to linguistics. As in other branches of applied mathematics, the influence of the empirical subject matter is somewhat indirect: theorems are often proved more for their inherent mathematical value than for their applicability.

Nevertheless, the internal organization of linguistics remains the best guide for understanding the internal subdivisions of mathematical linguistics, and we will survey the field following the traditional division of linguistics into → Phonetics, → Phonology, → Morphology, → Syntax, and → Semantics, looking at other branches of linguistics such as → Sociolinguistics or → Language Acquisition only to the extent that these have developed their own mathematical methods.

Phonetics The key structures of both mathematical and phonetic interest are → Hidden Markov Models (HMMs). Their importance stems from the way their structure is set up: discrete, psychologically relevant underlying units as hidden states coupled with continuous, physically relevant output. Though phoneticians routinely use the mathematical apparatus of ACOUSTICS ever since the pioneering work of Helmholtz, neither DIFFERENTIAL EQUATIONS nor HARMONIC ANALYSIS are considered part of mathematical linguistics, because they enter the picture only indirectly, as part of the physics of the medium carrying the linguistic signal. HMMs, on the other hand, remain equally applicable if the modality is changed from spoken to written or signed language (see → Speech Recognition, → Optical Character Recognition, → Sign Language).

The HMM idea of discrete structural units (typically → Phonemes or → Words) coupled with continuous phonetic phenomena inspired the LAFS(Lexical Access From Spectra) model, the first explicit → Psycholinguistic model incorporating the modern apparatus of SIGNAL PROCESSING.

Though their structure is well suited for continuous phenomena, NEURAL NET models (→ Cognitive Science) generally shy away from any attempt at detail phonetic modeling: the influential TRACE model is typical in this respect. The mathematical reason for this is to be found in the fundamental difference between the way temporal succession is handled in the two models. Without the additional expense of adding recurrence neural nets can only deal with inputs and outputs of a fixed dimension, and once recurrence is added, neural net training becomes extremely complex. HMMs, on the other hand, assume a Markovian underlying structure, which is, for the most part, ideally suited for modeling the succession of linguistic units.

Phonology and Morphology Starting with Bloomfield's postulates, the basic conceptual apparatus of mathematical linguistics — in particular, the idea of hierarchical structures composed of relatively stable recurrent items — was developed primarily on the basis of phonological and morphological phenomena. There are three theoretical models for the description of linguistic structure, one based on → Finite-State Automata (FSA), one based on → Context-Free Grammars (CFGs), and one on context-sensitive grammars (CSGs) and/or the even more powerful Unrestricted Rewriting Systems (URSs). The relation between these is investigated under the heading → Generative Capacity, and was the basis of much further work on formal language theory within computer science.

Regarding mathematical work on phonology, there were some logicians and linguists who worked on phonemic theory from a set-theoretic standpoint in the 1960s and 1970s, but such work had little impact on linguistic practice. By that time, it was well known that ordered sets of CSG or URS rules provide a good mathematical reconstruction of Panini's (morpho) phonological rules, and are superior to the neogrammarian SOUND LAWS both in descriptive detail and in predictive power. It there fore came as something of a surprise that a system of considerably weaker generative capacity, finite state transducers (FSTs), can apparently describe the same phenomena. This observation was not fully assimilated in models of → Computational Morphology until well over a decade later with the introduction of two-level phonology and morphology.

Until the mid-1970s, the internal structure of phonological representations, based on → Distinctive Features, could be formalized by embedding it in an n-dimensional cube. With the advent of → Autosegmental and → Metrical phonology, a considerably more involved formalism became necessary . While the representations retained this additional complexity, in the 1990s the whole notion of rules operating on such representations in sequence was abandoned in favor of → Optimality Theory which describes the relationship between underlying and surface units in terms of rank-ordered constraint systems. A number of mathematical linguists (including Jason Eisner, Robert Frank, Markus Hiller, Lauri Karttunen, Giorgio Satta) have shown that this mode of description need not imply an increase in generative capacity, inasmuch as FSTs, under various sets of assumptions, have sufficient power to model the interaction of systems of ranked constraints.

Markov's pioneering work is a contribution both to phonology and to → Statistical Linguistics, given the near-phonemic nature of Russian orthography. Historically, the development of Markov models took place largely in isolation from mainstream phonology and morphology, largely because these offer a rich storehouse of LONG DISTANCE and NON-CONCATENATIVE phenomena, which in a segmental framework appear as violations of the Markovian assumption. The autosegmental framework, by resolving these violations, helped to usher in a more mature understanding of the key technical issues, and it is fair to say that today the mathematical apparatus of phonology and morphology is centered on the study of deterministic, nondeterministic, and probabilistic FSTs.

Syntax Chomsky's first significant technical contribution to linguistics was his formalization of IMMEDIATE CONSTITUENT ANALYSIS by means of → Context Free Grammars. Though in the definition of CFGs he sacrificed some of the detail of the earlier work (in particular, his system did not provide for DISCONTINUOUS CONSTITUENTS or for BAR LEVEL SUPERSCRIPTS), from a mathematical perspective CFGs hit on a particularly sweet spot: just as FSA correspond to the rationals, CFGs correspond to algebraic numbers.

CFGs found an immediate application in the design of PROGRAMMING LANGUAGES, where they retain a central position to this day, in spite of the fact that it can be shown that a number of widely used programming languages go beyond the context-free in some respects. For example, if it is considered a syntactic requirement that each variable used be declared at the start of the program, that aspect of the syntax is likely not to be CFG-describable). In fact, much of the early work in mathematical linguistics concerned with efficient methods of parsing eventually found a better home in COMPILER DESIGN → Parsing.

The key idea of CFGs was to replace the symmetrical (equational) notation used in earlier formulations by the asymmetrical notion of string rewriting that had, up to that point, been applied only by logicians, and only in settings of considerably broader generality, recursively enumerable or recursive. Though distributional equivalence, which was the basis for the equational notation, remained an important technical tool, the focus shifted from mutual to unidirectional substitutability, which helped to clarify the effect of CONTEXT.

In a Markovian world, only context linearly to the left matters, and even that, only within a limited window: it is this limitation which makes it possible to state Markov's original ideas in the contemporary framework of (probabilistic) FSA. In a CFG, only hierarchical context (parent node in a tree) matters: string context, including immediate neighbors, is immaterial.

The resulting theory can be expressed in terms of finite TREE AUTOMATA. In a CSG, both hierarchical and linear context plays a role, and the resulting theory turns out to be equivalent to Turing machines with workspace linear in the size of the input. → Automata Theory.

In syntax, the appropriate choice of → Grammar Formalism is more of a contentious issue than in phonology/ morphology. Unsettled issues include whether COMPETENCE has any probabilistic aspects, and what → Generative Capacity is necessary and sufficient for the range of actual and potential natural languages. Though probabilistic CFGs are widely used in → Computational Linguistics, the theoretical necessity of a probabilistic component has been broadly accepted only in → Sociolinguistics, but even there, the dominant statistical model (LOGISTIC REGRESSION) has its detractors.

The issue of generative capacity played a key role in GENERALIZED PHRASE STRUCTURE GRAMMAR (GPSG), which developed the idea that CFGs are sufficient. By providing a critical assessment of the earlier literature GPSG paved the way for subsequent work that resulted in the current near consensus that some power beyond that of CFGs is required. This development led to renewed interest in → Mildly Context Sensitive languages which are equivalently definable by at least four distinct grammar formalisms: TREE-ADJOINING GRAMMARS, HEAD GRAMMARS, COMBINATORY CATEGORIAL GRAMMARS, and LINEAR INDEXED GRAMMARS.

Semantics Early efforts to address linguistic semantics within generative grammar assumed that the meaning of expressions was to be given by providing them with translations into expressions in a representational system of some sort. Philosophers have objected that no such representation in any vocabulary can amount to a specification of meaning.

Since the work of Montague became known to linguists, attention has shifted to providing natural language expressions with actual model-theoretic interpretations, exactly as is done with formal languages in logic.

For reasons that have much to do with the still controversial AUTONOMY OF SYNTAX thesis, formal semantics is very often done in conjunction with nontransformational theories of syntax such as → Categorial Grammar.

On the whole, approaches to semantics based on → Information Theory are still largely restricted to LEXICAL SEMANTICS, though many tasks such as → Machine Translation that were originally believed to require sophisticated semantic analysis are now often performed by purely statistical models.

Model-theoretic syntax One recent line of research connects model theory to syntax by means of a logical theory that has well-formed structures in the language as its models.

Rogers devises a monadic second-order logic that characterizes the sets of trees generable by a CFG. The statements that context-free grammars make about sets of trees are made directly, without phrase structure rules. Blackburn and Meyer-Viol explore similar ideas using MODAL LOGIC on trees, and Rogers extends these ideas to structures more complex than trees.

Both in phonology/morphology and in syntax/semantics the choice of linguistic formalism is to some extent influenced by considerations that go beyond the primary issue of DESCRIPTIVE ADEQUACY. One important issue is → Recognition Complexity.

This concerns the complexity of the decision problem for membership in a language: it is assumed that a grammatical theory should have the property of guaranteeing that there is some reasonably rapid (polynomial in the lenght of the input) computation that will answer the question of whether a given sequence of words is a grammatical expression according to a given grammar. Human beings certainly do much more than this when they listen to an utterance and figure out the meaning of what was said, so a grammatical theory that cannot even guarantee reasonably rapid confirmation of well-formedness is probably not psycholinguistically realistic.

Another one is → Learnability, which concerns what sorts of mathematically definable procedures could in principle correctly guess the grammars for languages.

Chapter 19

History of Modern Linguistics

INTRODUCTION

This topic presents the history of modern linguistics, tracing developments in the theories, principles and methods of major figures and prominent schools as they relate to primary areas of investigation from semantics, syntax and phonology to pragmatics and discourse analysis.

WAYS OF DOING HISTORY

History as history of ideas
History as argument for a position
History as clarification from new perspective
History as comparison of theories
History as Kuhnian paradigm shift

- Prehistory as science, pre-paradigm period
- Paradigmatic science
- Normal science
- Crisis science
- Crisis resolution, return to normal science

MODERN LINGUISTICS

Scientific study of language begins in 19 century:
Reliance on data
Development of
Hypotheses
Accumulation of
Knowledge
19 century linguists developed perspectives and ideas

which lay the groundwork for 20 century linguistics: Language as a system of signs independent of individual speech habits and speech acts

We'll see how these concepts work themselves out in 20 century linguistics

LINGUISTICS IN THE 19 CENTURY

The Genetic Hypothesis

The relationship between a whole group of languages:

The *Sanscrit* language, whatever be its antiquity, is of a wonderful structure; more perfect than the *Greek,* more copious than the *Latin,* and more exquisitely refined than either, yet bearing to both of them a stronger affinity, both in the roots of verbs and in the forms of grammar, than could possibly have been produced by accident; so strong indeed, that no philologer could examine them all three, without believing them to have sprung from some common source which, perhaps, no longer exists. If languages are related, then what needs explaining is not their similarities, but their differences.

The *Genetic Hypothesis*: languages "sprung from some common source" belong together in a language family.

This *Genetic Hypothesis* raises a whole set of questions about the nature of language and relations between languages.

Consider first just English and German:

We see that English and German share cognates like:

mouse – Maus house – Haus

jeans – Jeans rock and roll – Rock and Roll

theater – Theater philosophy – Philosophie

To this point, the shared words might be explained by borrowing – maybe from each other, maybe from a third language.

But there are whole sets of regular relations like:

pole –	*path – Pfad*
Pfahl pipe	*pepper -*
– Pfeife	*Pfeffer*

and even parallel sets of inflected items like:

I me mine - ich mich/mir meiner

we us our - wir uns unser

the correspondences are so great that two languages must be related by more than borrowing.

Consider a whole group of languages

Old	English	Gothic	Latin	Greek	Sanskrit
eom	(am)	im	sum	eimi	asmi
eart	(art)	is	es	ei	asi
is	(is)	ist	est	esti	asti
sindon	(are)	sijum	sumus	esmen	smas
sindon	(are)	sijup	estis	este	stha
sindon	(are)	sind	sunt	eisi	santi

The Genetic Hypothesis:

- Languages as belonging to families: German and English are closely related to each other and ultimately to Sanskrit, but not to, say, Chinese or Thai
- Languages as living organisms that evolve through the generations (recall that Darwin's theory of evolution did not yet exist!)
- Mechanism of change as either progress or decay.

According to Friedrich von Schlegel, *Über die Sprache und die Weisheit der Indier*

Sanskrit and language decay

Organic vs *mechanical form*

Organic (inflectional) form: stems change, as in Latin:

esse (infinitive)

ero (1 person future I)

sim (1 person, present, subjunctive)

Mechanical form: stems combine without change, as in Turkish:

sevisdirilmek 'to be made to love one another'

sev- 'love'

is- 'reciprocal'

dir- 'causative'

il- 'passive'

mek 'infinitive'

Three-fold distinction of languages

- *Isolating* "without grammatical structure": each word consists of a single unchanging root as in Chinese, Vietnamese
- *Affixing* with unchanging roots and affixes as in Turkish
- *Inflecting* with changeable roots and affixes as in Sanskrit, Latin, German

Über das Conjugationssystem der Sanskritsprache: In Vergleichung mit jenem der griechischen, lateinischen, persischen und germanischen Sprache

Importance of inflections like verb conjugation in language comparison

Wilhelm von Humboldt

- *Agglutinating* replaces *affixing*
- Language classification and Romanticism
- Language structure as reflection of *Volksgeist*

Jacob Grimm *Deutsche Grammatik*

Ablaut vs *Umlaut* (as new inflectional principle)

Ablaut marking changes in verb forms was part of the Indo-European heritage, as in:

sing - sang - sung ride - rode - ridden

but *Umlaut* was a new process in the Germanic languages marking other alternations, e.g.

Mund - Münder - mündlich Schloss - Schlösser - Schlösschen

Lautverschiebung = *sound shift*

Grimm's Law First (Germanic) shift:

T (Latin tu)	> TH (thu OE)
D (Greek daman)	> T (tam OE)
TH (Greek thugater)	> D (dohtor OE)

Second (High German) shift:

TH (thu)	> D (du)
T (tamjan)	> Z (zähmen)
D (dauhtar)	> T (tochter)

This leads to a recurrent set of correspondences:

T > TH > D > T The standard textbook version of Grimm's Law is:

First Sound Shift (Grimm's Low)	
IE bh, dh, gh ⟶	(Respectively) Gmc β, ð, γ ⟶ b, d, g
IE p, t, k ⟶	(Respectively) Gmc f, θ, x (→ h initially)
IE b, d, g ⟶	(Respectively) Gmc p, t, k

Sound shift takes place in the mass, but never neatly in the individual words, and exceptions occur, e.g.

Latin dies and Gothic dags (English day)

Law-like nature of sound shift aligns linguistics with *Naturwissenschaft* by contrast with *Geisteswissenschaft*

- recurrent process

mass phenomenon outside human control

Confusion of letters and sounds

Isolating, Agglutinating, Inflecting structures not *nebeneinander*, but *nacheinander*

Language as evolving organism

Linguistics as *Geisteswissenschaft* because it's historical and diachronic, but linguistics as *Naturwissenschaft* in its methods and statement of natural laws

(Comment: Distinction of *Geisteswissenschaft* vs *Naturwissenschaft* often makes the wrong division for linguistics. More appropriate is distinction between physical (experimental, predictive) sciences and biological (taxonomic, descriptive) sciences)

The Regularity Hypothesis

"Eine Ausnahme der ersten Lautverschiebung"

No exception without a rule

There must be a rule for irregularity

Verner's Law: differential stress in Indo-European accounts for exceptions to Grimm's Law, thus:

Sanskrit bhrátar > OE brothor (as per Grimm's Law)

Sanskrit pitár > OE fæder preceding stress

Apparent exceptions form a pattern just as predictable as the primary pattern

Verner extended his law to [s] in medial and final positions:

—After stressed syllables, [s] was voiced to become [z], and this [z] later shifted to [r],

explaining the alternation between was and were

([s] in past plural wesan shifted to [z] then [r], while voiceless [s] in was shifted only later to voiced [z]);

cf. Engl lose, lost but forlorn

Engl choose G gekoren (veralt. kiesen)

Engl hare, G Hase

Note: though described later, the shifts in Verner's Law must have preceded those in Grimm's Law

Die Declination im Slavisch-Litauischen und Germanischen

Sound laws admit no exceptions

Die Junggrammatiker

Language does not have a character of its own independent of its speakers language change as ongoing process can be studied in languages today Sound laws as fundamental mechanism of language change

Analogy and *Borrowing* always factors in change

dove replaces dived in AE in analogy to rode, wrote

It was generally assumed that:

sounds in transition always remain distinct

sound change never interferes with understanding

speakers are unaware of change in progress

each language is a discrete, rigid system

dialect variation is irrelevant in change

Meaning Change

Karl Christian Reisig (1825) "Semasiologie"

as study of meaning to find principles governing development of meaning along with syntax and etymology in Latin Philology e.g. narrowing: OE fugol 'bird' ModE fowl widening: OE brid 'young bird' ModE bird

Hermann Paul (1880). *Prinzipien der Sprachgeschichte* gave prominence to matters of meaning

Arsène Darmesteter (1887). *La vie des mots étudiée dans leurs significations* for general public

Michel Bréal (1883). *Les lois intellectuelles du langage* first used the term "semantics" i.e. "sémantique" laws psychologically motivated, e.g. by the principle of least effort and the tendency to generalize, but also by goals of communication like desire for clarity intentionality at work in language change.

The Sociological Approach

Durkheim (1895) founded sociology as distinct from the physical world and the psychological domain.

Recognized a *collective consciousness* (*âme collective*) at work in society, transcending any individual member social facts are ideas within this collective consciousness which govern our behavior without our explicit awareness, e.g. dietary preferences, proxemic behavior, habits of dress etc.

Society consists in a complex web of social facts institutions like the judicial system are highly structured social facts: thus certain acts like car theft count as crimes, lead to arrest, trial, sentencing and imprisonment, and we act accordingly. For Saussure, language was also a *fait social,* a sort of mean or average not complete in any individual.

Saussure (1916) Cours de Linguistique Générale: Lectures from 1906-1911

"It is the viewpoint that creates the object" synchronic versus diachronic: Primacy of synchronic description

The place of language in the facts of speech

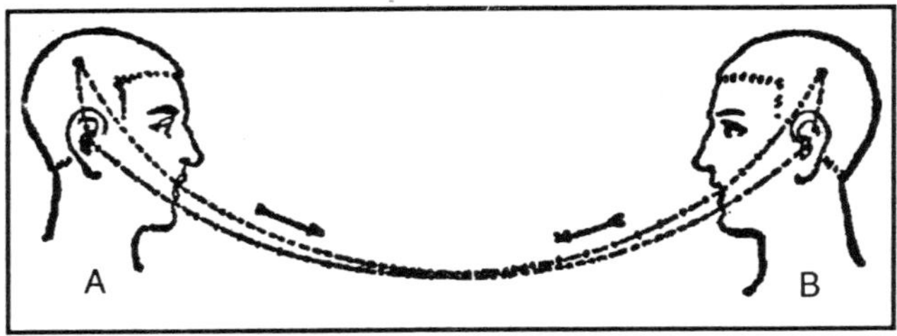

Individual execution of the speech act is *parole*

Note: *Parole* includes sounds, wording and grammar

Language (langue) "can be localized in the limited segment of the speaking circuit where the auditory image becomes associated with a concept."

It is outside the individual, who can never create it or

modify it by himself.

"Language is not complete in any speaker; it exists perfectly only within a collectivity."

Language, Speech, Speaking: really a 3-way distinction

"Language is speech less speaking"

Individual and dialectal variation disappear in the *collective consciousness* of the community

Hence: no interest in group variation, register, style etc.

Overarching System as independent of individual speakers with inertia of its own: Mutability and immutability

"The linguistic sign unites, not a thing and a name, but a concept and a sound-image"

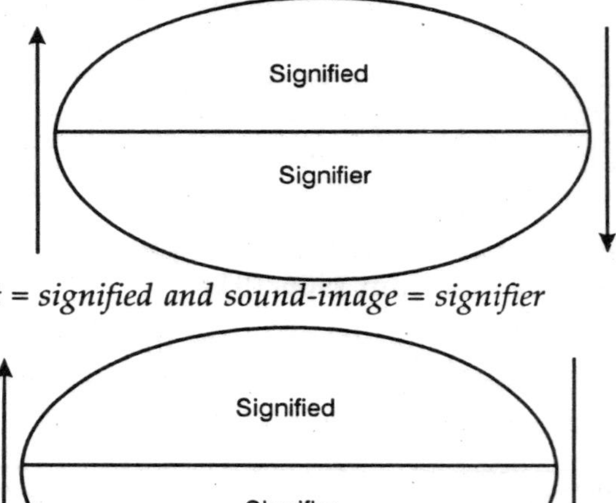

concept = signified and sound-image = signifier

The sign is a psychological entity independent of its manifestation: phonemes suggest activity and apply to the spoken word only.

Language as a system of *arbitrary* signs with *value* in system.

Determined by contrast with all other signs.

The sign relation is not an event but only "the momentary relation of terms" in the system. "Phonemes are above all else opposing, relative, and negative entities":

Not constituted by substance, but only by differences

which separate it from all other units not characterized by positive quality but by the fact that it is distinct same as letters:

we can write T t T t *T t* T t, all that counts is distinctiveness

The Saussurian relation of sounds and ideas

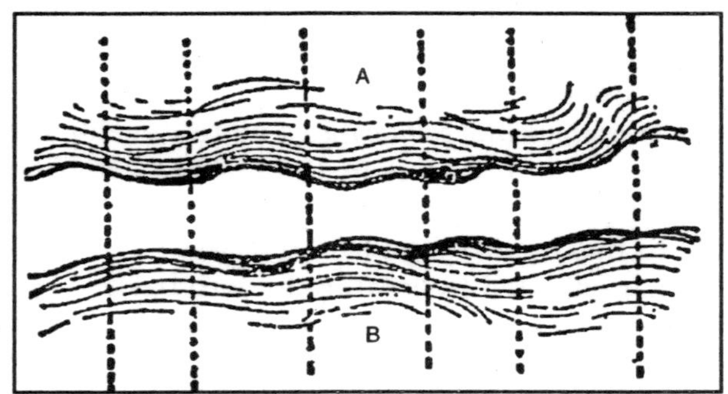

A modified diagram clarifies distinct segmentations of phonic substance and thought.

Meaning justifies delimitation of the sound chain phonemes do not provide a basis for analysis mois = [mwa] in le mois de Septembre but: mois = [mwaz] in un mois après cf. knife [nayf] vs knives [nayv]+ Plural [z] esp. since *sign* is not equivalent to *word* e.g. porte-plume 'penholder' s'il vous plaît 'please'

Syntagmatic and *Associative* (later: *Paradigmatic*)

Relations between words generate two classes of values in the language system:

In discourse, words acquire *Syntagmatic* relations based on the linear nature of the speech chain

Outside discourse, words acquire *Associative* relations based on diverse links in memory

The sentence is the ideal type of syntagm, and the sentence belongs to speaking, but the syntagm itself belongs to the language system, because:

- Many set phrases must count as independent signs, e.g. take offense, by dint of, there's no need for
- Certain syntagmatic types recur e.g. intolerable, impossible, indefatigable
- Associative relations on borderline between language

system and speaking e.g. assignment, judgment, payment (due to suffix) assignment, duty, job (due to meaning) assign, malign, refine (due to sound-image)

"In reality the idea evokes not a form but a whole latent system that makes possible the oppositions necessary for the formation of the sign"

Both the *syntagmatic solidarities* a word develops with the other words surrounding it in the spoken chain and the *associative* relations it contracts with other forms *in absentia* contribute to making the sign less arbitrary.

Baker is motivated by relation to verb bake

And by relation to other deverbal nouns with –er suffix, e.g. player, hunter etc

Assessment

Saussure's description of language as the psychological link between the concept and the sound-image is so general that it fits any semiotic system.

Saussure's treatment of value and systematic relations laid the groundwork for linguistics as the synchronic study of the language system. But Saussure's linguistics renders language abstract, independent of its manifestation in sound and its function in human interaction, due to his principled dichotomy of *langue* and *parole.*

The definition of phonemes as "negative entities" independent of substance is disturbing, and the comparison of phonemes with written letters is simply wrong, since variants of phonemes are conditioned by phonetic context, while shape of written representation is choice of font, printing vs script etc.

Saussurian Semantics:

e.g. Jost Trier (1931) *Der deutsche Wortschatz im Sinnbezirk des Verstandes*

First synchronic semantics based on Saussure's work. Still concerned with diachronic meaning change, but as a structural phenomenon, i.e. meaning determined by adjacent items: theory of *semantic fields,* e.g.

horse, cow, sheep, pig

Walter Porzig (1954) "Wesenhafte Bedeutungsbeziehungen"

Purely synchronic approach to meaning, opposed to Trier's paradigmatic word fields, concerned instead with syntagmatic relations, e.g.

horse–whinny horse–ride hair-blond

PRAGUE SCHOOL

Vilém Mathesius (1911) "Potentiality of the phenomena of language"

Recognizes Variation as basic in language: individual, dialectal, societal, diachronic

Language as a whole functional system, not fragmented as in Neogrammarian approach to sound shift

Linguistics as search for laws of language

Appeal to functions of language and within language

No sharp line between synchronic and diachronic

No sharp line between speech and language

Inclusion of dialects and functional varieties

Functional Sentence

Perspective:

theme-enunciation (later: *rheme*)

The sentences below express similar information, but each *thematizes* a different element

Theme	**Rheme**
The kid	left three marbles in the bag.
Three marbles	remained in the kid's bag.
The kid's bag	still contained three marbles.

Also quantitative analysis to compare productivity

functional load (or *yield*) of affix or phoneme and combinability of units in system

Nikolaj Trubetzkoy (1929) phoneme divisible into *distinctive features*

/f/ = [+C] [+labio-dental] [+fricative] [-voice]/v/ = [+C] [+labio-dental] [+fricative] [+voice]

Neutralization:/f/ is [+voice] just like/v/ in plurals like knives and lives

Archiphoneme combines features of neutralized variants:

[+C] [+labio-dental] [+fricative]

labio-dental fricative in knives, lives etc is not [+voice] as such, simply *unmarked*, realized phonetically as [-voice] in word final position and [+voice] before plural morpheme

Markedness Theory: generalizes the concept of Markedness within language system and across languages

Marked items: neutralized in certain positions less frequent across languages often missing in dialects acquired later by children

Karl Bühler (1933) "Organon Model": functions of language

Language as a tool

Roman Jakobson (1960) expands Bühler's model

Language realizes multiple simultaneous functions

Prague School interest in literary language, poeticity, style from the beginning

Assessment

Major influence through functional approach, esp. functional sentence perspective (Theme-rheme); distinctive feature theory, later applied in semantics as well as phonology; markedness theory, later applied in many areas of linguistic description; influenced structural descriptions of literary texts, esp. poetry.

AMERICAN STRUCTURALISM

Franz Boas (1911) Handbook of American Indian Languages

Language as key to understanding culture

There are no primitive languages

In every language certain categories must be expressed, while other categories are left unexpressed, e.g.

Russian: singular/dual/plural English: singular/plural Chinese: no number marking language description in cultures with no written tradition, so:

No need to distinguish synchronic and diachronic no point in distinguishing *langue* and *parole*

Languages can "differ from each other without limit and in unpredictable ways"

The search for linguistic universals must proceed via slow accumulation of data

Linguistic description as a workable model of behavior not a reflection of mind

Hocus-Pocus vs *God's Truth (Householder 1952)*

Related question: Can you correctly describe a language you don't speak?

Edward Sapir

Edward Sapir (1921, 1929, 1949) Benjamin Lee Whorf (1945, 1956) proposed relationship between language, meaning, culture, and personality

"Sapir-Whorf Hypothesis" states that our language determines our perception: This remains open issue even today

Sapir (1933) proposed psychological reality of phoneme, rejected purely physical, mechanistic description of language

Sapir also studied the poetic effects of rhyme

Sapir's "Formal completeness" and the "Sapir-Whorf Hypothesis":

Language is like a number system with a specific digit for each item. Gaps and deficiencies appear only in contact, e.g. efforts to translate. From formal completeness, he concludes that speakers are "at the mercy of their language."

But human language is not formally complete. Languages have standard gap fillers like thingamajiggy and je ne sais quoi. Grammars are full of indeterminacies like: it is I/it's me and funner/more fun as well as sets of options like:

We saw a place where/at which/which/ö/ we could stop (at)

We all acquire a set of words for talking about the things we deal with. Basic level shifts with interest: bug/weevil or tree/beech. Nobody knows or uses the entire vocabulary with whatever gaps and dense areas it contains, and thus nobody's "at the mercy" of it.

Leonard Bloomfield (1926, 1930): Linguistics as Science

Again: Linguistics as *Naturwissenschaft* as opposed to *Geisteswissenschaft*

Physicalism (vs. mentalism) based on:

Logical Positivism: only true/false statements meaningful

Operationalism: definitions must include test conditions

Monism: no distinction between body & mind

Behaviorism: only observable behavior counts; no appeal to mind or reason for explanation

Human language behavior (indeed: all communicative behavior) explicable in terms of physics and biology

Even human conduct such as belief systems, ethics, law, science can be understood monistically—given the unique role of language

Refusal to use reports of introspection Rejection of teleological statements

Not: the flower turns to face the sun

But: the movement of the sun makes the flower turn

Or: the flower turns as the sun moves

Human and animal behavior; thought as speech

Stimulus and *response, substitute stimulus* and *response*

S > r ... s > R Jack and Jill

Given: world – concept – image - utterance

define language as linking world & utterance where world is network of knowledge, custom etc all describable in physical terms with no appeal to psychology or mind

(cf. Saussure: language as linking concept & image)

If we had sufficient knowledge of the physical world and the complex workings of human behavior, we could predict what people would say in given context

Meaning and expert knowledge: salt = NaCl

effectively removes semantics from mainstream linguistics

No recourse to semantics in analyzing structure

No recourse to morphology in analyzing phonemes

In general, no level mixing:

(Units defined by position in system, as for Saussure)

Phonemes and allophones below word level,

in morphemics we ignore allophones, in syntax we ignore allomorphs

Discovery procedures:

begin with sound, identify phonemes to determine words,

minimal pair test for phonemes

pet – bet tap-tab

but reconsider: knife-knives

we can't say singular knife [nayf] becomes plural [nayv] then adds voiced form of plural suffix [z], since this description includes morphological data: singular/plural

Even the ordering implicit in this statement is a convenient fiction:

the descriptive order . . . is a fiction and results simply from our method of describing the forms; it goes without saying . . . that the speaker who says knives, does not "first" replace [f] by [v] and "then" add [-z], but merely utters a form (knives) which in certain features resembles and in certain features differs from a certain other form (namely, knife).

And from the hearer's perspective, it's a matter of recognizing the knife and plural in the speech chain

Immediate Constituent (IC) analysis to describe sentence Pauses, insertions, permutations as tests

The little dog will chase the big cat The little dog will chase the big cat The little dog will chase the big cat The little dog will chase the big cat The little dog will chase the big cat

IC analysis yields constituents and hierarchy [[will$_{Aux}$] [chase$_{V}$] [[the$_{Det}$][big$_{A}$][cat$_{N}$]$_{NP}$]$_{VP}$]

IC analysis resolves structural ambiguity

old [men and women] [old men] and [women]

Bloomfieldian Linguistics concentrated on phonemics:

(Comment: Recent, psycholinguistic research shows that other features are salient than the ones linguists identify for systematic purposes: thus aspiration is more salient than voicing for stops; the real acoustic distinction if *voicing onset time (VOT)*. Moreover, we recognize words before or simultaneous with phonemes in top-down processing. Hence, much argumentation over phonemic systems and perceptions was based on false premises.)

Some Bloomfieldians went beyond phonemics:

Goal: describe all elements in the sound sequence, not just to distinguish words (as Bloomfield & Saussure), to yield a complete description of elements, variants and combinations

Hockett (1954) explicitly distinguishes two methods of description:

item-and-arrangement:

bake [beyk] infinitive

bakes [beyks] 3 person, present tense

baked [beykt] past tense

item-and-process:

infinitive bake [beyk] plus s => 3 person, present tense bakes [beyks] infinitive bake [beyk] plus t => past tense baked [beykt]

go back to description of knife-knives above:

item-and-arrangement grammar:

knife singular [nayf] plural [nayv]

Plural [s] after voiceless Consonants

[z] after voiced Consonants

hence: [nayvz]

item-and-process grammar: knife + singular > [nayf] + plural > [nayv]

Plural > [s] after voiceless Consonants > [z] after voiced Consonants

hence: [nayvz]

phonotactics

- Phoneme distribution

e.g. velar nasal [n] written ng only syllable-final, h only syllable-initial

- allophone distribution

e.g. preglottalized, unreleased t only word-final flapped [D] only word-internal

- combinations

e.g. Consonant clusters

syllable-initial CCC: str, spr, skr, spl, skl

Hockett (1968, 1983) argues that phonetics-phonotactics differs in kind from morphemics, syntax, semantics, pragmatics:

Like sound changes, phonetics-phonotactics has physical correlates and is generally beyond consciousness, while morphemics, syntax, semantics and pragmatics are "mental constructs" accessible to conscious attention

Thus phonetics-phonotactics counts as *Naturwissenschaft* while the rest count as *Geisteswissenschaft*

Charles Carpenter Fries (1952) *The structure of English*

Telephone conversations as data eschewing traditional syntactic terms, develops system of word classes and arrangements e.g. introducers like well, oh

Zellig S. Harris (1951, 1952) sentences in discourse

Linguistic theory should account for systematic relations like those between active and passive sentences

Transformations express such relations among sentences which can occupy the same slot in a text as part of the analysis of discourse

Harris proposes equations for constituent analysis which Chomsky later formalizes as *Phrase Structure Rules*

Pike 1945-1967 Language in Relation to a Unified Theory of the Structure of Human Behavior

Levels of description: *etic* vs *emic*

Focus may be narrow/wide, deep/shallow e.g. football game or family breakfast

Functions of language within behavioral units,

e.g. in greetings, leave-taking, meetings etc

And functions of behavioral units within language

e.g. wave, handshake, nod, shoulder shrug etc along with or instead of language units

Method: not just ethnographic but *monolingual*, working directly in the language to be described

Pike rejects any dichotomy of language and behavior or of language system and its realization (*langue/parole)*

Pike questions binary oppositions as especially distinctive, or as advantageous in linguistic description or as fundamental in language acquisition

Language is a set of units and relations, not oppositions

Pike rejects any functional dichotomy of form and meaning: Meaning must be manifested in language no necessary separation of phonemic and other levels,

Thus native speaker intuitions on meaning are admissible as "one kind of data"

And we must recognize that the morphemic system can differ from one speaker to the next

Triadic view of language: as *particle,* as *wave,* as *field* Reflecting: *item, process, arrangement*

Form & meaning always both co-existent in different modes

e.g. not is 'negation' in the *feature mode*

not or n't in the *manifestation mode*

unique in the *distribution mode*

because only n't occurs in the *slot* was__it?

This relation between a unit and its slot-occurrence is the most basic in language: *tagmeme* Structural meaning overcomes morphemic meaning, e.g. awfully tasty, damned nice, terribly good

where the slot overcomes negative meaning

Slot occurrence locally conditions semantic variation

e.g. drive a car vs drive a horse

Language is hierarchically structured from phonological level through morphemes, phrases, sentences and discourses with *Portmanteau levels*: single phoneme as word, word as sentence, sentence as discourse etc.

Meaning is inherent in the whole system from the morphemic level on upwards

Pike allows for potential indeterminacy at any point in the language system, just as in other areas of human experience.

GENERATIVE GRAMMAR

Chomsky (1957, 1965): Standard Theory

Linguistic theory describes an *ideal speaker-hearer* in a

completely homogeneous speech community, who knows its language perfectly, and is unaffected by such grammatically irrelevant conditions as memory limitations and errors in applying his knowledge of the language in actual performance

Hence distinction: *competence* vs *performance* language as a set of sentences use of introspective judgments of grammaticality and rejection of real discourse as data

Universal Grammar (UG) as innate property of human mind

Language Acquisition Device (LAD) based on *UG* enables child to acquire native competence so fast

Generative Grammar formalizes IC analysis as *Phrase Structure Grammar*

Re-write rules

S > NP VP NP > Det (A) N VP > Aux V (NP)

But Phrase Structure Grammar can't account for:

- *Discontinuity*
  Judy must have driven have + en for *Perfect*
  Judy must be driving be + ing for *Progressive*
- Underlying relation of distinct structures
  Sue put out the cat - Sue put the cat out
  Sue told the kid a story – Sue told a story to the kid
- Underlying distinction of similar structures
  Judy is eager to please - Judy is easy to please
- Disambiguation of structures
  Flying airplanes can be dangerous

Transformations solve all these problems by relating *surface structures (SS)* to *deep structures (DS)*:

Transformations move, add and delete elements

Elements together in DS can be moved by transformations to end up apart in SS and vice versa, e.g.

DS Sue [put out_V] the cat

Particle Movement Transformation

SS Sue [put___V] the cat out

Similar or identical SSs can have different DSs, since transformations can delete elements, e.g.

DS_1 Judy is eager to please [someone]

DS_2 Judy is easy [for someone] to please *Indefinite Deletion Transformation*

SS_1 Judy is eager to please [__]

SS_2 Judy is easy [__] to please

Transformational Grammar as *item-and-process* description (as opposed to item-and-arrangement)

PS Rules generate base phrase markers,

Words are inserted into base phrase marker from Lexicon to create Deep Structure (DS),

DS provides basis for Semantic Component,

Transformations change DS into Surface Structure (SS), SS provides basis for Phonological Component

SS > Phonological Component

>| | Transformations > | |

>| |

PS Rules -> DS <- Lexicon | | Semantic Component

Only the Syntactic Component is strictly *generative*, Phonological and Semantic Components are *interpretive*

So-called *Generative Phonology* has process rules which work from underlying forms to phonetic forms, e.g.

write [rayt] > [rayD/r]

more generally:

[t] > [D] between Vowels even more generally, since [d] is flapped as well:

[+alveolar][+stop] > [+flap]/ V__V

Phonological process rules seem to describe the speaker's generation of speech from forms in memory, just as syntactic transformations seem to describe the speaker's generation of a sentence from an underlying plan;

the hearer has to work from the spoken alveolar flap in [rayDFr] back to the t in writer (or the d in rider); but Chomsky insists that TG implies no directionality and works equally well as a speaker or hearer model.

Generative Phonology postulates underlying forms which may be quite abstract and differ from anything ever pronounced by native speakers; In order to make the general rules work, underlying forms may reflect historical forms like [x] no longer realized.

Generative Phonology uses phoneme notation only as a convenience;

Sounds are really just bundles of features, and feature representation reveals *natural classes,* classes determined by fewer features than required for any member, e.g. class [p t k] = +stop, -voice

while [p] = +stop, -voice, +bilabial

[t] = +stop, -voice, +alveolar etc

Semantic Component of Generative Grammar:

Syntactically oriented semantics based on feature theory syntactic markers vs. semantic distinguishers

mare +N +common +count +equine +female +adult

die +V -transitive (X (become (not alive))) Compositionality and projection rules

Semantic interpretation simply combines markers

The mare died

([+equine +female +adult] become not alive)

Katz extended feature theory to describe such semantic notions as anomaly, contradiction, tautology, synonymy, antonymy, paraphrase etc.

Chomsky and followers continued to develop GTG, seeking general principles reflecting *Universal Grammar (UG)*

Languages differ in setting of *parameters*

e.g. English is *right-branching language,*

so all heads precede complements:

Verb Phrase > V Comp

Prepositional Phrase > P NP

but Japanese is *left-branching language,*

so all heads follow complements:

Verb Phrase > Comp V

Postpositional Phrase > NP P

Transformations as principles of UG: move á

PS rules redundant given lexical information:

X-bar theory: Verb heads VP, noun heads NP etc

Case theory: Verb assigns case features to terms, ensuring that they must contain nouns

è- theory: verb assigns semantic roles: agent, patient, goal etc to determine sub-types of nouns

Logical Form (LF) and Phonological Form (PF) are interfaces for successful derivations:

SS -> PF move á -> | | Lexicon -> DS -> LF

In newest *Minimalist* theory:

no DS or SS

LF and PF

operations apply anywhere derivations may be *convergent* at otherwise they *crash*

Assessment:

Generative Grammar is clearly *God's Truth* linguistics

Chomsky claims generative grammar reflects human mind

GTG has progressively assimilated positive aspects of other theories, viz. feature representation, case theory, semantic roles in è- theory, *theme-rheme* sentence organization and modal logic in LF.

In the *Minimalist Program*, grammar is built around words, especially verbs which determine the syntax and semantics of sentences. move á works as a universal operation requiring language-specific limits.

This avoids redundancy and suggests constraints, which become the principles and parameters of *UG*.

And this allows strong claims about universals and about language acquisition with *LAD*.

But GTG sees grammar as a disembodied abstraction, separate from production, comprehension and interaction; syntactic derivations take place without contexts or goals. Generative Phonology posits long series of rules and abstract underlying forms leading to wildly complex derivations, seemingly unmanageable for kids acquiring their native language.

The idealization of language as rigid *competence* with consequent focus on intuitions about grammaticality and the exclusion of real data from natural discourse limits GTG to an account of special mental processes and disqualifies it as a theory of language

LONDON SCHOOL

Henry Sweet includes *a popular exposition of the Principles of Spelling Reform* model of Henry Higgins in Shaw's "Pygmalion" pioneered theoretical and practical phonetics e.g. interest in spelling reform systematized phonetic transcription *phoneme* as unit in ideal orthography.

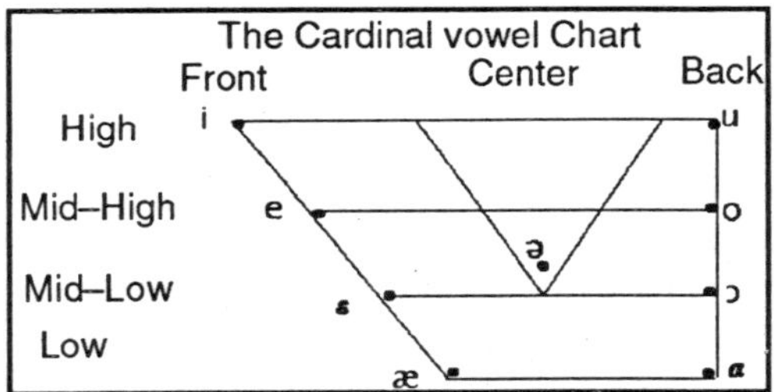

Main interests Semantic theory and Phonology
Rejects dichotomy of synchronic vs diachronic
Concerned with variation from the start:
Styles (including literary)
Regional dialects
Registers for special purposes

We must take our facts from speech sequences, verbally complete in themselves and operating in contexts of situation which are typical, recurrent, and repeatedly observable. Such contexts of situation should themselves be placed in categories of some sort, sociological and linguistic, within the wider context of culture.

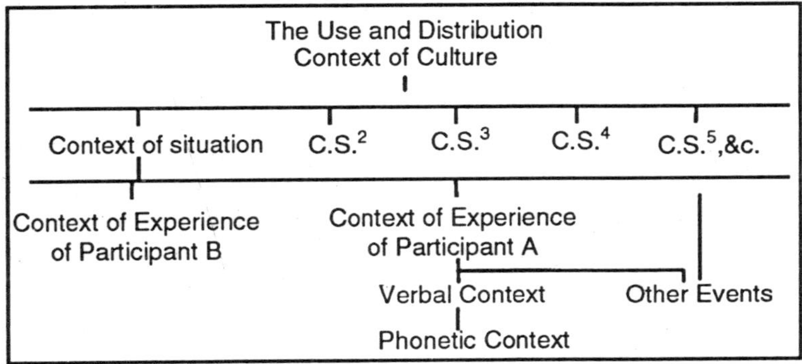

Meaning inheres in all levels of language organization

- In type of text:

Monologic vs *choric*

Creating rapport in *Phatic communion*

Coordinating a job of work

- *In grammar*: Sentence form declarative/imperative sentence mood active/passive
- *In phonology*: certain consonant sequences signal juncture e.g. in bring her and is she?

Leads to Firth's *Prosodic Analysis*

Polysystemic phonology expressed as plurality of systems of interrelated phonematic and prosodic categories

More than inventory of phonemes; different systems of sounds contrast at various points in system

Not all sounds occur in all positions e.g. no final [h] or [tw] in English

> essentially integrates phonotactics into phonology

Sounds may contrast only in certain grammatical categories

e.g. voiced th only in group of mostly deictic words: this, these, them, there, then etc

> occurrence of [wa:] can naturally be limited to borrowed words like:

coiffure, boudoir, bourgeois

Alternations don't necessarily occur everywhere

e.g. Am Engl [d],[t] distinct word-initial: dip, tip and word-final: pat, pad but not medially: rider, writer

> troublesome [f]–[v] alternation in knife-knives can be described as system only operative in word-final position for a certain set of native English words—with no consequences for the whole system

Prosodies may extend across whole syllable, word, phrase, even sentence, esp. in marking initial, final, juncture

e.g. voicing in breadwinner lip-rounding in soup-spoon

> agreement of negative prefix with initial sound in stem receives natural statement

indirect imperfect irregular illogical etc

Firth begins "empirical analysis of meaning at the

phonetic, morphological, syntactical, and semantic levels" with "the simplest context—a purely phonetic context," e.g.

[b.:d] with initial voiced bilabial stop [b], back round vowel [.:] and voiced alveolar stop [d]

note prosody: voicing extends over whole word

"function or meaning" at this stage just differentiation from e.g. bid, bed, bad, bard, bought, port, pot etc

but [b.:d] is a *neutral* (i.e. ambiguous)

asked for contexts of experience, speakers may say:

which [b.:d], [b.:d] of studies, [b.:d] to death

then associate various forms in *formal scatters*:

- Board, boards
  Bawd, bawds
- Board, boards, boarded, boarding
- Bore, bores, bored, boring

The scatters identify the form as: 1. a singular noun, 2. a simple verb form, 3. a –d form of a verb

Then try to eliminate the neutrality by extending the scatters:

- Room and board, boarding school etc
- Bawd, bawdy, bawdiness etc
- Boarding ramp, boarding pass etc
- Crashing bore, bored to tears etc

But still:

- Final [d] has no semantic function, since it fails to distinguish various forms
- Even syntactic frame on the [b.:d] shows only that the form is a noun semantic function appears only in context of situation, e.g. when I ask: [b.:d]? in a lecture, and you reply yes or when I ask: Does the price include [b.:d]? of a hotel manager

The meanings of complex words and speech acts are built up through *contextual elimination*.

"The rest of the contextualization is in the province of sociological linguistics."

"The central concept . . . is the context of situation, in which, in a sense, whole stretches of personal biography and cultural history are involved."

Parallel to *polsystematic* approach and view of speech as simultaneous realization of meaning on various levels is Firth's famous treatment of the origins of language :

Firth's terms make light of speculations that language had some single origin:

- *bow-wow* or *cuckoo* theory claimed language originated in onomatopoeia
- *pooh-pooh* theory claimed language originated in emotional interjections caused by pleasure or pain
- *yo-he-ho* theory claimed language originated in muscular and rhythmic efforts accompanying group work; the social character of this theory could include group activities such as eating, celebrating and mating, hence words like: yum-yum, ta-ra-ra-boom-de-ay, and hey baby
- *ding-dong* theory claimed language originated in our harmony of sound and sense with all sentient nature: as if we all *ding-donged* phonetically to our environment
- *ta-ta* theory claimed language originated in pantomimic gestures, whereby the movement of the tongue in pronouncing ta-ta mimics the movement of the hand in waving goodbye

Firth predictably maintains that all these sources contribute elements of meaning to language reflected in various parts of our vocabulary

Assessment

The practical basis of Firthian linguistics and its grounding in text and context, along with its rejection of the dichotomies *synchronic-diachronic* and *competence-performance,* naturally lead to interest in discourse, style and variation as well as to pedagogical applications.

Firthian semantics has been repeatedly criticized—just as Bloomfield's has. Both are monistic, physicalist in method, and critics have failed to understand how they ultimately include cultural knowledge through the context of situation and the context of culture; cf. sociolinguistic analysis of speech events in Hymes, which divides the context of situation into setting, participants, goals, key, medium, genre etc

Polysystemic Prosodic Analysis allows most natural description of certain phenomena like alternations in small sets of words and *prosodies* stretching across segments.

HALLIDAY (1967-68, 1973, 1975, 1978, 1985) HALLIDAY & HASAN (1976), HALLIDAY, MCINTOSH, STREVENS (1964)

Systemic Grammar as extension of Firthian linguistics

Systemic Grammar also *polysystemic* in Firth's sense:

posits set of systems describing choices at various points in syntactic structure of a language

Systemic Grammar as taxonomic, not generative

Systemic Grammar as functional and contextual (by contrast with abstract, mental TG)

Systemic Grammar naturally hooks up with sociology (while TG hooks up with psychology)

since language reflects cultural categories

Hence: *Language as social semiotic*

In Householder's terms, Systemics is *hocus pocus* linguistics (by contrast with the *God's truth* attitude in TG)

Halliday rejects *competence-performance* (*langue-parole*) dichotomy sees meaning potential in terms of culture, not mind asks what speakers can do and mean, not what they know sees meaning as a way of behaving "mean is a verb in the doing class"

Develops general concepts *Field* (activity, subject matter), *Mode* (channel, genre), *Tenor* (social relations) for describing how Firth's *context of situation* determines types of meaning expressed

Linguistic features associated with configuration of situational features constitute a *Register* (personal narrative, oral, among friends)

Register coupled with *context of culture* determine choices in discourse

- major functional-semantic components:

Ideational

Experiential: reflecting *context of culture* Logical: abstract

Interpersonal: social, expressive, appellative

Textual: coherence in text and context

e.g. every clause involves choice in system of *Theme*, dividing content into *theme-rheme*

and: every spoken *tone* group involves choice in system of *Information Structure*, dividing it into *given-new*

Thus: Hallidayan Systemics naturally applies to texts, and supplies special category for spoken discourse

Consider the system for *Person*

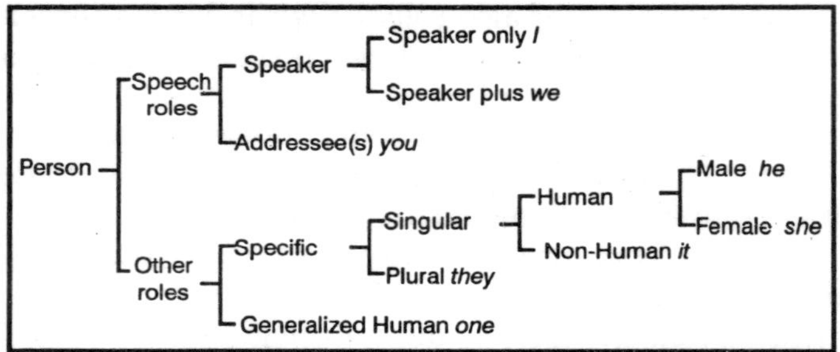

Systemic Grammar provides ever more *delicate* description down to word level, where it distinguishes even similar words like boy and girl, based on collocational differences (only recently with computers and large corpora can we confirm such delicate *semantic prosodies*, whereby girl occurs much more frequently in collocations with nice or little) compare: nice little girl - nice little boy.

Halliday's concerned with language acquisition in real-life context (instead of merely positing LAD as in TG)

kids must first learn the modes and conditions of meaning

- First just one meaning per utterance utterance form related to meaning system becomes more arbitrary through time
- Then comes grammar, allowing combination of various types of meaning in a single utterance
- In adult language, most utterances realize multiple meaning.

This ontogeny recapitulates phylogeny of human language

Assessment

By contrast with most other work in semantics, the functional-systemic linguistics of Halliday recognizes not only ideational and interpersonal meaning, but also textual meaning. Thus, systemic linguistics has operated with the goal of describing discourse meaning all along, and offers tools for handling cohesion, coherence, anaphora etc.

Halliday presents integrated theory of language acquisition, text and context, sociolinguistics, variation, semantics and grammar.

Critics fault Halliday for inflation of terminology, reliance on intuition, lack of empirically testable and potentially universal hypotheses about language.

Labov and Sociolinguistics

As Labov puts it: sociolinguistics is "a somewhat misleading use of an oddly redundant term"

Since language always exists in varieties and is always changing, any adequate linguistic theory should be sociolinguistic in its description of variation by speaker, class, region and time; failure to account for variation and change should render a linguistic description useless

Labov questions Saussurian/structural assumptions:

The distinction between synchronic and diachronic linguistics became a program for ignoring the fundamentally dynamic nature of language

Like binary distinctions generally, this dichotomy privileged one half of the pair, namely synchronic linguistics;

The distinction of langue and parole similarly privileged langue, the language as a system, and marginalized parole, language in use; this distinction became a program for ignoring the fundamentally social and behavioral nature of language

New York dialect sounds impolite and tough; Bostonian sounds refined and snooty; Southern drawl sounds lazy and ignorant, etc

- Those who use highest degree of stigmatized form also condemn it most
- Pre-adolescents are aware of prestige and stigmatized

forms, and they monitor their speech accordingly; but they usually settle back into established class patterns

- Indeed, lower class groups know prestige forms, but choose not to use them, and they continue to use forms they know to be stigmatized in most styles,
- Apparently covert norms opposed to those of the middle class attribute positive values to use of the vernacular

Language change as positive influence

- Language change as deterioration and leveling of distinctions is only half the story; change also introduces new distinctions and features
- Language change must have value for the group, because it requires extra learning and monitoring of forms; change from below strengthens position of vernacular
- Language change appears dysfunctional only if we view language as a purely ideational system; for language to serve as a social marker, it must have variation and undergo change

"The actuation problem" = what sets change in motion?
Social factors account for change in a general way, e.g.

- Pressure from new group produces greater solidarity in original group, and members signal this through distinctive behavior, including speech patterns
- Commuters accommodate speech patterns to focal point, usually a major city, and introduce patterns at home
- "Linguistic missionaries" return from living in focal point city with high status new speech patterns

Linguistic factors may favor certain changes, e.g. regularizing a pattern like/ay/ causing parallel change in/aw/ but even taken together they can't predict that change will occur or in which direction

Even knowing the linguistic and social matrix doesn't explain why one specific feature changes and another doesn't, e.g.

- Why has the pronunciation of the vowel in words

like craft changed from [æ] in OE to [a] in ME, back to [æ] in EModE and back to [a] in the 18 Century (in southern England, but not in America or northern England)?

- Why do speakers in southwest England drop -r in posh pronunciation, while careful speakers in New York City are reintroducing the sound?
- How can historically stigmatized constructions like the comparative and superlative forms funner and funnest become standard in the course of a single generation (in AE)?

To account for variation, Labov postulated "Variable rules"

Assume full forms are stored in memory and reduced in speech, e.g. by rules for contraction:

She + is > she's we + have + been > we've been

> las' time as in las' time:

and by rules for deletion:

we've been > we been last + time

Phonological rule for final consonant cluster simplification,

C > f/ C ___ ## C

Read: delete a consonant following a consonant at the end of a word, if the next word begins with a consonant.

Some dialects allow consonant cluster simplification even if the next word begins with a vowel, as in las' of all, so we could write:

C > f/ C ___ ##

This rule fails to say that deletion is far more likely before a consonant than a vowel—in every dialect; so we need variable rules, relating differences in application to differences in the environment, as in:

C > <f>/ C ___ ## <C>

Read: delete a consonant following a consonant at the end of a word, more often before a consonant than a vowel.

In addition, the rule is far less likely to apply if the consonant to be deleted represents the past tense suffix -t,d, as in:

liked (pronounced [laykt]) and seemed (pronounced [simd])

This suggests a revision of the rule as:

C > <f>/ C <~#> ___ ## <C>

Read: delete a consonant following a consonant at the end of a word, more often if there's no morpheme boundary between the consonants, and more often before a consonant than a vowel.

Further, deletion is more likely for speakers of Black Vernacular than for white speakers, and more likely for younger speakers than for older speakers and so on.

Cognitive Linguistics

Recall that Chomsky's original GTG: Accepts traditional grammar categories (though based on Latin grammar) accepts and formalizes IC Analysis and basic Structuralist viewpoint

But TG also seeks universals

Assumes universal deep structure

Chomsky's own students, esp. Postal, Lakoff, Ross, McCawley, tried to make TG work to achieve stated goals by attempting to capture semantic relations like:

X please Y -Y like X

X reminds Y of Z - Y finds X similar to Z

Reducing grammatical categories

PrepP as NP, since both contain Noun Phrase

Adj as V, based on e.g.

Sue resembles Al - Sue is similar to Al

decomposing complex lexical items, e.g.

dead = 'not alive'

die = 'become dead' = 'become not alive'

kill = 'cause to become not alive'

All had effect of:

rejecting traditional categories

deepening Deep Structure (DS),

making DS more semantic

making DS more adequate as universal level

In the "Linguistic Wars" that followed, Chomsky rejected semantic claims of GS and borrowed much of its syntax in

avoid abstract, psychologically unreal forms *synchronic-diachronic,* so that a single construction may receive both synchronic and diachronic explanations, e.g.

it is I vs it is me

literal-figurative, since imagery is basic to the extension of prototypes in grammar and semantics *grammar-lexicon,* since: even so-called function words can have elaborate meanings, e.g. modals like can, must and prepositions like up, over, esp. as compared with e.g. thing, have, function words may be less abstract than lexical items, e.g. entity, proximity so-called *closed classes* of function words can gain new members, e.g new coordinator: plus in She's old, plus she's crazy and personal pronouns: you-all

Cognitive Grammar may provide both synchronic and diachronic explanations, and a construction may appear in lexicon and follow morphological rule, e.g.

stapler <= staple + er but additional meaning

Personal, temporal, regional differences in prototypes in semantic categories, but also in grammatical categories, degrees of centrality and entrenchedness, provide natural approaches to linguistic variation as well.

Assessment

By rejecting the standard (Saussurian) dichotomies, Cognitive Linguistics has a chance of providing adequate descriptions of real, scalar, fuzzy linguistic phenomena. Cognitive Linguistics also at least has a chance of providing a psychologically valid theory of language by taking into account research in cognitive psychology.

By viewing language as real, physical, embodied, evolved and acquired by complete organism in cultural context (like Firth), Cognitive Linguistics avoids the abstraction and narrow scope of Generative Grammar; by incorporating the results of research in cognitive psychology, it avoids the charge of "bad Behaviorism" leveled at Firth and Bloomfield. This inclusion of psycholinguistic considerations also entitles Cognitive Linguistics to claim a "God's truth" description of language.

By allowing multiple explanations of a phenomenon from

different perspectives, Cognitive Linguistics avoids the pitfalls of claiming the one single absolutely correct description.

Cognitive Linguistics also shows promise as a tool for the description of linguistic variation and discourse in the cultural context.

Toward Discourse Analysis

Partially as reaction to Chomskyan TG, abstract syntax, mentalism

Partially ongoing tradition in anthropological linguistics going back to Boas, Sapir, Bloomfield (and Pike)

Anthropological, functional, ethnographic

Includes context of situation & culture

Speech events

Gumperz Intercultural communication

Speech styles, stylistic differences Contextualization cues

Presupposition entered linguistic semantics from philosophy

Indexicality and anaphora as aspects of meaning requiring inferences about speaker beliefs and intended referents, beyond truth-functional semantics proper.

Chapter 20

Ideology, Power and Linguistic Theory

Our aim in this paper is to discuss an intensely complex cluster of interlinked concepts involving distinctions between (i) descriptive and prescriptive grammar, (ii) constitutive and regulative rules, (iii) conservative and liberal attitudes, and (iv) standard and non-standard dialects. We cannot hope to be comprehensive, but we will try to be clear.

Sometimes it seems to me that the issues we are dealing with here have been mired in the same controversies for a good forty years. Other times it seems more like a hundred and forty. There are few signs of any knowledge about grammar dating from after 1900 having become known to a broad cross-section of the general public or having had an impact on education. Perhaps it is time to attempt to understand the situation better, rather than simply to deplore it.

CORRECTNESS CONDITIONS

We begin by taking it for granted that there are conditions we might call correctness conditions for natural languages. (Whether they are standard languages, non-standard dialects, or undescribed tribal languages of preliterate peoples does not matter: all have correctness conditions.) And we will also assume that it is possible in principle to be perfectly explicit about such conditions. In terms of the distinction drawn familiar, thirty-five years ago by John Searle, They are constitutive, not regulative. They do not regulate the use of the language, in the sense that one could use it either in ways that comply or in ways that don't; they constitute the language, in the sense that not respecting them amounts to not using it at all but doing something else instead.

Modern descriptive linguists try to figure out from the available evidence the principles that constitute the language being described, and to give explicit, and potentially falsifiable, formulations of them.

Linguists often make little effort to distinguish the conditions themselves (the subject matter under study, the conditions as they truly are) from proposed statements of the conditions (hypotheses about the grammatical structure of expressions in the language).

They often rely on a 'systematic ambiguity' that lets such terms as 'the grammar of English' refer either to the conditions that actually do constitute English or to the linguist's current effort at making a statement of them, whichever the context may call for. But the difference is important. For one thing, arbitrarily many different strongly equivalent statements of the correctness conditions for English could be given, but that doesn't imply that there are arbitrarily many different objects of study.

Suppose a linguist states it as a condition that in Standard English an independent declarative clause beginning with a preposed negative adjunct must have a tensed auxiliary before the subject:

- Never before had we seen such a thing. *Never before I had seen such a thing.
- At no time did he leave the room.

*At no time he left the room.

The claim being made is not that speakers of Standard English OUGHT to position subjects of independent clauses before the tensed auxiliaries when there is no preposed negative adjunct, as in the (a) examples; the claim is that they actually DO position them thus (setting aside unintentional failures like typing or editing errors that sometimes prevent people from doing what they intended).

This of course implies that you would be well advised to position them thus if you want to be regarded as using

Standard English; but no one is telling you that you SHOULD speak Standard English.

The correctness conditions of a language, by definition, provide full justification for any true claim to the effect that some expression is or is not well formed in the language. But it's important that justification of a quite different sort is needed for the higher-level claim by a linguist that a certain set of statements captures the RIGHT correctness conditions for a given language. The linguist can be wrong about whether some proposed statement of conditions is accurate for some language, even when it is the language that the linguist speaks natively. Hence the phrase 'potentially falsifiable' above.

It should be obvious that different dialects have (at least slightly) different correctness conditions. If an elderly British speaker says Have you a pen? and a young American speaker could never say that (but would say Do you have a pen? instead), it is not sensible to assume there is just one answer to the question of what is grammatical, and one of the two speakers is wrong. The American and British varieties of English exhibit a very close similarity, but they are not quite the same. They differ very slightly in what correctness conditions hold.

This claim on its own is quite enough to spark controversy in some circles. William Labov pointed out to linguists forty years ago that it can be applied, and should be applied, to African American Vernacular English (henceforth, AAVE). When a linguist says that in AAVE a tensed auxiliary may begin a declarative clause if that auxiliary is marked with the negative suffix (like ain't, in sentences like Ain't nobody gonna tell me what to do), the claim is not that if you speak AAVE you OUGHT to position your negative auxiliaries before your subjects, but that if you speak AAVE you often DO position them thus. The expressions defined as grammatical in AAVE are not the same as the ones defined as grammatical in Standard English.

It really didn't take any more than a restatement of that observation to prod the world's press into excoriating the governing board of the Oakland Unified School District when it made its infamous declaration of December 1996 concerning the distinctness of AAVE from Standard English and the appropriateness of using AAVE in the classroom. The furore will be recollected by most professionals in the fields of language and education (though we should keep in mind that it was long enough ago that many of our students will not even have heard of it). The most striking thing about it the furore in my view was that the excoriation of the school board proceeded in the absence of any real understanding of what the dialect under fire was like as a language, or what the school board had actually intended to propose as a matter of linguistic policy.

It isn't irrational to propose teaching AAVE speakers how to use Standard English. But it is irrational to go into paroxysms of fury about the very idea of taking AAVE seriously as a separate linguistic system with its own somewhat different syntactic correctness conditions. And anyone who thinks that is not what the press commentators did simply hasn't read the press cuttings from late 1996 and early 1997. Eldridge Cleaver, in the Los Angeles Times, compared acceptance of AAVE to condoning cannibalism.

GRAMMAR AND STYLE

Grammar — the principles constituting the syntactically and morphologically permissible expressions of a language — is not at all the same thing as style. Style involves skill. It involves making choices between alternatives that the grammar makes available. Those choices can make the difference between using the language brilliantly or using it ploddingly. This is the sort of domain in which the notion of regulative rules makes sense. Indeed, what are known as 'house style' guides issued by publishers of books, journals, and newspapers may lay down rules that are in effect mandatory (there can be job-related consequences if the rules are not followed). But other sources (language teachers; writing tutors; books on how to write) offer discretionary advice. When a style guide or writing tutor tells you that adjuncts are not placed between to and the head verb of an infinitival clause, the claim is not that this never happens in Standard English prose. Far from it: the matter would not be worth mentioning unless people often placed adjuncts in that position! Rather, the claim is that you are doing wrong if you position adjuncts thus: you are doing something that you shouldn't.

This is what is meant by a prescriptive rule. Construed as having descriptive intent, prescriptive rules seem hopelessly silly, easily refuted hypotheses about the correctness conditions. They seem less worthy of being taken seriously than the absurdly obvious warnings printed on the packaging of nearly every kind of tool or other consumer durable you can buy in America. We swear we purchased a folding windshield-sized cardboard screen for protecting the inside of my car from getting overheated in the hot California summer sun, and on the back were the words "Do not drive with screen in place."

But at least that is advice that everyone seems to follow, and a good thing too. Prescriptive rules seem even dopier than that, because they warn against doing things which (a) everybody does all the time, and (b) are not harmful or inadvisable anyway.

But of course prescriptive rules are not intended to be constitutive. They are intended to be regulative. English is assumed to be already defined in some other way, or not to need any definition. The prescriptivist's rules are deliberately making recommendations about the ways in which you are recommended to use it or not to use it.

The received view of AAVE appears to be that it is just glaringly in contravention of prescriptive rules: it is bad Standard English, sullied and impaired by ignorant mistakes. This is not a defensible view. It makes a readily testable claim: that white English speakers should be able to do convincing impressions of AAVE speakers simply by injecting random mistakes. They should be able to write scripts for AAVE speakers in films, for example. Try it. You won't do well as a scriptwriter for films with young urban African American characters. There are well described systematic features of the syntax and morphology of AAVE that you would need to learn if you wanted to pass as yourself off as knowing it. Some African Americans seem to think there is no possibility of your succeeding at the task, incidentally. We gave some examples of a few elementary rules of AAVE syntax during a lecture to teachers in Santa Clara County, California, and later a black teacher came up to me and explained that there aren't really any constitutive correctness conditions for AAVE: it's entirely a matter of personal style, intuitive rather than governed by constraints; rather like jazz. It's a black thing, he wanted me to understand.

Of course, in one respect the suggestion he made actually goes beyond the received view: by saying that a special improvisational skill is involved, and tying it to the ethnic identity, culture, and even musical ability of African Americans, he did offer a tentative explanation for the inability of white speakers to create convincing AAVE dialog simply by injecting errors. But as it happens we have evidence of the falsity of that tentative explanation.

William Raspberry, the distinguished African American columnist for the Washington Post, published a column of mockery attacking the Oakland school board ('To Throw in a Lot of 'Bes,' or not? A conversation on Ebonics'), and included some invented dialect in AAVE. We wrote to him to point out that within the 32 words of dialogue he had crafted there were at least four clear errors of AAVE grammar, and he had also included a false claim about the phonology. We got no reply. Even for an African American, the notion that AAVE might have rules, so you might get things wrong, is an idea that lies beneath the realm of comment or even acknowledgment.

Raspberry tried to simulate AAVE by injecting a few cases of be where am or is would be appropriate in Standard English, using ain't a couple of times, and leaving the g off the ends of some words. The attempt is painfully silly to those who have even a trivial amount of knowledge about AAVE. He got nowhere close. The reason is that there is nothing random about it. Merely being acquainted since birth with African-American style and culture (Raspberry was born black in a Mississippi town that we assume was rigidly segregated by race) will not equip you to construct even trivial-sized utterances in it with any conviction; to speak AAVE or write it you have to have to have an up-to-date active acqaintance with its correctness conditions. Raspberry either never knew them or had forgotten them.

What has to be understood about AAVE is that it does have its own correctness conditions, sharply different from those of Standard English. But to say that is not the same as saying it is in any way standard, or that it should be. It is a non-standard dialect of English. We happen to (mostly) understand it, and enjoy hearing it spoken; we don't regard it as having anything wrong with it. But we recommend against using it in an interview for a job in a bank. In many jobs employees are expected to use Standard English. That is just a social fact, and railing against it will not change it. It is entirely orthogonal to the linguistic fact that Eddie Murphy does know how to speak AAVE and William Raspberry apparently does not.

PRIVILEGED DIALECTS

In complex societies it is common for there to be a privileged dialect, privileged over others in the sense of being more prestigious or more widely admired or more generally employed for public communication or perhaps religion. Certainly this is true of the Anglophone world, where although phonology (accent) and lexicon (words) differ regionally quite a bit, there is a dialect known to linguists as Standard English that has a remarkably stable and consistent syntax worldwide.

Saying which of a selection of dialects is the prestige one is, of course, no part of what is done by either constitutive rules of grammar or regulative rules of style. We formulate statements of those for application to a dialect of English we identify independently.

The dialect known as Standard English originated during the last two to three hundred years, evolving out of a dialect used around London. Its syntax lacks the negative concord that was a feature of Middle English: negation is marked just once in a negated clause, either in the tensed auxiliary (verbal negation) or in the morphology of some nonverbal constituent of the clause (nonverbal negation):

- People didn't like it. [verbal negation]
- Nobody liked it. [nonverbal negation]

and indefinite NPs beginning with some- (like someone or something) are replaced by alternate versions beginning with any-:

- Standard English
  - People didn't like anything.
  - Nobody liked anything.

It is possible in Standard English to use both two distinct negations, but semantically they cancel out to none:

- Standard English
  - People didn't like nothing. [a" "People did like some things."]
  - Nobody liked nothing. [a" "Everybody liked something."]

To say (5a) is to deny that people liked nothing; to say (5b) is to claim that the set of people who had an empty set of things they liked is itself empty. This much is just a summary of some of the constitutive correctness conditions for Standard English. We can do likewise for some of the non-standard dialects.

In the dialects of English that retained negative concord (these include the dialects of most of the working classes in Britain and Australasia as well as AAVE and many white American dialects), a negated clause always has verbal negation (a negative auxiliary, or a use of not with a finite auxiliary) and in addition all the indefinite NPs with the initial element some- are replaced by their negative counterparts:

- Various non-standard English dialects
  - He didn't like nothing [a" Standard English "He didn't like anything."]
  - Nobody didn't like nothing. [a" Standard English "Nobody liked anything."]

In these dialects, the meanings of sentences with an even number of forms that have negative morphology may be the direct opposite of what the same word sequence means in

Standard English. (A point that has hardly ever been made is that in cases with an odd number of negations the word sequences may come out with the SAME meanings as in Standard English, though the meanings may be extremely difficult to compute.

For example, in Standard English, liking nothing means disliking everything; so means that nobody did other than dislike everything; which means that everyone disliked everything; in other words, nobody liked anything, which is the same meaning that we have more straightforwardly in the non-standard dialects.)

Neither set of conditions says anything about the other dialect being WRONG. And certainly neither set of conditions can tell us which dialect is inherently fit to be accorded a prestige place in Anglophone society. As it happens, accidents of history accorded such prestige to a southern British dialect that had lost negative concord. But there is no reason things had to be that way. Modern Polish and modern Italian are standard languages that have negative concord. It is purely an accident that English developed in a way that had the dialect that lost negative concord eventually coming out on top and used in government.

Of course, in complex societies it is also usually the case that some people or classes of people have tangible power (e.g., political or economic) over others. Typically the prestige dialect is associated with such power. That might not be a necessary connection. (Think of a poverty-stricken British lecturer being admired for his accent by a Brooklyn-raised professor earning five times as much. Or think of a great

English-speaking country in which a politician given to the use of the informal register of a non-standard Texan dialect wins the White House.)

Nevertheless, it is a very natural association. When a linguist attempts to give a statement of the constitutive correctness conditions for Standard English, the project may be mistaken by some for a recommendation about how people should talk, because the advantages of learning to use Standard English are (for some purposes) fairly clear, it is taught in schools, and so on. One can see where this error comes from. But it is an error.

PRESCRIPTIVE IDEOLOGUES

The Anglophone world incorporates within its intelligentsia a very vocal class of people we will call prescriptive ideologues whose avocation, or even in some cases profession, is prescribing for others how they ought to write and speak, and lambasting the linguistic incorrectnesses and infelicities of those who do not follow the prescription. They do this, naturally enough, on behalf of the prestige dialect: there are no signs of prescriptive ideologues advocating for the non-standard dialects.

There is a link between the stance of the prescriptive ideologues and actual political conservativism. Geoff Nunberg has remarked that English grammatical usage "has become a flagship issue for the cultural right: the people who are most vociferous about grammatical correctness tend to be those most dismissive of the political variety." The question that concerns me is whether there is any other valid rationale for the connection. It is extraordinarily hard to locate one.

The prescriptive ideologues appear to be tacitly adopting some form of realism that grammarians generally do not endorse. Louis Menand (politically a liberal, by the way), expanding on what he meant by remarks in a review about how there should be more grammatical usage advice in The Chicago Manual of Style, stated in an email to my friend Arnold Zwicky that all regulative rules of usage "are fundamentally arbitrary, and thus sometimes feel as though they exist only to trip up even the most careful writer." Yet he made it clear that he felt they nonetheless defined solecisms for us, and were to be obeyed, since a writer should be careful to avoid solecisms. This is not just a common attitude; it is the standard one. A colleague of Zwicky's posted a remark to a newsgroup to the effect that violations of a certain prescriptive rule were indeed ungrammatical. Zwicky writes: "I mailed him an example [that violated the rule] from his own writing" but all that happened was that "he was inclined to think that he should just be more vigilant." There is more than a hint in this of a realist attitude to regulative usage rules — as if they exist independently of us.

But what kind of realism could this be? It can hardly be moral realism, aesthetic realism, or scientific realism. Realism is the view that there are external, objective bases for assessing proposed theories, principles, judgments, etc. Thus, for example, moral realism claims that there is a fact of the matter about what really is morally right and good, independent of our practice in calling this right or that bad, and that proposed systems of moral principles can be assessed by how they stand in respect to that external fact of the matter. A realist stance on prescriptive rules for English would claim that there is an external, objective basis — external to the use actually made of the language — for saying what really is correct. What could that basis be? What external first principles could yield the correctness conditions for Standard English?

There are a number of candidates. Let me run through all those we can discern in the literature. (Don't take the labels seriously; they're just ad hoc one-word mnemonic pointers, not technical terms to look up in a dictionary.) Following each putative basis for justifying prescriptive claims we will try to give an indication of what it appears to be designed to help us avoid.

- Nostalgia. Justificatory basis: The past glory of some vanished golden age, an imagined linguistic utopia in which people spoke correctly. To avoid: Change — decay and deterioration, either linguistic or social.
- Classicism. Justificatory basis: The standing of other higher-prestige languages such as Latin. To avoid: Adoption of an inferior form of human language.
- Authoritarianism. Justificatory basis: Subordination to the established authority of high-prestige masters of the language. To avoid: Social disgrace from using low-grade English.
- Aestheticism. Justificatory basis: Beauty and aesthetic responses. To avoid: Ugliness and awkwardness.
- Coherentism. Justificatory basis: Consistency and

order of patterning. To avoid: Chaos, randomness, disorder.

- Logicism. Justificatory basis: Logic in the strict sense. To avoid: Irrationality.
- Commonsensism. Justificatory basis: Common sense. To avoid: Silliness.
- Functionalism. Justificatory basis: Efficiency of the communicative function. To avoid: Ambiguity, misunderstanding, redundancy, etc.
- Asceticism. Justificatory basis: Discipline and self-control. To avoid: Laziness and sloppiness.

Some of these may seem distinctly 19th-century. But in grammar the 19th century never really went away. Mott Media still markets Thomas Harvey's textbook under the title Harvey's Revised English Grammar, Harvey was born in 1821, and his grammar was published soon after the Civil War (1868). It still treats English as having a number distinction in the second person pronouns (thou vs. you). But the massive home school industry to which Harvey's grammar and the McGuffey readers are still sold ignores little things like whether the textbook describes a language that nobody speaks any more.

And of course Strunk and White's toxic little compendium of bad grammatical advice, The Elements of Style, is still a best-seller, despite the fact that for nearly a hundred years it has been treated as a holy text and only very slightly revised, even in 1957 when White's name was added to the by-line and the fifth chapter was added.

Even the page breaks have stayed the same for decades. Both authors were already born when the 20th century began. Strunk was born seven years before Custer's last stand. The relevance is that Strunk's attitudes on usage and grammar and how to describe syntactic phenomena were formed long before the 19th century ended.

The Elements of Style sometimes illustrates all of the putative external bases for usage judgments we suggested above on a single page, or even within a single paragraph. Take this appallingly dogmatic entry, which actually does not stem from the 19th century like most of the book, but is due to White, who added it in his revision in 1957:

Hopefully. This once-useful adverb meaning "with hope" has been distorted and is now widely used to mean "I hope" or "it is to be hoped." Such use is not merely wrong, it is silly. To say, "Hopefully I'll leave on the noon plane" is nonsense. Do you mean you'll leave on the noon plane in a hopeful frame of mind? Or do you mean you hope you'll leave on the noon plane? Whichever you mean, you haven't said it clearly. Although the word in its new, free-floating capacity may be pleasurable and even useful to many, it offends the ear of many others, who do not like to see words dulled or eroded, particularly when the erosion leads to ambiguity, softness, or nonsense.

Look at the multitude of ways in which White justifies his wild hostility to the use of hopefully as a modal adjunct in clause structure.

He says the word has been "distorted" — an aesthetic judgment, apparently. He says the new use is "silly" — an appeal to common sense. He says that if you use it you will be talking "nonsense", which seems to appeal to logic — though in fact the appeal to logic is immediately forgotten, for the examples that follow do not illustrate contradiction, but merely the possibility of a word having two senses. For White, anyone who uses a word with two senses to say something hasn't "said it clearly" (he has strayed from logic to communicative efficiency.

But there is more. The suggestion that "the word in its new, free-floating capacity may be pleasurable" suggests a disdain for hedonism, and a favoring of discipline and self-control. The modal adjunct use may be "useful to many", but that makes no difference; after all, it may be useful to have an elevator, but the active man has the discipline to take the stairs — a hint of asceticism there.

But no (he changes his mind again), the real thing is, it "offends the ear" we're back to aesthetics. Or is it is that the original word has been "dulled" — like a misused knife blade — and "eroded" — like an unmaintained protective dyke?

These kinds of damage are bad because may lead to "ambiguity" (communicative efficiency once more), or "softness" (masculine toughness is being favored here — being vague is just one way to be wimpy), or maybe "nonsense" (in his wild searching for terms of opprobrium White has cycled around and come upon this word a second time, heedless now of the Strunkian maxim he values so much, to "omit needless words").

There is something distinctly parental about this outburst of hints, allegations, and redundant abuse. You're being silly, you're talking nonsense, you're offending the ear of your betters, you're being sloppy, you're acting soft like a girl — for goodness' sake pull your socks up!

And it is perhaps even more reminiscent of the vacillating motivations for old-fashioned sex advice to the young. Don't touch yourself down there, it's dirty, you'll go blind, it saps your strength, it'll ruin you for marriage, it's unhealthy, it's immature, it's immoral, it's forbidden in the Bible.

It is not a new observation that one can draw relevant parallels between the politics of language and the politics of sexual behavior. John Sherwood drew the parallel in a fascinating 1960 article in College English, connecting traditional grammar ("the old grammar", as he terms it) to a whole slew of value-laden issues. The article appears to have been motivated by a reaction against Charles C. Fries's The Structure of English in 1952, a very explicit representative of the tradition of American scientific structuralism, with its refusal to use terms like 'noun' or 'verb' (they stemmed from the bad old days of traditional grammar, and had to be replaced by category names like 'Class 1' and 'Class 2'), with the two Kinsey reports on sexual behavior not very far in the past.

The "new grammar" — the modern 'scientific' linguistics represented to college English teachers in 1960 by Charles C. Fries — is a very different kettle of fish):

As a Sprachansschauung, if not as a science, it stands for democracy; for spontaneity, self-expression, and permissiveness; for nominalism; for skepticism; for a social-scientific view of life; for progress and modernity; for nationalism and regionalism. It is "other-directed," seeing the proper standard of conduct as conformity to the mores of the group. It represents a linguistic Rousseauism, a belief that man's language is best and most real when most spontaneous and unpremeditated and that it is somehow tainted by the efforts of educational systems to order and regularize it. Just as the old grammar tried to take its values from above, the new tries to deduce them, in the manner of Dr Kinsey, from the facts.

It is hard not to see here the liberalism that was to become dominant in the sixties that lay ahead: democracy, spontaneity, self-expression, permissiveness, skepticism, social science, progress, and modernity. This is a list of just about all of the conservative's worst nightmares.

And as for the 'old grammar', once we separate the issue from structuralist claims to offer a "scientific" linguistics, Sherwood claims:

the old grammar is seen to stand for values that are often a good deal more defensible than their opposites. It stands for order, logic, and consistency; for the supremacy of the written language and of the literate classes and of the literate classes in setting linguistic standards; for continuity, tradition, and universality–for what is common to older and modern, British and American English, to the whole body of European languages rather than for what is local and singular; for discipline and self-control; for the practice of an art, a system developed by tradition and the authority of masters rather than statistical study. . . . Loving logic and order, it opposes oddity and irregularity, and at times may have the coldness that goes with order and regularity. It is not resigned to the chaos of experience but wishes to impose its own order upon it; it believes, with Orwell, in man's power to master his linguistic environment . . . it attempts to raise the illiterate to the level of the literate, not to average everyone out to a common level.

One could hardly miss the buzzwords of political conservatism here: order, continuity, tradition, discipline, self-control, authority — and the inherent supremacy of the literate classes. And it is also not hard to see allusions to a number of putative external bases for prescriptive regulative rules: at least coherentism, logicism, authoritarianism, classicism, and asceticism.

FAILING JUSTIFICATIONS

Why do the prescriptive ideologues' various external criteria of justification fail? Because none of them have any foundation: the things they presuppose just are not so. Let's briefly run through the reasons, familiar though most of the objections are.

Nostalgia There never was, of course, a golden age. The linguistic utopia of widespread proper usage never existed. In particular, many constructions that people imagine are banned by the laws of proper English grammar — preposition stranding, split infinitives, and they with singular antecedents, for example — have been attested in much admired English writing throughout the entire 700-year history of the language. Even if all change WERE decay and deterioration, use of these constructions has gone on since the earliest days of anything recognizable as English.

Classicism: It might have been sensible in the 16th or even the 17th century to look to Latin, despite its typological dissimilarity to English, for a developed theoretical vocabulary for grammar and a literature in which complex thoughts were expressed with accuracy and conceptual rigor. But it is absurd today, when English has a far larger literature of careful scholarly and analytical writing than Latin ever had, and the tradition of writing grammars of English is some four hundred years old.

Authoritarianism Respect to the established authority of high-prestige masters of the language is just fine, but subservience to the personal whims and hatreds of a self-anointed language controller is not. Notice, we are not undercutting the idea of standards for judging the use of the English language, because — let's not be coy about this — there can be no doubt that some people use the English language brilliantly and their writing gives us pleasure, while others use it abysmally and the ineptness of their fumbling phrases makes us wince. There is a difference between the writing skills of G. K. Chesterton and those of Dan Brown.

One common objection to linguistic authority as a basis for usage decisions is that it involves dependence on a selected canon, and too often canon selection has been done by near-dead white males selecting thoroughly-dead white males — the unspeakable in pursuit of the unreadable. I'm objecting to authoritarianism, but that isn't the right objection. The real trouble is that the prescriptive ideologues turn out not to know what even their favored canon really contains.

Stanley Fish wrote a column in The Chronicle of Higher Education attacking President Larry Summers of Harvard for a remark allegedly couched in poor English. The remark was this:

- We regret any faculty member leaving a conversation feeling they are not respected.

One of the two alleged syntactic errors was a non-genitive subject of a gerund clause (Fish thought it should have been any faculty member's leaving); Fish appears not to know that it is the genitive subject that is the innovation, and it took a while to achieve its present status of being an acceptable alternative in most but not all contexts. The other is a case of they with a singular antecedent. But Fish, though a Milton scholar, was apparently not aware that even Milton uses they with singular antecedents.

Such cases could be multiplied arbitrarily, as Merriam-Webster's Dictionary of English Usage will confirm. So the point is that if you actually take a look at what the great masters of English literature write, you will find that the dicta of the prescriptive ideologues are simply not confirmed as trustworthy guides to good style. Generally acknowledged fine writing does exemplify gerund-participial clauses with accusative subjects, and they with distributive singular antecedents; clauses do end in prepositions in great literature; infinitives do get split.

Aestheticism: The adage that beauty is in the eye of the beholder is surely more applicable in the area of linguistic beauty than anywhere else. White says that hopefully is "distorted" and "offends the ear" if it is used as a modal clause adjunct. How could it be? Moby Dick contains an instance of the clause other leviathans might be hopefully pursued, where hopefully is a manner adjunct. If we shift the adverb one word to the left we get other leviathans might hopefully be pursued, where hopefully is today more naturally interpretable as a modal adjunct (that is, we can imagine it meaning it is to be hoped that other leviathans might be pursued). How could that be so much uglier that it would offend the ear? The whole appeal to offense of a generic ear (which White appeals to repeatedly in his contributions) is disingenuous. White should simply have said, "I don't like this usage." To which the obvious answer is, then don't use it. What is going on here is a dishonest attempt to universalize one's personal taste without admitting to having done that.

Coherentism: It is really remarkable to see Sherwood proposing that traditional grammar champions order, logic, and consistency, "opposes oddity and irregularity," and aims to "impose its own order" on "the chaos of experience." English is not ordered, logical, or consistent; and willing it to be cannot make it so. The Cambridge Grammar offers thousands of pages of evidence. Let me summarize just a snippet or two.

- English has nearly two hundred verbs that are inflectionally irregular in a variety of ways (Swahili, by the way, has none). There are verbs with one, two, three, four, and five inflectional shapes, and one extraordinary one (be) with twelve.
- There are two functional types of relative clauses, integrated and supplementary, and while the integrated ones can be bare (anyone you like), or introduced by the subordinator that (anyone that you like) or a pronoun (anyone who likes you) or a preposition phrase (those to whom it is important) or a noun phrase with whose as determiner (anyone whose car is stolen), other noun phrases are not permitted (*anything the wrapping of which is

damaged). The supplementary ones, on the other hand, can be introduced by a pronoun (Bob, who likes you), a noun phrase with whose as determiner (Bob, whose car was stolen), or other kinds of noun phrase (a gift, the wrapping of which was damaged), but they cannot be bare (*I've invited Bob, you like) or introduced by a subordinator (*I've invited Bob, that you said you liked). Where's the consistency?

- The relativized element in a relative clause can be the subject with any of the above types, except for one: the bare relative. So we get Anyone who (/that,/ whose partner) wants to come is welcome, but not *Anyone wants to come is welcome.
- In interrogatives, the words who, which, where, when, why, and how can all be used as interrogative words. In relatives, the words who, which, where, when, and why, can all be relative words, but how and whose on its own cannot (*the way how you do it is non-standard).
- The word whose can have a non-human antecedent in a relative clause (a card table whose legs are wobbly) but not in an interrogative clause (*I left repairing the tables to you because I didn't know whose legs were wobbly), and can be used without a following head noun in an interrogative clause (Whose is this?) but not in a relative clause (*the man whose was stolen).
- There are nine reflexive pronouns in Standard English, all compounds formed with the suffix ·self, and two are based on accusative forms (himself, themselves), two are based on plain case forms (itself, oneself), and all the others are based on genitive forms (myself, yourself, herself, ourselves, yourselves). Dialects that regularize this to the genitive throughout (*hisself, *theirselves) are regarded as non-standard.

One could list any number of such examples. No one who had worked over English carefully could possibly think that there was order, logic, or consistency to be found amongst the vast array of exceptions and puzzles found in the English language. Despite all the system and regularity that makes it possible for us to learn, it is riddled with disorder, illogic, inconsistency, oddity, irregularity, and chaos — everything Sherwood says traditional grammar stands against. And I'm referring to Standard English, the kind the prescriptivists wish to prescribe. This part of his thesis has no foundation at all. If you seek regularity and consistency, good luck, but neither descriptive correctness conditions nor prescriptive rules for Standard English can help you.

Logicism. Very similar remarks can be made about basing grammatical principles on logic. We will not dwell on the point for long, since it is so familiar, but consider one small illustrative point. There is disagreement about the preposition that should head the preposition-phrase complement of the adjective different. The most frequent is different from; second ranked is different than; and least popular but still very commmon is different to. Different than has been criticized for centuries, and American usage books say that different to is restricted to British. And perhaps one could imagine developing an argument that differentness is a matter of separation, not convergence, so that from is more logical than to: difference is the opposite of similarity, and we say similar to, so it should be different from.

But consider the word dissimilar. It too is an antonym of similar. But it is also derived from similar. Should it follow the derivational morphology, yielding dissimilar to? Or should it follow the sense, yielding dissimilar from? How can logic settle such a question? It does not, of course: Webster's Third gives two examples with dissimilar followed by a preposition phrase complement: one has from and the other has to. Take your pick. Current Google statistics show about 8,000 pages in the .edu domain (which perhaps reflects prevailing American academic usage) with uses of dissimilar from, and about 20,000 with dissimilar to. Use that as a guide if you like, but logic won't help you. In logic, dissimilarity and difference are the same, but dissimilar is tending to get its syntactic selectional behavior more from its derivational origin than its truth conditions.

Commonsensism: The appeal to common sense (often put by White in terms of using one's "ear") is a pervasive feature of The Elements of Style. But if anything is silly, it is imagining that one's notions of silliness are objective and independent of one's spatiotemporal location.

A 1937 New Yorker cartoon of two American women shopping in London has one of them saying:

"I have to do all the buying, because George won't say tuppence ha'penny. He says it's silly."

This on its own should be enough to remind us of the parochiality of silliness judgments: in 1970 it did not seem silly to any British English speaker to say tuppence ha'penny. A year later, with decimalization, it became strictly meaningless, and by 1980 British teenagers didn't even understand it. Of course what is not current will often sound silly. But that is an argument for sticking to what's current as a matter of today's common usage whatever it is; it's the opposite of what the prescriptive ideologues actually seek.

Functionalism: Efficiency of the communicative function is perhaps the commonest putatively external and objective justification offered by the prescriptive ideologues, but it is also one of the easiest to rebut. Take ambiguity. To begin with, the fact that ambiguity might arise if some grammatical feature were this way rather than that way cannot possibly be parlayed into a reason why the grammar should or must be that way. Losing the distinction between thou wouldst and you would has led to ambiguity between 2nd singular and 2nd plural, but that doesn't mean that use of you with singular reference is wrong. The sentence We saw her duck is profoundly ambiguous, but that doesn't mean either that the verb duck or the noun duck has been wrongly used.

Allegations about what will lead to ambiguity are often thinly supported if supported at all, and sometimes are demonstrably false. It is asserted that use of phrases like any museum which charges an entrance fee will lead to ambiguity because we don't know if we are to interpret the relative clause as integrated or supplementary; but that is not true here: the determiner and head noun tell us it cannot be supplementary, and the lack of a comma before the relative clause also tells us that. One can look through dozens and dozens of relative clauses without finding a single one where ambiguity would arise from use of which rather than that.

Similar remarks can be made about misunderstanding, redundancy, and the other things that are cited in connection with problems for communication. It just is not true for most points insisted on by the prescriptive ideologues that communication is at risk unless their prescriptions are followed.

Asceticism. We come finally to discipline and self-control. And here we think we might be a little closer to some important genuine connections between the grammatical and the political.

At first sight it seems fantastic that Sherwood can think he sees a link between grammatically correct writing and self-discipline. Has he no knowledge at all of the biographies of great literary figures who have written classics in Standard English? Coleridge, the opium addict? Wilde, with his addiction to Bosie and his pathological inability to pay his bills? Fitzgerald and his disastrous love affair with alcohol? One can hardly think that the ability to write great and memorable Standard English goes along with jogging before breakfast, a clean life, avoidance of addictions, and disciplined control over one's own evil or debauched urges.

But of course, what's more relevant is Sherwood's references to descriptive structural linguistics as allied with democracy, spontaneity, self-expression, and permissiveness. The notion is that left to ourselves, we would naturally all want a share of power; we would all want to do whatever we felt like whenever we felt like it; we would all want to do things our way, linguistically and in every other sphere of life; and we would indulge in all sorts of naughty stuff. In language we would be just the same: we would each be in control of our own language; we would alter syntax unwisely and idiosyncratically, collapse meaning distinctions, slur pronunciations, and invent ugly and unintelligible jargon; it would be anything goes. Wanna ignore verb agreement? Have another doughnut. Fancy using the accusative instead of the nominative in one context, and the nominative instead of the accusative in another? We're cool with that. If it feels good, do it.

The role of traditional grammar, as Sherwood seems to imagine it, is to keep us in check, to rein in our unseemly impulses. Yet it does it only by providing a code that we can follow if we choose. The ones who follow that code will be the ones who have the discipline and self-control to do so. The ones who don't will be the ones whose self-expression combines with their permissiveness to yield bad results like double negatives and failure of verb agreement. Average over them, and you will have something we do not want to set up as the model for the linguistic behavior of the young. That is what Sherwood seems to be suggesting.

All we can do is bluntly disagree. Just as people in general do not always do wicked things just because they can, it simply isn't true that human languages fall apart if not defended through the analogue of vigorous training, constant maintenance, and regular cold baths. Human language is systematic and stable to a degree that is quite astonishing.

Negative concord provides an excellent example. It was clearly present in early Middle English (there is evidence in Chaucer). It has survived to this day among millions of speakers all over the world despite the fact that their dialects are not just recognized as non-standard but often condemned as sub-standard. Think how robust the negative concord phenomenon must be to last 700 years and spread among working people all over the world in defiance of the authority of the high-prestige speakers of the standard dialect.

Standard English will of course be even more robust. It is represented in more permanent media — millions of books, newspapers, and magazines. It is spoken by prestige speakers at NPR, the BBC, Buckingham Palace, MLA meetings. It is taught to billions of people in schools and language classes around the world. It is in absolutely no danger of deterioration whatever. Don't worry; be happy: Standard English will survive.

So the issue regarding purported rules like the one saying that a pronoun can never have a genitive antecedent is not about whether we ought to find the discipline to sustain obedience to it. It is about whether we have the intelligence to recognize that it never was one of the correctness conditions of Standard English, and never will be, and the time spent on teaching it, and testing that it has been properly learned, is time utterly wasted.

CONCLUSION

It is a complete caricature of linguists' attitudes to usage that they think anything goes and regard everything that occurs as grammatical. They don't. Quite to the contrary, they insist that there are constitutive correctness conditions for natural languages, conditions that define the difference between right (grammatical) and wrong (ungrammatical) for individual languages. Grammaticality is not to be confused with choice of formal style, though: informal style is grammatical too.

Correctness conditions provide sufficient justification for saying that something is grammatical or ungrammatical, provided they are the correct conditions; but they need their own justification. Linguists seek to justify formal statements of proposed sets of correctness conditions by means of a basically scientific investigative methodology — it based on attention to evidence.

Prescriptive ideologues tacitly take the descriptive work to be already done (they do not spend any time on order of subject and predicate or preposing of relative pronouns, where there is no disagreement); their concern is solely with a superstratum of particular points on which usage is controversial and they have a view to present.

The regulative rules that the prescriptive ideologues advocate need their own justification, if they are to have any force. If the justification offered were to be simple compatibility with the facts of usage in uncontroversially admirable exemplars of good English prose, the prescriptivist project would collapse with that of the linguists, so that is never the justification cited. Instead an array of external sources of justification are vaguely alluded to.

These are very diverse, but what is clear is that none of them can be taken seriously. The prescriptive ideologues do not know what is found in the texts they take to illustrate good usage; they do not even know what their own usage is. Jacques Barzun, and then opens a paragraph on the next page by using one with which. E. B. White does not even get through the second paragraph of his Stuart Little without using an integrated relative with which, which in The Elements of Style he deprecates.

Unjustified and perhaps unjustifiable, the rules of the prescriptive ideologues, dimly grasped and often misunderstood, nonetheless form the backbone of what the general public understands and believes about English grammar.

The clearest fact about the spirit of the regulative rules the prescriptive ideologues advance is that they are genuinely linked to conservative ideology: the mistrust of ordinary people and the pessimism about what they would get up to if left to their own devices is palpable. This makes it not so surprising that, as Geoff Nunberg has observed, attention to grammatical correctness correlates to some extent with contempt for liberal-style political correctness.

It is a familiar pattern for people to reify an unjustifiable set of regulative rules that are supported mainly by the taste of the person making the proposal, to treat them as if they were the constitutive correctness conditions for some language that people do not speak but should, and to call that language English.

As long as asking for justification of the proposed rules is treated as some kind of radical crankery or impudent challenge to power, and proposing that the rules lack justification and are not defining features of English can be portrayed as "lowering standards," irrationality will prevail in this area. And matters like the attitude adopted by the press and public to the Oakland school board's policy on 'Ebonics' can hardly be treated rationally at all. Even Standard English is not being treated rationally. It is hard to imagine anything in the field of linguistics being clearer than the fact that Standard English, the prestige syntactic dialect of the whole global family of English dialects, has preposition stranding, singular-antecedent uses of they, infinitival constructions with an adjunct between to and the verb, and so on — and has had them for literally hundreds of years. Yet people pointing that out are treated as if they were proposing that masturbation should be taught in the public schools.

We see all this writ large in the application to the strikingly divergent African American Vernacular dialect with its unusual syntactic features. People wildly confuse constitutive correctness conditions for a specific non-standard dialect with regulative rules for appropriate usage in the standard, and confuse slang with the linguistic system of which it forms a tiny subpart, and dishonestly express hostility toward black people and their way of speaking as if it were defense of the language that we all speak . . .It all makes the Oakland 'Ebonics' brouhaha one of the worst and most tangled instaweces we have ever seen of the confusions that we have been trying to disentangle here.

Chapter 21

Pre-Juncture Lengthening and Foot Binarity

INTRODUCTION

Pre-juncture (or pre-boundary) lengthening refers to the phenomenon where the final syllable before a major syntactic juncture is longer than a similar one in other positions. The phenomenon has also been called 'phrase-final lengthening' and 'pre-pausal lengthening'.

Phrase-final lengthening may suggest that all XP final positions have a similar lengthening effect, which is not the case. Pre-pausal lengthening may suggest that the lengthening takes place only before a pause, which is not the case either. To avoid such ambiguities, we use the term 'pre-juncture lengthening' in this article.

In this study we compare pre-juncture lengthening in Chinese and English, with an emphasis on the phonological perspectives. Is there a phonological basis for pre-juncture lengthening? In what ways is a difference in pre-juncture lengthening between two languages related to their phonological systems? Given a difference in pre-juncture lengthening, what other phonological differences can one expect?

PHONETIC EXPERIMENT

It has been noted in the literature that there is considerably difference in pre-juncture lengthening between English and

Chinese. While previous studies showed consistent results, they were based on fairly small numbers of speakers. In addition, these studies were primarily designed either for English or for Chinese, and not for comparing them directly. It will be helpful, therefore, to see whether the same result obtains with more speakers and under direct comparisons. For this purpose an experiment was conducted to compare pre-juncture lengthening in English and Chinese in controlled environments.

Method

Test Sentences

Three sentences were used in English, shown in (1), with phonetic transcription.

(1) a. an1 an2 an3
[tɛn plus tɛn taimz tɛn]
'(Ten plus ten) times ten.'

b. bn1 bn2 bn3
[tɛn plus tɛn taimz tɛn]
'Ten plus (ten times ten).'

c. [hi bot e fæn but ai bot e kar]
'He bought a fan, but I bought a car.'

Three corresponding sentences were used in Chinese, shown in (2), with phonetic transcription, characters, tone, Pinyin transcription, word-for-word gloss, and translation. The tonal markings are: H = high (the First tone), R = rise (the Second tone), L = low (the Half-Third tone), F = fall (the Fourth tone), and 0 = toneless.

In choosing test sentences, factors that could affect duration were taken into consideration. The target syllables in the (a) sentences were the three numbers, indicated as an1, an2, and an3. The target syllables in the (b) sentences were also the three numbers, indicated as bn1, bn2, and bn3. (1a,b) and (2a,b) were modeled after the test sentences '(A plus E) times O' vs. Phonetically, [t[n] 'ten' in English and 'three' in Chinese are the two digits that are closest in segmental and syllabic compositions, which was why they were chosen.

(an2, an3, and bn3) on the other. This result reconfirms the well-known fact that stressed pre-juncture rimes were significantly longer than stressed non pre-juncture rimes in English.

There was no significant difference between non pre-juncture rimes, or among pre-juncture rimes. On the other hand, there was a significant difference between pre-juncture rimes and non pre-juncture rimes, as there was in English.

Next we compare English and Chinese. The non pre-juncture rimes in English (an1 = 169 ms, bn2 = 168 ms) had similar durations as those in Chinese (an1 = 162 ms, bn2 = 170 ms). In addition, in both languages pre-juncture rimes were significantly lengthened. However, it can be seen that the size of lengthening was greater in English than in Chinese. To determine whether the between-language differences were significant, Repeated Measures ANOVA was performed on the averages of non pre-juncture rimes (an1 and bn2) and the averages of pre-juncture rimes (an2, an3, and bn3). First, in both English and Chinese a significant difference was found between pre-juncture and non pre-juncture rimes. Second, the difference between pre-juncture and non pre-juncture rimes was significantly dependent on the language. Third, non pre-juncture rimes did not differ in the two languages.

Let us now consider whether the extra lengthening in English was due to tonal complexity. The lexical tone for the Mandarin word 'three' was H, which was maintained throughout. Of the 180 tokens of pre-juncture English rimes, 121 had F, 28 had FR, 2 had H, 17 had L, and 12 had R. The majority of them (F, H, L, and R, or 84%), therefore, did not need more than two moras. The Mandarin syllable [sæn] also has two moras. In addition, there is little durational difference between H, R, and F in Mandarin. Thus, tonal complexity could not have contributed to the extra pre-juncture lengthening in English.

Finally, consider pauses. After an1 and bn2, the average silence durations were under 30 ms in both English and Chinese, which should belong to the closure of the following stop. Thus, there was no obvious pause after an1 and bn2. After an2, however, the average silence duration was above 100 ms in both English and Chinese, which means that there was some pause besides the closure of the following stop or affricate. This shows that both English and Chinese can use a pause in addition to pre-juncture lengthening at a syntactically and/or semantically contrastive juncture.

Summary

The present results are consistent with those of previous studies and give the following conclusions. First, both English and Chinese are subject to pre-juncture lengthening. Second, English exhibits significantly more pre-juncture lengthening than Chinese does. Third, Chinese has a greater tendency to use pauses at syntactic junctures than English does. It will be helpful, of course, if more experiments are carried out on other rime pairs in English and Chinese. But the consistency in the results obtained so far provides good indication that further results will point to the same way. In what follows we will assume that the present conclusions are essentially correct.

PHONOLOGICAL ANALYSIS

Let us now explore the reason for the difference in pre-juncture lengthening between English and Chinese. First, consider the idea that Chinese lacks pre-juncture lengthening because it is a tone language in which every regular syllable has a lexical tone. Since a tonal contour is a function of both pitch height and time, changing the duration of a syllable will presumably change its tonal contour. And since tonal contour is a distinctive property of every regular Chinese syllable, it is plausible that changes in tone are generally avoided. However, this proposal has three shortcomings.

First, it is not the case that there is no pre-juncture lengthening in Chinese; we have seen that there is significant pre-juncture lengthening in Chinese, just as there is English. Second, although lengthening a syllable may change its tonal contour, the distinctions among tonal categories need not be lost. For example, Mandarin has four tones on full syllables, which are often described as high level, high rise, fall-rise, and fall. If we interpret them as H, MH, MLH, and HL, and assume that the lengthened syllable has three moras, the resulting tones, over the moras, will be HHH, MHH, MLH, and HLL, where the four categories remain distinct. Third, changes in tone do occur in Chinese, despite the loss of tonal contrast. For example, the well-known Mandarin Third Tone Sandhi changes the Third tone into the Second, which can introduce ambiguities. For example, [mai3] 'buy' has the Third tone and [mai2] 'bury' has the Second tone. In [mai2 ma3] 'to buy a horse', [mai3] has changed to the Second tone because of the following Third tone in [ma3] 'horse'. As a result, the expression sounds identical to 'to bury a horse'. Thus, the fact that a pre-juncture Chinese syllable lengthens less cannot be attributed to the need to preserve tonal distinctions.

What else then is the explanation? We suggest that pre-juncture lengthening is not a homogeneous phenomenon, but is sensitive to both phonetics and phonology. Let us call the former phonetic lengthening and the latter phonological lengthening. The former is probably due to a 'slow-down' tendency at the end of a structure. We assume then that both English and Chinese are subject to phonetic lengthening, in accordance with the fact that pre-juncture rimes were longer than non pre-juncture rimes in both languages. However, unlike phonetic lengthening, phonological lengthening is not universal, but requires specific conditions. We will argue that these conditions are met in English but not in Chinese. Consequently, phonological lengthening occurs in English but not in Chinese, which leads to the fact that English pre-juncture rimes are longer than those in Chinese.

Consider first the motivation for phonological lengthening in English. A fundamental property of stress and rhythm is the alternation between strong and weak beats. To realize such an alternation there needs to be a minimum of two beats (syllables). In phonology this is known as foot binarity. In earlier literature foot binarity was thought to be a soft requirement, but recent research suggests that it is stronger than has been realized.

Nevertheless, there remain two questions about the null

vowel. First, what is the motivation for it? Second, how is it realized? For the first question, Burzio suggests a cross-linguistic constraint that all words must end in a vowel. This may explain why 'fan' is analyzed as (fan.nø) (ignoring consonant gemination), but not why 'bee' should be analyzed as (bee.ø). For the second question, one would expect the null vowel to be realized as a silent pause, perhaps. But there is no such evidence. A better analysis, therefore, is not to posit the null vowel for English, yet still preserve Burzio's key insights. We suggest that instead of analyzing 'fan' as [faen.nø] and 'bee' as [bi.ø], they be analyzed as [fææ.n] or [fae.aen] and [bi.i]. In other words, they are disyllabic, but without the null vowel. Because the disyllabic forms contain more segment slots, they are expected to be longer than non pre-juncture and [bi]. This analysis preserves the binary foot minimum, a key in Burzio's analysis, and avoids the difficulties with the null vowel. In addition, this analysis accounts for the fact that a stressed pre-juncture English syllable is significantly lengthened (beyond the amount of phonetic lengthening observed in Chinese), as shown in the present experiment and previous literature.

Let us now turn to the lack of phonological lengthening in Chinese. First, consider stress in Mandarin. Unlike English, where many words are polysyllabic and where intuition for stress is reasonably clear, Chinese is a monosyllabic language in which the question does not arise as to where stress falls on a simple word. There is, instead, a fairly clear distinction between full syllables, which are usually content words, and unstressed (toneless) syllables, which are usually functional words or particles. The question of stress does arise in compounds (and phrases) made of two or more full syllables, whereas there is a good degree of agreement on which syllables are unstressed, opinions differ in regard to relative degrees of stress among full syllables of a compound. Still, some linguists made an attempt to capture the nuances.

But there is some evidence that Mandarin has left-headed stress, just as English does. Most people agree that duration is a primary indication of stress in Chinese. The second syllable of a disyllabic Mandarin compound is longer than the first, the final syllable of a trisyllabic Mandarin compound is longer than the other two.

However, the first syllable is longer in both disyllabic and trisyllabic compound. One may wonder why there is contradicting evidence. A close look at the methodology suggests that Wang & Wang's result is more reliable. Further evidence for left-headed stress in Mandarin compounds comes from the distribution of unstressed (toneless) syllables. In disyllabic compounds there are many cases where the second syllable is unstressed, but there is no case where the first syllable is unstressed. Similarly, in four-syllable compounds there are many cases where the second and third syllables are unstressed, but there is no case where the first and the third syllables are unstressed.

It appears then that Mandarin has left-headed feet after all, just as English does. But then we are back to the original question again: why is there more pre-juncture lengthening in English than in Mandarin? We suggest that the answer lies in syllable inventory. English has a wide range of syllable structures. Preceding the vowel there can be from zero to three consonants.

The vowel itself can be short (lax), long (tense), or a diphthong. After the vowel there can be up to four consonants. Although there are some constraints on the English syllable, such as sonority (for onset and coda clusters) and place of articulation (for coda clusters), there is still a large inventory of syllable types.

The C represents a consonant or a glide (the consonant can also have a secondary articulation, which is traditionally written as a separate glide). The V represents a short vowel, the first mora of a diphthong, or the first mora of a long vowel. The X represents either the second mora of a long vowel, or the second mora of a diphthong, or a nasal coda.

The richness of the English syllable inventory allows it to turn a monosyllable into a disyllable easily (when called upon by foot binarity).

For example, [t[n] 'ten' can turn into [t[.[n], [t[[.n], or [t[[.[n], without creating ill-formed syllable types. In Chinese, however, such freedom is not available, because CVX is the only syllable structure.

For example, one cannot turn [sæn] 'three' into [sae.aen], [saeae.n], or [saeae.aen]; in the first case both syllables are ill-formed and in the second and third the second syllable is ill-formed. Thus, although a stressed pre-juncture syllable is subject to foot binarity in both English and Chinese, English can satisfy it by lengthening, but Chinese cannot.

Lengthening is not the only way to satisfy foot binarity, however. Ironically, while the idea of null syllables did not seem appropriate for English, it works fine for Chinese. In particular, I suggest that a stressed pre-juncture syllable in Chinese is followed by a silent beat, and together they form a binary foot.

This analysis directly accounts for the two differences between English and Chinese, which have so far remained unexplained: first, English had greater pre-juncture lengthening than Chinese, and second, the pause after a stressed pre-juncture syllable is often absent in English but rarely absent in Chinese.

In English the pre-juncture syllable is turned into two syllables through lengthening, made possible by the flexibility in syllable structure.

In Mandarin the same lengthening is not available, owing to the rigid CVX syllable structure. Instead, Mandarin satisfies foot binarity by using a silent beat (pause) after a stressed pre-juncture syllable.

This analysis accounts for the three phonetic results reported in here: (i) there is pre-juncture lengthening in both English and Chinese, (ii) English shows more pre-juncture lengthening than Mandarin, and (iii) a pause after the pre-juncture syllable is optional in English but required in Mandarin.

CONCLUSIONS

We have given experimental results that English shows more lengthening in a stressed pre-juncture syllable than Chinese. To explain the difference, we propose that pre-juncture lengthening is influenced by both phonetics and phonology.

Phonetic lengthening is present in both English and Chinese. Phonological lengthening is present in English but not in Chinese. Phonological lengthening in English is motivated by the need to satisfy foot binarity; in particular, a stressed final syllable does not form a binary foot, and to satisfy foot binarity, it will split into two syllables.

Thus, [fæn] 'fan' is turned into [fae.aen] or [faeae.n]. What appears to be syllable lengthening, therefore, is in fact the result of syllable split. Like English, Chinese also obeys foot binarity, but owing to its rigid syllable structure, syllable split is not available.

In particular, CVX is the only structure for full Mandarin syllables (Duanmu 1993); a syllable like [faen] 'rice' cannot be split into [fae.aen], [faeae.n], or [faeae.aen]; in the first both syllables are ill-formed, and in the second and third the second syllable is ill-formed. As a result, Chinese needs to satisfy foot binarity in other ways, such as using a pause (or a filler word) as the second syllable of a foot.

The present analysis raises a range of questions. For example, is there independent evidence that a lengthened English syllable counts as two syllables? Is there independent evidence that a pause can count as a syllable in Chinese?

Can the present analysis be extended to other languages? Will a stressed monosyllabic word be lengthened in nonfinal positions? Are there other consequences of the difference in pre-juncture lengthening between English and Chinese? Are there exceptions to the present claim that Chinese syllables can not be lengthened? Is phonological pre-juncture lengthening categorical, i.e. either present or absent? For lack of space, these issues will not be addressed here.

Chapter 22

Language Comprehension in Ape and Child

People have always been fascinated with the possibility of "talking with the animals. Many have observed that their pets seem to understand language, and others claim that theirs can actually talk. However, the scientific community has been less willing to grant nonhumans the ability to comprehend and emit language. The recently published monograph, presents a research project designed to provide further evidence to the scientific community that "apes have a heretofore unrecognized capacity for language").

The Rumbaughs' research has also led to a number of important human applications. For example, their work has been instrumental in the successful development of symbol and picture communication systems for nonverbal humans. Many aspects of their research, such as the lexical system, the specific training procedures, and the data collection systems, have benefited this human population. This type of verbal behaviour, and its distinction from topography-based verbal behaviour, has several important implications for speech pathologists and for those attempting to teach verbal behavior to nonverbal humans.

The Rumbaughs' primary interest with this research has been to demonstrate that humans' biological kinship to apes carries over to complex learning, specifically language. The Rumbaughs have long campaigned for granting linguistic competence to the ape. However, as the authors point out in the abstract of the monograph, this position is controversial and is often met with skepticism because "popular theories of human language acquisition suggest that the ability to process syntactic information is unique to humans and reflects a novel biological adaptation not seen in other animals" v). Furthermore, "claims of cognitive contiguity between ape and human still evoke in many scientists a quick reaction of disgust, as if humankind in general is not yet comfortable with the image of itself being part ape".

The study addresses several of the criticisms leveled against ape language research by other language researchers. Specifically, the current project was designed to (a) demonstrate that an ape could comprehend novel and compound spoken English commands (b) without visual or imitative prompts or (c) specific training procedures involving contingent reinforcement, and that (d) the ape's acquisition of these linguistic skills occurs in a manner similar to that of a typically developing human child. The project is presented in the standard form of method, results, and discussion, and will be briefly described below.

METHOD

An 8-year-old male bonobo named Kanzi and a typically developing 2-year-old female human named Alia served as subjects. The formal study took place in a laboratory where Kanzi was raised and in a double-wide mobile home 300 feet away where from 3 months of age onward Alia visited each weekday afternoon.

The arrangement of the interior of the mobile home was similar to Kanzi's environment, and many of the same daily activities that were conducted with Kanzi were conducted with Alia (e.g., games, eating, watching videos, outings, cleaning). One of the experimenters was Alia's mother, who worked in the morning with Kanzi and in the afternoon with Alia. During both of these periods, Alia's mother (as well as the other experimenters) always used speech and the lexical system while interacting with the 2 subjects. Alia and Kanzi, however, did not interact with each other.

Prior to the current experiment, both subjects had

extensive histories with the experimenters, spoken English, and the lexical system. Alia was exposed to the lexigrams beginning at 3 months of age, and Kanzi was exposed to human speech and the lexigrams beginning at 6 months of age. Kanzi accompanied his mother, Matata, while she was receiving training on the lexical system. Sessions were frequently conducted in the forest surrounding the area, as well as in other places around the compound. During Matata's training, caretakers typically talked to Kanzi in natural English and pointed to lexigrams as they spoke; however, no specific training was provided for Kanzi. Matata failed to acquire the symbols, but Kanzi excelled, and by 5 years of age he was producing multiple responses in correct English word order. Kanzi learned so fast that the authors state that "more than any previous ape, the nature and the scope of Kanzi's language acquisition has paralleled that of the human child".

Kanzi spent each day with one or more human caretakers (experimenters) who treated him much like a typical human child. As a result, Kanzi, like Alia, became "accustomed to cooperating with [the experimenters] on a daily basis, and the experimenters were accustomed to determining their moods and facilitating a cooperative attitude" These locations were replenished daily. Kanzi's caretakers always attempted to do things that were of interest to him and talk to him in a natural manner. They also carried with them a large symbol board and pointed to symbols as they spoke to Kanzi. If the words that they were saying were not on the symbol board, they simply continued talking without pointing to any symbols. (Indoors, Kanzi's symbol board was attached to a speech synthesizer so that he could "talk" aloud by pressing the symbols.) Kanzi spent a great deal of time outdoors during the warm months of the year, traveling and playing in the woods. In the winter, he played with toys, painted, helped cook, watched television, visited people in the other indoor parts of the building, played with the other apes at the facility, and even traveled by car (to keep warm) through the woods. All of these activities were accompanied by language in a way that seemed natural to the caretakers.

Testing Procedures

The dependent variable in the formal study consisted of the subjects' response to 660 different verbal instructions. The instructions consisted of a series of novel, and often odd, spoken multiple commands (e.g., *Pour the water on the vacuum).* Prior to the presentation of the multiple commands, both subjects were tested to ensure that they could comprehend the individual words to be used in the sentences.

There were 13 different types of verbal commands that generally increased in complexity as the experiment progressed (e.g., from *Turn the vacuum on* to *Go get some cereal and give it to Rose).*

There were two phases of the study: non-blind trials (Trials 1-180 for Alia and Trials 1-244 for Kanzi) and blind trials (Trials 181-660 for Alia and Trials 245-660 for Kanzi). During the nonblind trials the experimenter presented the subjects with an array of nonverbal stimuli and a verbal command such as *Put the pine needles in the backpack.*

During the blind trials the experimenter presented similar stimuli and verbal commands but was positioned out of the subject's sight.

During many of the blind trials, the human recipients of specific actions wore radio headphones, so they could not hear what Kanzi or Alia were told to do by the experimenter (e.g., *Give Liz a shot),* thus ensuring that humans were not inadvertently providing prompts to the subjects.

Correct responses were specifically not followed by the delivery of food for both blind and nonblind trials. Incorrect responses were followed by a correction procedure that consisted of repeating the command, varying specific words, and providing verbal praise and reprimands.

Most of the trials were videotaped, and a scoring system was employed to record correct, partially correct, and incorrect responses.

After the experiment was completed, a more complex scoring system was developed to score the responses from videotape. These scores, and the complete transcripts of the interactions between the experimenter and subjects.

RESULTS

The results showed that Kanzi not only acquired a complex comprehension repertoire but acquired it in a pattern similar to that of a typically developing human child, and in many cases outperformed the human child. Kanzi was correct on 72% of the total trials (nonblind and blind), and Alia was correct on 66% of the total trials. The transition to blind trials, during which the speaker was out of the subject's sight, initially resulted in poor responding and confusion for both subjects, but they quickly improved. Over the whole set of blind trials, Kanzi was correct on 74% of the trials, and Alia was correct on 65% of the trials.

DISCUSSION

The results clearly demonstrate that an ape and a child can correctly respond to a wide variety of novel and complex verbal instructions. In addition, the results of the blind condition show that these responses were not a function of imitative or visual prompts that were inadvertently emitted by the experimenters. However, the issue of how Kanzi and Alia acquired this linguistic behavior has not been answered by the data. The authors propose that these novel responses emerged, as in humans, not as a function of reinforcement or specific training but rather as a function of the ape's human-like cognitive and abstractly specified physiological characteristics. The authors conclude that "the lack of contingent reward, the novel nature of the requests, the absence of previous training to perform these specific requests, and the unique nature of each trial countermand simple explanations that depend on the conditioning of responses".

When faced with the question of how Kanzi came to understand the complexities and nuances of human speech, when apes generally do not, the authors state that "the answer is to be found in how the neural networks of a highly complex and relatively plastic brain ... become organized ... during infancy and early development", and that the subjects learned these comprehension skills because they observed "competent speaking models and began to decode the speech signal into its components as well as assign meaning to those components". As a result of these views, the authors conclude that although "psychologists historically have emphasized the role of reinforcement as regards learning, we suggest that observation and perceptual learning processes are far more important to the infant for the learning of complex systems such as language".

The book includes a commentary by Elizabeth Bates, whose primary focus concerns the issue of comprehension and its relation to verbal production. Bates is largely supportive of the authors' work and concludes that she is convinced that "the bonobo ... is capable of language comprehension that approximates ... the abilities of a human 2-year-old". Bates presents an interesting overview of the research on comprehension, and the current methods for assessing its development in human children. She frequently compares these findings with those of Savage-Rumbaugh et al. and suggests several possibilities for additional research with both humans and apes. Bates also points out the many ways in which comprehension differs from production and searches for a biological explanation of these differences. She concludes her commentary by pointing out the general difficulty of giving up the notion that apes and humans are similar and recommends that it is time to learn to live with these similarities.

In the reply to Bates, Savage-Rumbaugh discusses some new techniques currently being developed with apes to assess comprehension. Savage-Rumbaugh suggests that these new techniques will "provide an increasingly sophisticated understanding of the behavioural and neurological relation between man and ape". Savage-Rumbaugh then goes on to discuss the discrepancy between Kanzi's comprehension and production repertoires. She takes issue with Bates's proposal that this dichotomy is related to differences in the brain's right and left hemispheres and proposes that "the productive-receptive discrepancy itself results from a more basic dichotomy, one that characterizes many activities in addition to language". The remainder of the reply primarily focuses on, like Bates's commentary, a search for biological explanations of the differences between comprehension and production.

A BEHAVIORAL INTERPRETATION OF THE DATA

The authors' primary objective for their study was to demonstrate that an ape could acquire language comprehension in a manner similar to that of a human child. That objective was accomplished; however, the authors' analysis of the variables responsible for this acquisition can be questioned. The authors take the position of traditional psychology and attribute the causes of the learning to cognitive and physiological variables while deemphasizing the role of the environment. However, there are a number of possible environmental variables that have not been identified and methodologically controlled by the authors. These variables will be identified here, and four major issues raised in the monograph will be addressed: (a) performing without rewards, (b) providing no specific training, (c) novel verbal stimuli evoking novel responses, and (d) the relation between verbal comprehension and verbal production.

Performing Without Rewards

A major theme emphasized throughout the monograph and in the recorded presentation of this work at the 1994 Association for Behavior Analysis (ABA) convention was that the subjects acquired the targeted behavior without contingent reinforcement. The authors wanted to eliminate reinforcement as a causal variable so they could argue that the ape's acquisition of language comprehension was more like that of an "untrained" human child rather than that of a "trained animal." (The prevailing psycholinguistic view, of course, is that human children acquire language comprehension without reinforcement) In addition, by ruling out reinforcement, the authors argue that human-like cognitive and physiological variables are responsible for the ape's emerged behavior.

The authors' procedure to control for reinforcement consisted of not following correct responses with food. When

any specific training. The authors wanted to eliminate specific training for the same reasons that they wanted to eliminate reinforcement; to argue that the ape's acquisition of language comprehension was a cognitive and physiological process and was more like that of a typical human child than that of a "trained animal.

The "no-training" procedure consisted of having the caretakers simply interact with the subjects in a manner that seemed typical of that of a mother and child interacting during the course of a day, except that they pointed to the symbols as they talked. Although it is true that the "no-training" conditions were very different from the formal training given to the dolphins and sea lions (and perhaps were a procedural improvement), it is unlikely that environmental contingencies were irrelevant to the emergence of the observed behavior. The daily interaction with the subjects in their natural environment, although not considered training by the authors, contained many of the previously identified behavioral contingencies that were probably relevant to acquisition.

For example, in her ABA presentation, although arguing that Kanzi's behavior was acquired without training or programmed reinforcement contingencies, showed a videotape of Kanzi and his caretakers making hamburgers over an open fire in the forest. In making the hamburgers Savage-Rumbaugh said to Kanzi "Put the hamburgers in the pan, no we're not going to eat it, put it in the pan. In the pan! In the pan! ... No. No, it's not done yet." "From a behavioral point of view, there is no question that training is occurring by using verbal prompts and conditioned punishers. The fact that training was not systematically programmed is irrelevant to whether processes of reinforcement, punishment, and extinction are involved in the language acquisition that resulted. The focus on these natural environmental contingencies for language training has long been the subject of research in the applied behavioral literature.

The formal study was begun after both subjects had long histories of daily contact with these types of natural environmental contingencies. They also had successful histories of following verbal instructions given to them by the experimenters, as would be expected with a typical 2-year-old child, and as demonstrated in pretests with each subject. Therefore, not only did the experimenters have stimulus control over the subjects' behavior, but the comprehension of the individual words was already strong in the subjects' repertoires (i.e., the subjects had already acquired an effective listener repertoire). These independent variables can be clearly identified in the following description of a correction procedure: After Kanzi failed to correctly respond to Request *(Give me Rose's cereal. Get Rose's cereal Rose's cereal.).*

The use of *That's right, Go ahead, Yes,* and *No, Put that down, Not the milk* strongly suggests the presence of verbal prompts, praise, and reprimands in the shaping of successive approximations to receptive discriminations. Praise and reprimands were probably effective as conditioned reinforcers and conditioned punishers, because both the child and the bonobo had extensive histories of these verbal stimuli being paired with other effective consequences. The occurrence of these consequences following specific behavior would also then begin to establish several different forms of stimulus control and functional equivalence, while reducing the evocative strength of the relevant establishing operations (including reflexive conditioned establishing operations. Although a good percentage of responses did occur in the absence of prompts and consequences, it does demonstrate how nonprogrammed prompts and differential reinforcement, punishment, and extinction were used to shape instruction-following behavior. One also wonders what role the banana and the stolen food item may have played in Kanzi's responding.

Novel Forms of Stimulus Control and Novel Responses

The formal testing conditions consisted of the presentation of novel combinations of the known verbal stimuli (e.g., *Take the doggie to the bathroom),* Thee ape is not just a trained animal that emits specifically shaped behavior, but rather is an organism with human-like cognitive processors and neural networks that organize novel stimuli and produce creative and novel behavior.

The authors state that novel and untrained behavior cannot be explained by behavioral concepts, and in fact, that novel behavior negates behavioral explanations. This view, which was repeatedly emphasized by Savage-Rumbaugh (1994) in her ABA presentation, reveals the common misconception that behavior analysis is predicated on specifically established stimulus-response relations and cannot account for variability or novelty of behavior. However, a fundamental aspect of behavior analysis is that operant behavior consists of functional correlations between classes of stimuli and responses rather than structural bundles of specific stimulus-response relations.

Unfortunately, the research methodology employed in the study, although effective for showing that the subjects could comprehend novel verbal stimuli without human imitative or visual prompts, was insufficient for identifying the critical independent variables responsible for the emergence of the observed behavior that constituted comprehension. It is inadequate to simply say that Kanzi and Al-ia's "activities were accompanied by language in a way that seemed natural to the caretakers"), and as a result, the subjects "began to decode the speech symbol into its components as well as assign meaning to these components on their own"). The authors were not clear on the specific identification and experimental control of what "seemed natural." Therefore, it would be difficult to replicate this experiment given this limited information, and even taken at face value, the observation does not justify their assertion.

Furthermore, no data were reported (or apparently taken) on variables such as levels and frequencies of prompts, schedules of reinforcement and punishment (which surely were intermittent), the relative strength of establishing operations, or the frequency of daily trials (other than the targeted trials). In addition, there was no experimental manipulation to separate reinforcement from non-reinforcement, punishment from nonpunishment, extinction from nonextinction, pairing from nonpairing, and so on. It seems quite possible that the true absence of any of these variables would indeed affect acquisition. For example, when Kanzi attempted to take an item from Rose's lap, but when he reached for it Rose gave "no indication that he [was] permitted to take it", it appears that extinction was used to weaken incorrect responses. In order to clearly identify the role of this behavioral principle in the acquisition of the comprehension repertoires, conditions involving extinction and no extinction would have to be compared.

In order to determine more precisely how Kanzi and Alia acquired their comprehension repertoires, these potential independent variables would have to be further identified and partitioned using standard behavioral methodology. The law of scientific parsimony suggests that it would not be prudent for the authors to attribute the causes of their subjects' behavior to autonomous cognitive processors and neural networks until all these easily specifiable environmental sources are experimentally controlled. The research presented in the current monograph made no such attempt to account for any of these potentially potent independent variables.

Comprehension and Production

The final topic to be addressed is the authors' position on verbal comprehension and its relation to verbal production. The authors' view of comprehension is that "comprehension precedes production in the language development of normal children, and it may indeed guide production" v). In addition, "the fact that comprehension did *not* require reinforcement supports the view that comprehension is the driving force underlying all of language acquisition". Behavior analysts, of course, argue that comprehension does indeed require reinforcement as well as the other behavioral principles and procedures, and that it is these environmental variables that are the primary basis for language acquisition. Behavior analysts also assert that comprehension does not cause production; rather, it is a functionally independent repertoire, because mands, tacts, and intraverbals are functionally independent repertoires at the time of acquisition. The authors' focus on comprehension alone seems to be a function of a number of variables.

In addition to their view that comprehension caused production, the authors suggest that other ape language research suffered because "no systematic, controlled measures of receptive capacities were taken by the Gardners or by Terrace and his coleagues". Perhaps the most significant reason, however, was that "popular theories of human language acquisition suggest that the ability to process syntactic information is unique to humans and reflects a novel biological adaptation not seen in other animals"). By demonstrating that comprehension could be acquired by apes in a manner similar to humans, the authors could argue that the ape possesses cognitive and biological equipment similar to that of humans. In addition, they could then argue that the emergence of expressive behavior in apes is due to the same variables that are responsible for its emergence in humans.

However, there are no data in the monograph that show the transfer to production. Thus, it is not clear, despite the authors' assertions, how this research supports the view that comprehension causes production. Also, in the video of Kanzi, the majority of his responses were receptive responses, and there is a striking absence of expressive behavior (i.e., mands, tacts, and intraverbals). This seems odd because one would expect a wider variety of verbal responses (like Alia often emitted), given the size and strength of his comprehension repertoire, if indeed comprehension caused production.

In summary, the authors' claim that the subjects learned the behavior without reinforcement or training does not hold up to a behavioral analysis of the subjects' history or to an analysis of the procedures, transcripts, and videos. Their view that the subjects' acquisition of comprehension was not due to "simple explanations that depend on conditioning of responses" 98) is true, not because behavioral explanations are simple, but because simple explanations are inadequate to analyze the emergence of behavior as complex as language comprehension. In fact, the behavioral analysis of comprehension is quite complex, involving much more than one principle of behavior and one formal training procedure. Finally, in order to scientifically determine how the subjects acquired a comprehension repertoire, a more rigorous research methodology that controls for the many potential independent variables should be employed.

THE VALUE OF THE AUTHORS' POSITION: ADVANCES AND APPLICATIONS

It should be pointed out, however, that a cognitive view with appeals to abstract physiological mechanisms is especially important to the authors because it reflects the current views of mainstream psychology and child language development. This compatibility with the prevailing views is critical for their cause of demonstrating that apes learn complex behavior in a manner similar to humans. At this time, a strong behavioral position would probably hurt the Rumbaughs' cause of demonstrating the similarities between apes and humans, because explanations in behavioral terms such as reinforcement, prompting, and shaping often evoke pejorative comments by critics such as "rote responding" or "just a trained animal." The authors' ability to show that simple behavioral explanations, such as imitation and reinforcement, are not responsible for learning may be attractive to many members of the scientific community because it supports their views of cognitive and biological control (individuals who may become more willing to attend to ape language research and support the authors' cause of granting linguistic competence to apes). These authors cannot be faulted for the fact that a behavioral analysis is generally not understood or accepted in linguistics or psychology.

This monograph, despite its conceptual shortcomings, does advance ape and human language research in many important ways. In addition to showing that an ape can acquire language comprehension in a manner similar to a human child and that an ape can emit those skills in the absence of visual prompts, the research contains several procedural advances that have implications for both ape and human language research. For example, the authors' effective use of natural contingencies to develop Kanzi's basic comprehension and verbal repertoires could serve as a model for those attempting to develop verbal behavior in human subjects. The frequent outings to the forest and other places with Kanzi and the lexigram board made use of many naturally occurring stimuli, establishing operations, consequences, and so on, that helped to establish not only differential verbal stimulus control but also Kanzi's verbal response forms of pointing to the lexigrams. The use of these natural contingencies to teach verbal behavior to nonverbal humans has been shown to be a very important tool for language training. Language research with nonhumans offers several experimental advantages over research with humans, and it may be possible to examine more carefully a number of the parameters and variables involved in designing a natural environment to teach verbal repertoires in cases in which explicit teaching techniques are needed.

The authors' hierarchy of increasingly complex verbal stimuli could also provide clinicians with a method to assess a nonverbal person's comprehension skills. In addition, Kanzi's and Alia's performances on these different tasks could give the clinician some guidelines as to which types of comprehension to teach first. For example, the finding that it was more difficult for both subjects to go to a location and get an object than it was to select an item and take it to a location has interesting implications for language training. More research on the relative difficulty of these different types of comprehension tasks could improve die current methods of language instruction. The scoring system used in the study, especially the modified system used to score the videotapes, should also be of interest to researchers attempting to score and classify ongoing verbal interactions. This system was very useful in identifying potential antecedents and consequences that were relevant to the observed behavior. Applied behavior analysts could benefit from using such a system for recording the emission of verbal behavior by early language learners. Also, the authors' flexible approach to experimentation was similar to many aspects of the exploratory research strategies.

This approach to experimentation was termed *radical methodology* by Willard Day and his students, and it has led to several interesting behavioral findings. The most significant aspect of radical methodology is that the experimenters allow their behavior to be controlled by the subjects' behavior. The experimenters then analyze their behavior as a dependent variable that changes as a function of the subjects' behavior as an independent variable.

The authors of the monograph under discussion made several changes in the procedures as a function of their subjects' behavior, resulting in an interesting research project that produced important findings. This approach can be seen throughout the study. For example, the present study was not designed to determine whether the subjects could process sentences that utilized a recursive structure. Rather, our tests of this capacity evolved when it became apparent that the subjects were having difficulty with an ambiguous linear structure—only then was the recursive structure introduced to resolve this ambiguity.

Finally, the Rumbaughs' continued development of their computerized lexical system has significant implications for the development of symbol communication systems for nonverbal humans. Their study demonstrated advances by the development and use of portable boards, the use of a voice synthesizer for auditory output, and procedures involving constant exposure to the system. Research on these features may improve the methods currently being used for teaching language to nonverbal persons.

BEHAVIOR ANALYSIS AND NONHUMAN VERBAL BEHAVIOR RESEARCH

The field of behavior analysis has much to offer to research on nonhuman verbal behavior. Behavior analysts are not only experts in the use of the behavioral principles and methods for shaping new repertoires, but they also have long histories of working with various nonhuman species. In addition, and perhaps most significant, behavior analysts have a functionally based conceptual framework for systematizing the development of verbal repertoires. These conceptual and methodological resources, which are readily applicable to both human and nonhuman behavior, could enable substantial improvements in the methods of language assessment and intervention for the millions of humans who fail to acquire effective language skills. The involvement of behavior analysts in this exciting line of research could also advance the cause of granting linguistic competence to apes and other nonhumans.

There are two general lines of research that could be pursued by behavior analysts. The first involves the systematic identification and control of the relevant independent variables that are responsible for the emergence of linguistic repertoires in nonhuman subjects. A number of potential independent variables were identified above, but the precise roles of these variables can only be revealed by a thematic line of experimental research that carefully partitions these variables from one another. It is unreasonable to expect that a nonbehaviorist could accomplish this level of behavioral experimentation, especially because many of the behavioral explanations suggested above involve complicated concepts such as stimulus control, functional equivalence, conditioned reinforcement, and establishing operations. Determining, for example, the role of abstraction or functional equivalence in the emergence of novel behavior would require a number of sophisticated research projects with both basic and applied components.

The second general line of research suggested for behavior analysts involves the specific use of Skinner's (1957) analysis of verbal behavior as a conceptual framework for establishing verbal repertoires in nonhuman organisms. Most of the current language research with nonhumans (as well as humans) adheres to the traditional linguistic framework of receptive (comprehension) and expressive (production) language. As a result, language researchers often focus on establishing these two repertoires and studying the cognitive or physiological connection between them. Perhaps the most significant contribution of Skinner's analysis of verbal behavior is the distinction he makes between receptive language and the several different types of expressive behavior.

Skinner distinguishes among echoic, mand, tact, intraverbal, textual, transcriptive, and autoclitic repertoires as the basic components of expressive verbal behavior (note that Skinner's use of *verbal* includes all types of response forms such as speaking, signing, and pointing).

Interestingly, many of the disagreements over the years among researchers of nonhuman language is related to the fact that each one taught specific types of verbal behavior and none taught all the verbal operants under all the necessary and sufficient conditions. Unfortunately, this application of Skinner's analysis of verbal behavior has not been followed by other researchers, including Savage-Rumbaugh herself.

SUMMARY AND CONCLUSIONS

The research presented in the monograph by Savage-Rumbaugh et al. (1993) clearly demonstrates that an ape can acquire language comprehension in a manner similar to that of a human child and that an ape can emit those comprehension skills in the absence of visual prompts. The research also contains several procedural advances that have implications for both ape and human language research. These findings should contribute to the authors' long-term effort to convince the scientific community to grant linguistic competency to apes.

However, the authors' claim that the subjects learned such behavior on their own, without reinforcement or training, does not hold up to a closer examination of the subjects' history or to an anal sis of the procedures, transcripts, and videos. The training and testing procedures appeared to involve a number of possible independent variables that were not examined, including conditioned reinforcement and punishment, verbal prompts, stimulus control, establishing operations, and extinction. In addition, other behavioral phenomena, such as abstraction and functional equivalence, were not considered but may have been relevant to the emergence of the observed behavior.

Behavior analysts are in a unique position to make substantial contributions to this line of research; their concepts and methods might well have a major impact on the current state of research on nonhuman verbal behavior. Such research could also have significant implications for applied work with language-delayed humans. In addition, verbal behavior research with nonhumans provides behavior analysts with a valuable opportunity to bring together the conceptual, experimental, and applied aspects of behavior analysis in a single line of research.

Approximately 20 years ago Jack Michael took a small group of students to Hope College in Holland, Michigan, to see Duane Rumbaugh present his work on Lana. We were all fascinated by the movies of Lana and her rapid performance on the computerized keyboard, but we cringed when Rumbaugh presented his analysis of how Lana acquired her verbal behavior. After a few rounds of questions, Jack encouraged us to focus on what Rumbaugh was able to teach Lana and the specifics of his teaching procedures rather than on his cognitive analysis of how Lana learned the complex sets of behavior.

The behaviorist reader of the current monograph will benefit from a similar approach. The Rumbaughs may have a different explanation of the repertoires acquired, but they have been successful in generating a number of complex receptive and verbal skills in apes. Behavior analysts should support this work and advance it by contributing the tools of behavior analysis in general and the concepts from *Verbal Behavior* in particular. It was pointed out that behavior analysts should not expect others to make accurate use of our complex analyses until we have done so ourselves.

Chapter 23

Behaviourist Linguistics

THE INFLUENCES OF WATSONIAN BEHAVIOURISM ON LINGUISTICS AND ON THE TEACHING OF READING

Pavlov and Skinner are not the only 'behaviourist' psychologists whose work is relevant in the present context. Another influential researcher in this broad and complex tradition was J B Watson, an extreme antimentalist and epiphenomenalist, whose thought had a profound influence on the North American linguist Leonard Bloomfield. Prior to coming under the influence of Watsonian psychology, Bloomfield had worked largely within the tradition of the German physiologist and psychologist Wilhelm Wundt. Wundt was, like many psychologists, interested in intelligence and intelligence testing.

Under the influence of Watson, Bloomfield came to reject genetic explanations of individual differences in favour of environmental ones. He also 'led linguistics away from any consideration of meaning ... ' (Coulthard, 1985, p.1).

The example also illustrates the continuing relevance of 'behaviourist linguistics': the work of Bloomfield is still cited, with varying degrees of approval and disapproval, by those who believe strongly in the importance of phonics (that is, grapheme-phoneme correspondences) in the teaching of reading, and who object strongly to the use of 'whole word', and other methods. Sometimes 'meaning' is regarded almost as an irrelevance, an afterthought. The Rose Report on the teaching of reading seems to strike an uneasy balance in this when reading, and that deleting particular sections of a text encouraged readers to use develop and apply such strategies. Research, however, suggested that cloze exercises only improved comprehension when they were used for small group discussion. This is also how DARTS were meant to be used. There was no evidence that silently completing written gap-filling exercises improved comprehension.

On the other hand, cloze has been very popular in adult basic skills classes both as a teaching tool and as an assessment technique. An adult literacy teacher trainer guessed that 'cloze' must be named after someone called Mr Cloze. This suggests that those involved in initial teacher training might benefit from a little more background knowledge of Gestalt theory generally and of the origins of cloze procedure in particular.

And almost whatever the 'skill', one can, according especially to the draft adult literacy core curriculum, use gap-filling exercises - dignified or not, as the case may be, with the name 'cloze procedure' to teach it.

Cloze procedure, supported by statistical procedures as well as by theories of reading, has also been used as the basis for the development of language tests in the ESOL field and for assessment in adult basic skills work, another reason why some of its theoretical underpinnings might usefully have been spelled out with a little more clarity in this particular research review.

SOME ISMS: POSITIVISM, BEHAVIOURISM, AND QUALITATIVISM.

Let us now turn to philosophy(ies) of knowledge and of science. One can usefully distinguish methodological from philosophical and logical behaviourism. Skinner himself was a philosopher of science, of mind, and of psychology as well as an empirical researcher, though he liked to describe himself as being atheoretical and empirical. Behaviourism may be distinguished from both positivism (as variously defined) and from empiricism. Many social scientists will associate the term 'positivism' with the thinking of the French Philosopher Auguste Comte, who died in 1857. Comte has been left out of the NRDC story altogether. These concepts are often evoked in arguments about the relative merits of quantitative and qualitative methodology. We note at this point that some 'New Literacy Studies' work has asserted that the group is 'empirical' but not 'positivist', a thought-provoking distinction indeed, and a point that might have been clarified in this research report through discussion of relevant definitions.

THEORISTS OF SITUATED LEARNING AND COGNITION

We have often been struck by parallels on an abstract level between aspects of Skinner's thought and aspects of the work of the New Literacy Studies group. For example, Skinner shares their apparently rather determinist view that the environment (albeit that this is, apparently, differently conceived of by the New Literacy Studies in terms of strong 'practice' views) determines behaviour, their dislike of cognitive psychology, and their philosophical rejection of 'theory' in favour of empiricism and description.

Skinner's rejection of the concept of 'autonomous' man has parallels in modern critical references to the idea of 'autonomous literacy', the term 'autonomous literacy' is used in a number of quite different senses.

The reference by the theorist of situated cognition Bredo to the neo-behaviourist thinking of Rorty encourages me in this line of thought.

These parallels explain for me the way in which the New Literacy Studies have encouraged and prescribed the use of 'task analysis', a technique drawn from behaviourist occupational psychology, in the development of workplace based literacy, numeracy and ESOL courses at all levels up to and including degree level We return to this topic later.

We would have liked to see these parallels between some work bearing the New Literacy Studies label and the thinking of Skinner brought out and discussed in the work under discussion. Interesting here would have been a discussion and comparison of 'strong' and 'weak' theories of situated cognition, and rather more subject-specific discussion of transfer, especially for those beginning to learn how to read and write.

On this latter subject, we would refer readers to the literature review by Mikulecky.

Continuing the theme of links between educational traditions, we suggest that the report might usefully have drawn out some of the similarities between, for example, Knowles' approach to adult education and behaviourist approaches.

NORM REFERENCING AND CRITERION REFERENCING

One outcome of various lines of what might generally be called positivist, quantitative research was the tradition of psychometric testing. Initially, this developed separately from North American research on learning, with the Frenchman Binet being a key figure, though the two traditions later combined.

Central to much psychometric testing has been the concept of the normal frequency distribution. Many people think of this in terms of the familiar bell-shaped curve. Some statistical procedures may only be used if the assumption is made that the data is normally distributed.

Test results for individuals are often expressed with reference to their position on the bell shaped curve, or, in other words, in terms of how the position of the individual compares with others on the normally shaped distribution that would represent the whole population.

Therefore, such statistically based tests are often referred to as 'norm-referenced'.

The move to criterion-referencing is often attributed to a paper by the psychologist Glaser. Following the publication of this paper, the term became part of the educator's vocabulary.

A general trend away from norm-referencing resulted in the current fashions for standards-based reform and objectives-led teaching, which are reflected in the form of the present Skills for Life curricula.

BLOOM'S TAXONOMY OF EDUCATIONAL OBJECTIVES

Though the work of Gagne, often placed within the behaviourist tradition, is rightly mentioned in the review, a more important theorist as far as adult education in general, and the Open College Networks in particular, are concerned, is Bloom.

The repeated use of the words 'identify' and 'recognise' in adult basic skills materials (something commented adversely upon in one FEFC Inspectorate report in connection with assessment) may be attributed to an unreflective use by programme developers seeking to develop criterion-referenced qualifications and accreditations of terms from Bloom's taxonomy of objectives. These same words appear frequently in both the adult literacy standards and the core curriculum.

At least one widely used FE tutor training book set as reading on some Skills for Life professional development courses refers to Bloom's taxonomy. Its influence in FE is, like that of Gagne, significant. We discovered in the course of my own research that some Open College Network development officers recommend the use of Bloom's terms as 'starter verbs' for writing learning outcomes - irrespective of the subject matter of the accreditation. Some specifically state that the learning outcomes must use 'behavioural' verbs, so that a starter such as 'understand' would be unacceptable. Some behaviour, from which, presumably, understanding must be inferred (if understanding is seen as important), has to be specified.

The words 'identify' and 'recognise' appear crop up so often in basic skills materials because they come at the bottom level of Bloom's taxonomy, and not because Bloom, or anyone else, has ever argued that they were appropriate in the context of initial literacy, language and numeracy.

THEORIES OF ADULT LEARNING

We now move on to look at the overall form of the report. It is sometimes said that form and meaning are inseparable.

The main text of the NRDC research report is divided into two sections, entitled 'models from psychology' and 'models from adult education'. This division, we would argue, is understandable in the context, but the form of the report is potentially misleading on at least two counts.

The general dislike of many working under New Literacy Studies umbrella for much of psychology is well known. However, misrepresenting that subject, by, for example, suggesting or implying that it was irrelevant in the context of 'adult' education, would not, for me, be a good way to construct a persuasive argument against it.

The two fold 'adult-other' division adopted in the research review implies that models from psychology were developed 'in the context of children learning within a formal educational system'. Readers should be aware that this by no means true of all the psychological theories included in the first section. Behaviourism, as has been explained, developed from a line of philosophical enquiry into the nature of reality and human knowledge, and the techniques of control and behavioural shaping that it developed have been applied with adults and animals as well as with children. No one familiar with the works of Skinner and the ethical issues that his form of radical behaviourism raises could conclude that his thought was only relevant to, or based upon, children.

Much psychology, including a great deal of work on communication and reading and many modern psychometric assessment and educational testing techniques, was developed originally by psychologists employed by the United States military forces. It is, therefore, based on adults, though only on a sub-sample of North American adults, as the American forces used testing to exclude a proportion of the population from military service, including many who would be seen, broadly speaking, as at Skills for Life levels of achievement.

Psychologists in universities have, moreover, notoriously used their own undergraduate students – few of whom are children - in large numbers of their investigations and experiments, with resulting questions about the generalisability of their findings to other population groups.

Conversely, the division implies incorrectly that some of the approaches to learning outlined in the second section are specifically relevant to adults. This implies that similar theories have not been taught to or used by those teaching children. Again, this is not necessarily the case.

We do not think that any particularly strong arguments are presented that learning to read or count for an adult and for a child are so radically different. Both need to learn the same thing. We would suggest an Internet search using the name 'Perfetti' for those interested in research in this area.

That said, since a broad variety of social science work shelters under the New Literacy Studies' umbrella, it is not necessarily correct to identify the label with any particular approach to product development.

Another interesting question is whether or not one ought to indulge in 'grand narratives', a question brought out in the publication under discussion. However, here one runs straight into the same paradoxical problems about whether a refusal to engage in theorising or metaphysics is itself another totalising narrative or theory. This sort of question was discussed historically in commentary on Skinner's philosophy of science, just as it has more recently been raised in the context of postmodernism.

One problem with views of adult learning as self-directed and independent is that they often assume that the adult can read and can therefore find things out by reading about them. For many Skills for Life students, this is not an accurate assumption. Suggestions that they should independently find out how to read and write were memorably described by an adult educator with whom we worked as (more or less) the 'flirt off and find out' school of thought. One of the electronic references cited below follows this train of thought a little further.

SOME IMPLICATIONS OF REJECTING COGNITIVE PSYCHOLOGY

One distinguishing mark of much work within the New Literacy Studies area is, as has been said, its dislike of cognitive psychology. While accepting absolutely that my own thinking is riddled with contradictions, an inconsistency in this area struck me forcefully when we read an article by Barton on dyslexia in the RaPAL journal, in which the account given of dyslexia was clearly based upon the work of cognitive psychologists on memory. A core phonological processing deficit explanation, drawn from other areas of cognitive psychology, is a popular alternative to this view. Rejecting cognitive psychology has interesting consequences here: reject cognitive psychology and you are under pressure to reject the whole concept of dyslexia with it.

And there is very little in this review about how one might most usefully go about teaching a person who cannot read or write how to do these things beyond a general admonition to work with what interests them and make the work 'relevant'. There seems to be no reference to any empirical evidence about 'what works' and what does not.

SCRIBNER AND COLE

Despite the predictable reference to Scribner and Cole, we remain unhappy with the use of 'practices' as the basis for curriculum development, especially for beginning readers, and we shall presently cite Scribner and Cole's discussions of the term in support of this .

Others have questioned the New Literacy Studies' reading of Scribner and Cole. We would question the methodology of the original study. Instead of giving the same intelligence tests to all their subjects and then comparing the results, they devised different intelligence tests for each group of subjects and then compared results. One could question how far they were really comparing like with like. The research was, it should be noted, quantitative, and used regression analysis. This makes it paradoxical that those with a declared dislike of quantitative, positivist cognitive psychology should so often cite it approvingly.

Scribner and Cole's discussion of the term 'practice' shows - and to some extent acknowledges - that the concept of 'practice' is so elastic that it is almost as meaningless as

Skinner's concept of 'reinforcement'. It sometimes seems simply to state some sort of rather unhelpful truism. On the other hand, it seems incapable of accounting either for societal change or for creativity.

Stevens has commented that the New Literacy Studies underplay the importance of literacy in gaining access to the world of culture. We often read to learn. Underplaying this 'mentalist' aspect of the part literacy plays in our life seems to link with the use of behaviourist occupational psychology in the development of role-specific, task-based, literacy curriculum:

'By a practice, we mean a recurrent, goal directed sequence of activities using a particular technology and particular systems of knowledge. We use the term 'skills' to refer to the coordinated sets of actions involved in applying this knowledge in particular setting. A practice, then, consists of three components: technology, knowledge and skills. We can apply this concept to spheres of activity that are predominantly conceptual (for example, the practice of law) as well as to those that are predominantly sensory motor (for example the practice of weaving). But we may construe them more or less broadly to refer to entire domains of activity around a common object (for example, law) or to more specific endeavours within such domains (cross examination or legal research). Whether defined in broad or narrow terms, practice always refers to socially developed and patterned ways of using technology. Conversely, tasks that individuals engage in constitute a practice when they are directed to socially recognised goals and make use of a shared technology and knowledge system.

We are reminded of Barker's treatment of the nested character of purposeful behavior; smaller behaviour units are nested within larger units as boxes within boxes. How the investigator chooses to slice up activities, the size or level of the unit of practice depends upon the purpose of the analysis...'

An emphasis on 'practices' - seen as what people do with literacy - seems to lead to a relative lack of interest in how people learn to read and write, and what they need to know in order to learn to read and write. This is illustrated in statements to the effect that 'literacy is the uses to which it is put' - a formulation with many behaviourist characteristics (as well as totally unclear pronoun reference, this resulting in a lack of what is sometimes called 'textual cohesion'.).

Scribner and Cole refer to uses of literacy for specific purposes. This is reminiscent of the work of Halliday and of the genre theory developed from it which has influenced the school literacy curriculum. There is, however, very little reference to the work of Halliday in Skills for Life tutor training materials, or in the review, though he has written extensively on the use of language for learning. Terms such as 'register', 'semantic field' and 'tenor' are familiar to English teachers in this country, though not to those in the US, we understand. They are also taught on AS English Language and Language and Literature courses. (Specificity has its own limitations.) we wonder whether knowledge of this range of concepts might be of more value to those training to teach reading and writing than an introduction to 'practice' views of literacy. Such knowledge would facilitate a greater degree of continuity between sectors and curriculum framework tracks. More tutors in further education would be able to recognise the prior achievements of their students. Moreover, some literacy teaching strategies in both schools and adult education - including the use of 'writing frames' have been justified with reference both to the concept of scaffolding and to genre theory.

Before leaving Scribner and Cole, it is worth noting that none of the population groups they studied learned to read and write informally, or by osmosis, or by legitimate peripheral participation in a community of practice . Reading and writing were taught.

A view that learning to read is like an 'apprenticeship', was, according to some sources, widely espoused by teacher trainers before the introduction of the phonics elements of the national literacy strategy. Failure to teach phonics is, indeed, widely regarded as one of the ways in which dyslexia is 'socially constructed'. Moreover, in Scribner and Cole's study, schooling seemed to be linked with better performance on a range of the 'intelligence' tests that Scribner and Cole administered to their subjects. Their findings would, therefore, not support arguments that young people should be allowed to drop English and Maths at an early age and left to pick up further literacy and numeracy informally in the course of on-the-job training.

THE THEORY OF LEARNING UNDERPINNING THE COMPETENCE-BASED, ASSESSMENT-LED REFORMS, OF WHICH THE 'SKILLS FOR LIFE' INFRASTRUCTURE IS A PART.

Another area that it would have been useful to discuss in the present context is the English NVQ and GNVQ 'competence' movement. A crucial figure here is Gilbert Jessup, who was in turn influenced by Tyler's view on curriculum development. As a counter-balance, the work of Eraut is often cited. Again, we have put some helpful links in the footnotes. We have touched upon this area already. The confusingly used terms 'competence' and 'competencies' feature largely in the literature on adult literacy and have been used in connection with the promised new tests of 'functional literacy'. One can find suggestions, for example, that Wordpower set out 'competencies'.

Competence-based assessment was introduced as an assessment-led reform, which is why an engagement with assessment issues is crucial in the adult basic skills context. In this respect, the NRDC report is disappointing, and surprising. An opportunity to debate some important influences on Skills for Life h s been missed.

One f equent criticism that was made of the NVQ and GNVQ traditions is that their emphasis on 'competencies' led to a neglect of theory and to fragmented learning experiences for students. Critiques of behaviourist approaches within vocational teaching have been many. Such criticism often drew upon philosophical concepts such as epistemology and commented upon behaviourist aspects of the NVQ initiative. As a result of this criticism, more theory began to be taught, but with a continuing emphasis on relevance: theory had to 'underpin' competent performance, and it began to be called 'underpinning knowledge'.

Philosophical criticism of competence-based approaches also highlighted the contradiction in expecting learners to be self-directed and independent when the outcomes of their learning had been clearly specified in advance, in an attempt at achieving 'transparent' precision. Other criticisms of the competence-based assessment movement focused upon different philosophical areas, including the philosophy of language .

Oates sums up the fundamental assumptions that underpinned NVQ as follows:

- A precise language can be established for the accurate communication of competences and attainment '... approaching that of a science ...'
- Outcomes-based qualifications possess high levels of validity, credibility and utility since they are based on the content of work processes
- For the purposes of modern national VET systems it is enough to state desirable outcomes, since these provide the basis for recognition (that someone is competent) and for instruction (these are the outcomes to which the instruction should lead)
- Significant benefits accrue from assessment and certification being independent of the mode, location and duration of training, particularly a facility to accredit experienced workers as well as trainees who have qualified through initial VET programmes
- unitised qualifications allow more accurate and flexible arrangements for recognising competence since different combinations of units can be used to construct varying qualifications.

APPLYING FUNCTIONAL ANALYSIS TO ARRIVE AT LITERACY, NUMERACY AND ESOL CURRICULA

We would have liked to see in this report analysis of the use of frameworks originally designed for the application of behaviourist approaches to occupational analysis (as, for example, in the NVQ frameworks) as the basis for the development of literacy curriculum. The Open College of the North West, with which the University of Lancaster is closely linked, has pioneered and prescribed this particular approach.

This scheme chopped reading into large sections (units) which were then sub-divided into smaller sections (elements) and it did the same with writing. Each element had 'performance criteria' listed for it. This procedure and format was based firmly on the NVQ approach to occupational analysis, with the NVQ assessment framework specifically mentioned in the manual.

Reading and writing were, as a result, seen as almost wholly distinct. They were also divided off from speaking and listening.

The approach was thoroughly behaviourist and fragmenting. It was described as competency based and as operating on mastery principles. The 'bits' of learning were called either 'competences' or 'competencies' terms which, in the English context, mean 'a bit of knowledge, skill or understanding wholly unrelated to any other bit of knowledge, skill or understanding'. In the US, competence-based assessment means, more or less, multiple-choice tests. The key skills movement may be seen, broadly, as attempting to put back into North American education something of that which a strong focus on testing and test results squeezed out of it.

The culture associated with competence-based assessment explains why, after tutors had been on the BSA 3-day core curriculum training sessions, many of them drew up tick lists of elements so that they could check off when they had obtained 'evidence' in respect of each individual one.

The term 'discrete' is used in the adult basic skills standards to describe the performance criteria or descriptors listed at each level. This too implies a behaviourist approach to the subject, as if each element were a 'competency' to be ticked off in the traditional NVQ manner.

The curriculum uses the phrase 'underpinning' knowledge and skills, another term deriving, as has been explained, from developments in vocational education and training.

TRACING THE INFLUENCES OF COMPETENCE-BASED ASSESSMENT IN 'SKILLS FOR LIFE'

A number of terms in the new Skills for Life framework, including the term 'elements', and the idea that competent performance 'at a curriculum level' is supported by clearly specifiable 'underpinning skills and knowledge', derive, as has been suggested, from the approaches to vocational training imported into FE via NVQ courses designed for non-academic school leavers.

The influence of NVQ methodology would explain why the developers of the standards set out 'criteria' they were thinking of the performance criteria used to set out NVQ assessment schedules. The same 'criteria' become, to the conceptual confusion of anyone who studies the curriculum and the standards carefully, 'learning outcomes' in the curriculum. Most of these criteria seem to be regarded by assessment software developers as assessable using the performance criterion of whether a student can solve a multiple-choice puzzle purportedly 'mapped' to the curriculum. It is salutary, given the explosion of multiple-choice literacy teaching, teacher training, and assessment software within Skills for Life, to remember the long-standing links between behaviourist educational psychologists, including Skinner and Glaser, and 'teaching machines'.

NVQ-think also explains why the standards set out pass-fail levels of literacy. This aligns with the 'mastery' view of teaching popular with behaviourists. One prevents students from moving on in their courses until they have achieved 'mastery' in what they have learned so far. When tests are used, a 'pass mark' of 80% is often used as the cut score for deciding whether the student has 'mastered' the topic. Other characteristics of the mastery approach adopted in English vocational training have been a belief that every single element of the course should be assessed, with no sampling of knowledge, a burden which Wolf has argued has not necessarily resulted in the sort of rigorous, across the board, raising of standards that was intended. Another common summative assessment practice, the aggregation of marks on different papers, with pass or fail judged on the basis of the overall mark, is also disapproved of in some 'competence-based' systems.

The highly linear approach of some 'mastery' based courses has implications for one's approach to the teaching of initial literacy, and is often especially recommended for students of all ages with learning difficulties. Arguments about whether the approach is the correct one are sometimes referred to as 'the reading wars' and are linked philosophically with arguments between researchers called 'the paradigm wars'.

Specific approaches to teaching and learning linked with more broadly behaviourist ideas, including 'mastery' approaches to assessment, were recommended by Tomlinson in some of his discussions about the 'functional skills' as which 'basic skills' seem about to be reincarnated. Some authorities equate 'mastery' assessment with 'competence-based' assessment. To do this is arguably to confuse two different issues.

Translated into key skills, the 'mastery', pass-fail requirement means that if you make more than one or two tiny mistakes in your writing, you fail. This draconian and unique state of affairs is supposed to motivate learners. On the other hand, if one research finding is consistent in the area of key skills, it is that learners are not motivated to learn them or spend time developing evidence for them.

Another, and almost accidental, result of the application of 'mastery' ideas to the teaching of literacy, is the advice to be found in the adult basic skills literature that students ought be prevented from writing complex sentences until they have mastered compound ones. Given that linguists disagree quite sharply on how sentences should be categorised, this injunction would be difficult to explain, enforce or obey without a sophisticated degree of linguistic knowledge. One would need to know whose definition of compound and complex sentences one was expected to use. A moment's thought shows how many everyday words would be banned under such a regime, and how crippling the 'rule' would be for students attempting to obey it.

Two last similarities between the present infrastructure and the history of NVQ should be brought out. First, Wolf pointed out how when there were crises of confidence in the assessment system, the response was to add more and more detail in a vain attempt to achieve precision and rigour. We can see this process repeating itself within Skills for Life. Faced with concerns over the rigour of key skills assessment, we set out criteria, which we flesh out with elements, each of which is then further sub-divided into yet smaller underpinning sub sections. Secondly, testing was introduced to balance tutor and portfolio assessment cheaply. The same has happened in key and basic skills. In basic skills, not even the portfolio has been retained. The test is all.

COMPETENCE AND PERFORMANCE AND ENGLISH RESEARCH ON ADULT BASIC SKILLS

The original, NVQ, usage of the term 'competence' is not, it has to be emphasised, 'competence' in any Chomskian sense, but implies a behaviourist approach to learning as changing behaviour. Even Fairclough, the doyen of critical literacy, confuses the two different senses of the word. Though the article purports to deal with behaviourism, it barely touches the subject. And it does seem odd for linguists to leave Chomsky off a list that includes Skinner.

It seems to me that there are two main reasons there has been so little academic debate about the influence of NVQ upon adult basic skills work. First, until the availability of funding within the Skills for Life infrastructure, there was very little academic interest in the area. It is not a high status area of enquiry.

We were once told bluntly that there was no interest in literacy at the Skills for Life levels, only in 'academic literacies'. Secondly, there is a small literature on key skills (and this is mostly critical) but researchers studying literacy and basic skills seem not to have engaged with it and have therefore not debated the ways in which assessment frameworks within that area were influenced by NVQ.

Though the same techniques are often applied to first and second language teaching in FE, underpinned key skills literacy/communication development, and have been taken to their logical conclusion in the isolated, discrete, objective 'descriptors'/'elements' of the adult core curriculum and standards, nobody has sought to discuss or analyse their suitability specifically for first or second language teaching. We once tried, and contrasted behaviourist approaches with, for example, phenomenological ones, but my work was criticised, by an adherent of the New Literacy Studies (who unforgettably apologised to me for using 'big words'), on the extremely ironical grounds that we had not discussed 'my epistemology'. Phenomenology, we would have thought, is a reasonably 'big' word. We were also advised to be more reflective. This piece may be regarded as an attempt to follow both pieces of advice.

If it is the case that, as 'classic' works on grammar assert, language is a system, the parts of which cannot be understood in isolation, then the way in which the carefully listed and numbered 'elements' of the curriculum model language is deeply misleading, both for students and for trainee teachers working towards levels 2, 3 and 4. we would argue that the model provided by the infrastructure is deeply behaviourist in this respect.

On the other hand, sharing 'targets' explicitly with learners so that they may self-directly work towards them may be represented as conforming absolutely to the principles suggested by some popular models of adult learning and with principles of formative assessment.

For me there remain many unanswered questions and dilemmas. We are in favour, generally, of criterion, as opposed to norm, referencing, as we think that it facilitates better teaching and learning. Yet most criterion referencing will, we think, inevitably have 'behaviourist' elements of one sort or another, depending, of course, upon definitions. We are certainly strongly opposed to the use of what are basically norm-referenced 'item banks' for the assessment of literacy, as is happening within Skills for Life, and seems likely soon to happen by extension, despite a total lack of any evidence of any kind that this improves standards, in schools. On the other hand, applying criterion-referencing without being reductionist, or draconian ('strict criterion-referencing'), or unmanageable, or prohibitively expensive, is not simple.

The only strictly relevant material we have found on teaching people to read and write in the workplace contrasts behaviourist (Fordist, fragmented) approaches to occupational training with post-Fordist approaches in industrial organisation, bizarrely linking Freire with Total Quality Management, flattened management structures and active participation in quality circles.

This all has very little to do with teaching people to read and write at basic levels. This problem arises because the word 'literacy' is used in many very different senses, and in both singular and plural forms, so that quite divergent points can be strung together upon changing usages of it in the course of a single text, or even sentence. One can quickly get bogged down in 'semantic arguments'. It is possible to read widely within the academic literature on 'literacy' while encountering nothing about teaching people to read and write.

On the subject of 'evidence', there is no evidence of which we are aware that the teaching of initial reading and writing and numeracy is best when the curriculum is limited to tasks or activities or 'practices' however defined from the individual learner's own lives or from one particular social role.

Evidence that we have seen, in an English study of Progress in Adult Literacy , suggests that the factor of whether or not the teacher has a degree is significant. We am sure we all look forward to the results of ongoing empirical research by the NRDC into this area.

CONCLUDING REFLECTIONS

Now that a summary of differing social theoretical and psychological approaches to learning has been published within the Skills for Life initiative, we suggest that perhaps the publication of some basic Sociology for adult basic skills practitioners might be a useful next step.

Perhaps, too, knowledge of some of the basic 'ethical' frameworks used by educational researchers would be appropriate. Cohen, Manion and Morrison (2000) might be a good starter text here. The question of informed consent is a particularly thorny one for radical behaviourists.

On theories of learning and knowledge, one could list important thinkers at length. Descartes, Kant, Hegel, Marx, Comte, the logical positivists, Kuhn (one cannot expect people to grasp the idea of a paradigm war unless they know what a paradigm is), Popper, phenomenology, existentialism, Habermas's thinking on knowledge and interests, and the post-positivists are among the thinkers likely to feature on reading lists, though the choices available are many.

Finally, we would have liked to see the authors of this interesting and timely report discuss 'their epistemology'. We have learned vicariously by observing the behaviour of others that this is an acceptable way to respond to a paper in which theories of learning are discussed in the context of adult basic skills work. One popular menu of choices is between Comte, Husserl, Godamer, Derrida and Harding.

In these times, one expects a reflexive awareness of the social situatedness of definitions of epistemology. So to conform to the prevailing orthodoxy - for once – we end by reflecting that all this has been just my interpretation and that it's probably all relative anyway.

Chapter 24

Bilingualism and Multilingualism

Approaching bilingualism and multilingualism from a communication perspective sheds light on a phenomenon which otherwise would appear static and asocial. Merriam Webster's online thesaurus defines *bilingualism* as 'the ability to speak two languages: the frequent oral use of two languages' and *multilingual* as 'of, containing, or expressed in several languages' and 'using or able to use several languages'. The apparent simplicity of these definitions is, however, deceiving for a number of reasons. First, they fail to make the distinction between bilingualism as a collective characteristic defining nations and bilingualism as a person's competence in one or more languages. As we will see below, that distinction is crucial to our understanding of bilingualism as the product of the interplay between individuals and their context.

Second, defining bilingualism at a national level entails, in itself, a number of difficulties. Since there are approximately 5000 languages distributed in 200 countries, most would be characterized by a state of relative bilingualism. Qualifying a state as bilingual does not, however, follow from a simple head count. A key question, here, is how do we distinguish a language from a dialect? Normally, languages are not mutually intelligible. Dialects, however, as varieties of one language differentiated along grammar, vocabulary and accent may or may not be mutually intelligible. European French speakers would probably not understand the Creole dialect spoken in the French West Indies but they would probably understand the French spoken in Canada. Does that make Creole a language and French Canadian a dialect? Not necessarily. According to Weinreich, 'A language is a dialect that has an army and a navy'. This introduces the issue of power hierarchies in the definition of languages. Languages are not languages unless they are recognized as such by the state and this usually entails the obligation to support their acquisition, maintenance and use. Hence, state-level degree of bilingualism is heavily dependent on the political and social climate. The third set of definitional problems is related to individual bilingualism or *bilinguality*. A bilingual person could be the one that can speak two languages perfectly.

Others would, however suggest that even a minimal knowledge of both languages is enough to qualify as a bilingual. Adding to the confusion is the fact that a strictly linguistic definition may not be appropriate. This perspective buttresses the social and political under pinnings discussed above regarding societal bilingualism. It compels to view bilingualism as heavily embedded in its social context and communication practices.

The following elaborates on each of the questions raised by these definitional problems. To be sure though, when speaking of bi- or multilingualism, we not only speak of languages in contact, but also of the people from varied cultural origins using these languages. Bilingualism is, therefore, an intercultural communication (IC) phenomenon (Acculturation Processes and Communication). While bilingualism and multilingualism have not been themes exploited in the literature on IC. We will argue that the two fields of research share many concepts which are similar and that showing these would highlight their complementary characteristics (Intercultural and Intergroup Communication).

BILINGUALITY

Acquiring and using a language other than the first language learned is a matter of fact inmost areas of the world. A distinction is usually made between simultaneous and successive bilingualism. In the first case, both languages are acquired simultaneously whereas in the second case, the second language is acquired later in life. It is important to note, however, that achieving such a state of 'balanced bilingualism' is subject to the existence of contextual factors favoring the equal status of the languages, their equal valuing by the parents, the availability of a language community for each languages as well as individual factors such as positive attitudes toward bilingualism and the languages.

The factors affecting successive bilingualism (the acquisition of L2 after L1 has been established) are by and large identical to those affecting simultaneous bilingualism. Research results underline the importance of such factors as linguistic aptitude, learning strategies and personality factors such as introversion. These aspects find little correspondence in the IC literature. Pioneering work on the question of motivation does, however, cross many of the IC paths. Originally aimed at describing the Canadian situation, over three decades of research have shown that L2 motivation, as affectively based in intergroup attitudes, is a determining factor in L2 competence innumerous settings across the world. And this connects with aspects of the IC theories described above. Since the original research, many alternative motivational models have been created. In all cases, however, the affective basis of the motivation is linked to contextual factors (Language Attitudes in Intergroup Contexts).

Besides intergroup attitudes, the more recent literature has supported the importance of L2 confidence as a determinant of L2 behavior and competence. L2confidence corresponds to the belief in being able to react adaptively to situations involving the use of a second language. It is related to positive self-ratings of competence and a lack of anxiety when using the second language. It originates from situations where contact with the L2 community is both frequent and pleasant. Thus, while positive attitudes may orient the individual towards the L2 community, intercultural contact generates the confidence required for L2 interaction and, in so doing, promotes L2 competence as well as other aspects as well as others consequences of L2 acquisition to be discussed below .Anxiety and uncertainty are also concepts found in IC theories. Accordingly, reconciling intergroup and interpersonal communication hinges on defining as the 'stranger' any other person, whether that person is perceived as different culturally or not.

Specifically, it is suggested that the influence on communication effectiveness of the motivation to interact with strangers, the reaction to strangers, the social categorization of strangers and the connection with strangers are mediated (in part) by an anxiety management system.

SOCIETAL BILINGUALISM

Many descriptions of bilinguality may convey the impression that the phenomenon is individually based or at, best, relevant to dyadic interactions. The above reference to the attitudinal context of bilingual development and L2 acquisition, however, situates it at the intersection of individual and societal processes. This question has, therefore, come to bea key issue for government authorities in a number of countries. Language planning has been the political and administrative instrument used to promote and protect languages according to predetermined societal options.

Accordingly, the State may determine the goals of language education, the medium of interaction with government agencies, tribunals and schools, and the relative visibility of different languages in public and commercial signs – the linguistic landscape.

These actions are often premised on the idea that a minority situation will not only entail the loss of L1 but may also result in the disappearance of entire cultural groups. Under the concepts of additive and subtractive bilingualism. Associative verbal behavior would correspond to attempts at modulating messages adjusted to one's interlocutor whereas dissociative verbal behavior would seek to establish communicative distance. Although no mention is made explicitly of one's usage of a L2 to accommodate the interlocutor, that type of behavior would be considered to be associative. Kim's theory also describes the environment in terms of institutional equity, relative ingroup strength and environmental stress, all factors describing aspect of the context likely to influence associative/dissociative behavior, in a manner that is consistent with ethnolinguistic vitality theory.

SOCIAL AND COGNITIVE CONSEQUENCES

A relevant issue here is the idea that positive benefits from L2 acquisition and usage will only be achieved to the extent that the first language and culture are well established within the individual. This presupposes afamilial, educational, and social context which allows the development and transmission of the first language and culture. Although such conditions may be present for majority group members, they may not characterize the situation of minority group members, immigrants, refugees, and sojourners. The relative status of the first and second language speaking groups and the linguistic composition of the community are here key determinants of the linguistic and cultural outcomes of second language acquisition. Specifically, as suggested by identity-based IC theories, there is an intimate link between communicative processes and individual identity. To the extent that the context brings about a loss of the first language, it will also bring about a loss of the first cultural identity.

A similar argument may be proposed as concerns cognitive consequences of bilingualism. It was originally thought that bilingualism would produce negative consequences for cognitive functioning. The study by Peal and Lambert (1962), however, showed that the bilinguals scored higher than monolinguals on verbal and non-verbal intelligence tests and showed a more diversified intelligence structure. According to these authors, bilinguals have the ability to manipulate two symbolic systems and thus analyzesemantic features in greater detail. Subsequent studies have resulted in the conclusion that bilinguals have greater metalinguistic awareness and cognitive flexibility, that is, they are better able to distinguish the symbol from its specific meaning which gives them an advantage in most school-type cognitive abilities. Socio-cultural inter-dependence hypothesis, positive cognitive outcomes will result only in situations where both the first and second languages are valued. In conclusion, the picture emerging, whether taken from the perspective of IC theories or from the point of view of theories dealing specifically with bilingualism and bilinguality show a phenomenon that is tightly interwoven with social factors pertaining to the community at hand. Whereas IC theories are generally formulated in more abstract terms than bilingualism theories, they do not cover some specific aspects, such as linguistic and cultural attrition or cognitive enhancements, which have been the prime focus of interest in societies valuing cultural diversity. In either camp, most theories attempt, however, to explain these phenomena through complex multi tiered mechanisms. They vary in emphasis and epistemological style but none of them makes predictions that are diametrically opposite to the others.

MULTILINGUALISM

In the last fifty years, large numbers of people have moved around the world. Today, Bristol, like many cities, is a place where many languages are spoken (EMAS supports children speaking 52 languages). Many citizens of Bristol speak a South East Asian language, a language from Eastern Europe, an African language or a dialect of French from the Caribbean. A significant number of people within the Deaf community in Bristol have British Sign Language as a first language.

This policy addresses issues for the education of all children and young people, especially those who have access to more than one language as a result of their home or community experiences. In many cases, they will be competent in one or more languages and at the early stage of learning another. In some cases, they may be balanced bilinguals with equal access to two languages. Some may be literate in both languages. Some may have only oral skills, either because they have not yet reached a stage where literacy is taught or because they come from a tradition where there is no written form of the language.

The policy recognises that high quality English is a key to success in Britain and that English is the primary language of education in this country. It also acknowledges the fundamental part that language plays in people's perception of themselves and in their attitudes to learning and therefore recommends that all aspects of children's language repertoire should be valued in school.

RIGHTS AND RESPONSIBILITIES

Languages for All: Languages for Life, the National Strategy on Language Learning, states that 'Languages are a lifelong skill – to be used in business and for pleasure, to open up avenues of communication and exploration and to promote, encourage and instil a broader cultural understanding.'

The Race Relations Amendment Act requires schools to eliminate unlawful discrimination, to promote equality of opportunity and to promote good relations between different groups.

An aspect of this is that all languages of the school community should be valued and there should be equality of treatment for all pupils and staff, no matter what their first language.

Whatever their preferred language, all children and parents should have access to the services provided by the school.

PRINCIPLES

- English is the primary language of education and communication in this country and in the world. Therefore all children have a right to effective teaching of English and in English.
- Support in all the languages in a child's linguistic repertoire helps to ensure that children have the best access to new concepts and ideas and therefore to the highest possible achievement. It is essential that this starts with a strong foundation in the early years.
- Language is a fundamental aspect of identity. Denying children the experience of communicating in their home languages damages their confidence, but valuing and drawing on this asset builds self-esteem and belief in their ability to learn.

- All pupils should have access to a range of languages in order to increase social and community cohesion. An ability to communicate in more than one language is a social and life advantage.
- To value the whole child or young person their full language repertoire must be included.
- Continuing to develop the first language at home and at school while learning English maintains family and cultural relationships.
- Promoting home languages at school and within the school's community, including communicating with parents in ways which are accessible to them, builds community links and mutual respect. This encourages families and schools to work in partnership to develop children's full range of language competencies.
- Achievement in more than one language develops the capacity to enjoy being a confident and competent user of spoken and written language for an expanding range of purposes.
- The approach to language development is inclusive and values the language heritages and experiences of all pupils and adults within the educational community, whether they are monolingual, bilingual or multilingual.

A WHOLE SCHOOL APPROACH TO PRACTICE

Leadership

There is a need for governors and senior managers in school to be committed to valuing the linguistic diversity of the school, its community and the wider community of Bristol and beyond. Governors should consider the approach taken to multi-lingualism and language diversity as part of their curriculum plan and their action plans under the Race Relations Amendment Act.

School leaders are in a strong position to take a lead on multi-lingualism and linguistic diversity through relevant policies, the expectations they set for notices and displays, Acts of Collective Worship and assemblies, classroom practice and communication with parents and the wider community. School leaders have a role to play in establishing practices which give children opportunities to communicate in their first language as well as providing structured support for the development of high standards in English.

Governors and head teachers can promote the value of community languages by making these an essential or desirable characteristic in recruitment processes at all levels. They can also ensure that staff who wish to develop their skills in community languages have access to appropriate professional development.

Schools should consider their policies for Modern Foreign Languages to ensure that they give appropriate value to the languages of the community. Schools should also ensure that language skills learned in supplementary schools and out of hours classes are known about and celebrated within school.

Attitudes in the school to children and the languages they speak will influence their confidence in using both their first and other languages. Fostering the ethos and supporting the training that will lead to understanding of the value of all languages to the processes of cognition and in building a climate of respect is an aspect of good leadership.

Teaching and Learning, Including the Curriculum

Approaches to teaching should recognise that children learn most effectively where all their prior knowledge and skills are built on as an aspect of current learning. This includes their whole linguistic repertoire.

Opportunities to use a range of languages can be offered whether or not there are bilingual adults in the classroom. For example, group and pair work using a share language and whole class work like games and rhymes can be enjoyed by all children.

Bilingual and multilingual adults within the classroom can model community and target languages and provide a bridge between other languages and English. This can be through translating key words, explaining key concepts in the first language and enabling children to work in some language groups.

Children can be asked for the key terminology in their first language. If one knows, then this can be communicated to the whole group.

Where children are new to English and arrive mid phase, buddying can be very helpful to develop their security and ability to learn.

The Foundation Stage documents and the National Strategies, for both Primary and Key Stage 3 provide detailed guidance on supporting pupils for whom English is an Additional language.

The curriculum for English, Modern Foreign Languages, history and geography all provide opportunities to value linguistic diversity and the contribution which all world languages and peoples have made to English language and culture.

Schools should seek opportunities to develop literacy as well as oracy in first languages. A good range of fiction and non-fiction resources are needed to support this process

Assessment

Wherever possible, pupils who are in the early years of education or new to English should be assessed in their strongest languages as well as in English. It is also important to use the preferred language when a bilingual child is being assessed to determine whether there is a Special Educational Need or whether the child is still at the early stage of English language development.

Chapter 25

Articulatory Phonetics

This chapter teaches us the followings:

- List the differences in production and function of vowels versus consonants.
- Identify the three descriptive parameters that are used for vowel articulations, and classify the vowels of American English using those three parameters.
- Differentiate between monophthong and diphthong vowels.
- Define centering diphthongs.
- Differentiate between a phonemic and a non-phonemic diphthong.
- Identify the four parameters that are used to describe the articulation of consonants.
- Define the various manners of articulation.
- Classify the consonants of American English according to their organ, place, manner, and voicing characteristics.
- Define coarticulation and assimilation, and describe the different types of assimilatory processes.
- Understand the importance of syllable structure in the assessment process.
- *A*rticulatory phonetics deals with the categorization and classification of the production features of speech sounds. A thorough knowledge of how vowels and consonants are generated remains essential for successful assessment and remediation of articulatory and phonological disorders. Although contemporary phonological theories have provided new ways of

viewing assessment and treatment of these disorders, knowledge of the speech sounds' production features secures a firm basis for utilizing such procedures. Without this knowledge, phonological process analysis, for example, is impossible.

This chapter discusses articulatory-phonetic aspects of the speech sounds of General American English. The specific goals are

- To provide a review of the production features of vowels and consonants.
- To introduce the concepts of coarticulation and assimilation as a means of describing how sounds change within a given articulatory context.
- To examine the structure of syllables and their clinical applicability in the assessment and treatment of impaired articulation and phonology.

The production of vowels and consonants, and their subsequent language-specific arrangements into syllables and words, depends on articulatory motor processes. If these processes are impaired, speech sound production will be disordered.

Articulatory motor processes depend in turn on many anatomical-physiological prerequisites, which include respiratory, phonatory, or resonatory processes. For example, the speech problems of children with cerebral palsy often originate in abnormal respiratory, resonatory, and/ or phonatory prerequisites for articulation. The proper function of such prerequisites, therefore, must first be secured before any articulatory improvement can be expected. Articulatory motor ability is embedded in many different anatomical-physiological prerequisites, which are of fundamental importance to speech-language pathologists.

Basic knowledge in these areas is typically gained from courses and textbooks covering anatomy and physiology of the speech and hearing mechanisms rather than from those covering impaired articulation and phonology. This is because the clinical significance of anatomical-physiological knowledge and its application to articulatory and phonological disorders is not always recognized. The anatomical-physiological aspects of such disorders are not within the scope of this chapter.

VOWELS VERSUS CONSONANTS

Speech sounds are commonly divided into two groups: vowels and consonants. Vowels are produced with a relatively open vocal tract; *no significant constriction* of the oral (and pharyngeal) cavities exists. The airstream from the vocal folds to the lips is relatively unimpeded. Therefore, vowels are considered to be *open sounds.* In contrast, consonants are produced with a *significant constriction* in the oral and/or pharyngeal cavities during their production.

For consonants, the airstream from the vocal folds to the lips and nostrils encounters some type of articulatory obstacle along the way. Therefore, consonants are considered to be *constricted sounds.* For most consonants this constriction occurs along the sagittal midline of the vocal tract. This constriction for consonants can be exemplified by the first sound in *top,* [t], or *soap,* [s]. For [t] the contact of the front of the tongue with the alveolar ridge occurs along this midline while the characteristic s-quality is made by air flowing along this median plane as the tongue approximates the alveolar ridge. By contrast, during all vowel productions the sagittal midline remains free.

In addition, under normal speech conditions, General American English vowels are always produced with vocal fold vibration; they are voiced speech sounds. Only during whispered speech are vowels unvoiced. Consonants, on the other hand, may be generated with or without simultaneous vocal fold vibration; they can be voiced or voiceless. Pairs of sounds such as [t] and [d] exemplify this relevant feature. Pairs of similar sounds, in this case differing only in their voicing feature, are referred to as cognates. Voicing features constitute the main linguistically relevant differences that separate the consonant cognates such as [s] from [z] or [f] from [v].

Vowels can also be distinguished from consonants according to the patterns of acoustic energy they display. Vowels are highly resonant, demonstrating at least two formant areas. Thus, vowels are more intense than consonants; in other words, they are typically louder than consonants. In this respect we can say that vowels have greater sonority than consonants. Sonority of a sound is its loudness relative to that of other sounds with the same length, stress, and pitch. Due to the greater sonority of vowels over consonants, vowels are also referred to as sonorants.

Consonants		Vowels	
Symbol	*Commonly Realized In*	*Symbol*	*Commonly Realized In*
[p]	pay	[i]	eat
[b]	boy	[ɪ]	in
[t]	toy	[eᶦ]	ape
[d]	doll	[ɛ]	egg
[k]	coat	[æ]	at
[g]	goat	[a]	father
[m]	moon	[u]	moon
[n]	not	[ʊ]	wood
[ŋ]	sing	[oᵘ]	boat
[θ]	think	[ɔ]	father
[ð]	those	[ɑ]	hop
[f]	far	[aᶦ]	tie
[v]	vase	[aᵁ]	mouse
[s]	sun	[ɔᶦ]	boy
[z]	zoo	[ɜ]	girl
[ʃ]	shop	[ɝ]	bird
[ʒ]	beige	[ɚ]	winner
[tʃ]	chop	[ʌ]	cut
[dʒ]	job	[ə]	above
[j]	yes		
[w]	win		
[ʍ]	when		
[l]	leap		
[r]	red		
[h]	hop		

Due to the production features of a special group of consonants and their resulting sonority, certain consonants are also labeled so-norants. Sonorant consonants are produced with a relatively open expiratory passageway. When contrasted to other consonants, so-norant consonants demonstrate less obstruction of the airstream during their production. The sonorant consonants include the nasals, the liquids, and the glides. The sonorants are distinguished from the obstruents, which are characterized by a complete or narrow constriction between the articulators hindering the expiratory airstream. The obstruents include the stop-plosives, the fricatives, and the affricates. There are also functional differences between vowels and consonants. In other words, vowels and consonants play different linguistic roles. This has often been referred to as the "phonological difference" between vowels and consonants. The term *consonant* actually indicates this: *con* meaning "together with" and *-sonant* reflecting the tonal qualities that characterize vowels. Thus, consonants are those speech sounds that function linguistically *together with* vowels. As such, vowels serve as the center of syllables, as syllable nuclei. Vowels can constitute syllables all by themselves, for example, in the first syllable of *a-go* or *e-lope.* Vowels can also appear together with one or more consonants, exemplified by *blue, bloom,* or *blooms.* Although there are many types of syllables, the vowel is always the center of the syllable, its nucleus. A small group of consonants can serve as the nuclei of syllables. A consonant that functions as a syllable nucleus is referred to as a syllabic. These form and functional differences are summarized in the table.

Table. Features Differentiating Vowels and Consonants Articulation

Vowels	Consonants
No significant constriction of the vocal tract	Significant constriction of the vocal tract
Open sounds	Constricted sounds
Sagittal midline of vocal tract remains open	Constriction occurs along sagittal midline of the vocal tract
Voiced	Voiced or unvoiced
Acoustically more intense	Acoustically less intense
Demonstrate more sonority	Demonstrate less sonority
Function as syllable nuclei	Only specific consonants can function as syllable nuclei

Example: front versus back vowels.

The tongue's position relative to the palate. Example: high versus low vowels. The degree of lip rounding or unrounding.

Front Central Back
High i ɪ ɝ ɚ u ʊ High
Mid e ɛ ʌ ə o ɔ Mid
Low æ a ɑ Low

The degree of muscular activity involved in the articulation and to the length of the vowels in question. Therefore, tense vowels are considered to have relatively more muscle activity and are longer in duration than lax vowels. The vowel [i] is considered to be a tense vowel, whereas [i] is lax.

When contrasting tense versus lax, one has to keep in mind that these oppositions refer to pairs of vowels that are productionally similar, to vowel cognates. For example, [i] and [i] are considered to be "ee" type vowels, and [u] and [u] are "oo" type vowels. The terms *close* and *open* refer to the relative closeness of the tongue to the roof of the mouth. Again, only vowel cognates are usually characterized with these terms. Using the previous examples, [i] is more close and [i] more open, [u] close and [u] open.

There are two types of vowels: monophthongs and diphthongs. Monophthongs remain qualitatively the same throughout their entire production. They are pure vowels. Diphthongs are vowels in which there is a change in quality during their duration. The initial segment, the beginning portion of such a diphthong, is phonetically referred to as the onglide, its end portion as the offglide. Using this notation system, the following descriptions for the most common vowels of General American English are offered.

Front Vowels

[i] a high-front vowel, unrounded, close and tense.

[i] a high-front vowel, unrounded, open and lax.

[e] a mid-front vowel, unrounded, close and tense. In General American English, this vowel is typically produced as a diphthong, especially in stressed syllables or when articulated slowly.

[e] a mid-front vowel, unrounded, open and lax.

[ae] a low-front vowel, unrounded, open and lax.

[a] a low-front vowel, unrounded, close and tense. In General American English, the use of this vowel depends on the particular regional dialect of the speaker. In the New England dialect of the Northeast, one might often hear it.

All front vowels show various degrees of unrounding (lip spreading), with the high-front vowels showing the most. The lip spreading becomes less as one moves from the high-front vowels to the mid-front vowels, finally becoming practically nonexistent in the low-front vowels.

Back Vowels

[u] a high-back vowel, rounded, close and tense.

[u] a high-back vowel, rounded, open and lax.

[o] a mid-back vowel, rounded, close and tense. This vowel is typically produced as a diphthong, especially in stressed syllables or when articulated slowly.

[D] a low mid-back vowel, rounded, open and lax. The use of this vowel depends on regional pronunciation.

[a] a low-back vowel, unrounded, open and lax. There seems to be some confusion in transcribing [D] and [a], although acoustic differences certainly exist. One distinguishing feature: the [a] shows some degree of lip rounding, whereas [a] does not. Back vowels display different degrees of lip rounding in General American English. The high-back vowels [u] and [u] often show a fairly high degree of lip rounding, whereas the low-back vowel [a] is commonly articulated as an unrounded vowel.

Central Vowels

[j] a central vowel, rounded, tense with *r*-coloring. Rounding may vary, however, from speaker to speaker. [^] is a stressed vowel. It is typically acoustically more intense, has a higher fundamental frequency, and has a longer duration when it is compared to a similar unstressed vowel such as [a*].

[a*] a central vowel, rounded, lax with *r*-coloring. Again, lip rounding may vary from speaker to speaker. This lax vowel is an unstressed vowel.

[3] a central vowel, rounded, tense. [3] is very similar in pronunciation to *[J-]*, but it lacks any *r*-coloring. This vowel is heard in certain dialects. [3] might be found in a Southern dialect pronunciation of *bird* or *worth,* for example. Also, it could be heard in the speech of children having difficulties producing the "*r*" sound.

[A] a lax, unrounded central vowel. It is a stressed vowel.

[a] a lax, unrounded central vowel. It is an unstressed vowel.

CLINICAL APPLICATION

Do Children Have Difficulties Producing Vowels

Vowel errors in children developing phonological skills in a normal manner are relatively uncommon. However, children with phonological disorders may show deviant vowel patterns. Several studies have documented the presence of specific vowel problems in phonologically disordered children. Although certain vowel substitutions seem to be articulatory simplifications that could also occur in normal development, other errors appear to be idiosyncratic. Assessment of vowel qualities should be a portion of every diagnostic protocol. This can easily be achieved with any formal articulation test by transcribing the entire word rather than just the sound being tested.

Diphthongs. As previously defined, a diphthong is a vowel sound that demonstrates articulatory movement during its production. Its initial portion, the onglide, is acoustically more prominent and usually longer than the off-glide. Common diphthongs in General American English are rising diphthongs. This means that in producing these diphthongs, essential portions of the tongue move from a lower onglide to a higher offglide position; thus, relative to the palate, the tongue moves in a rising motion. This can be demonstrated on the vowel quadrilateral as well

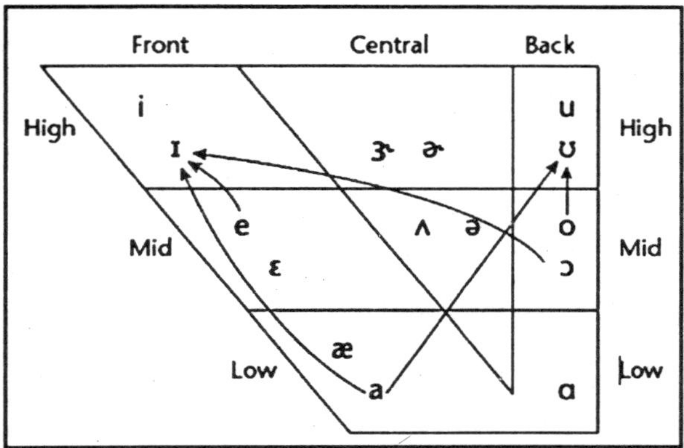

There are several different ways to characterize diphthongs as single phonemic units in contrast to two separate vowels. Some transcribers use a bar or bow either above or below the two vowel symbols—[el], [el], or [ei], for example. The author has chosen to use the transcription that elevates the offglide portion of the diphthong to indicate its typically lesser intensity and length.

Discrepancies may be noted between the transcriptions of diphthongs offered in this text and the ones in other books. Because phonetic transcription is purely *de*scriptive, never *pre*scriptive, any transcription will, of course, vary according to the actual pronunciation.

[e^1] a nonphonemic diphthong

It is nonphonemic in the sense that the meaning would *not* change in a particular word if the vowel were to be pronounced as a monophthong [e] versus a diphthong [e^1]. Therefore, the meaning would not change if just the onglide was realized. Words pronounced [be'k] or [bek], for example, would be recognized as the same word.

[o^u] a nonphonemic diphthong

[a[1]] a phonemic diphthong

It is phonemic in the sense that the meaning *would* change in a particular word if only the vowel onglide was produced. Therefore, the vowel was realized as a monophthong. A realization of

[a] instead of [a] will change the meaning in General American English as the words *sod* [sad] versus *sighed* [sad] demonstrate.

[T] a phonemic diphthong

The opposition [dT], *jaw,* versus [dT], *joy,* exemplifies its phonemic value as a meaning-differentiating sound feature of English.

[a$^{\tilde{o}}$] a phonemic diphthong

Oppositions such as [mas], *moss,* versus [ma$^{\tilde{o}}$s], *mouse,* exemplify its phonemic value.

Analyzing the Vowel System of a Child

Occasionally, the vowel system of a client may be restricted or show deviant patterns. In this case, a more in-depth analysis of the vowels produced may be necessary. Vowel systems can be analyzed using the vowel quadrilateral and knowledge of the diphthongs as guiding principles. Front, back, and central vowels as well as diphthongs can be checked in relationship to their accuracy and their occurrence in the appropriate contexts. George, age 5;3, is an example of a child with a deviant vowel system.

George was being seen in the clinic for his phonological disorder. He was a gregarious child who loved to talk and would try to engage anyone in conversation who would listen. The only problem was that George was almost unintelligible. This made dialogue difficult, possibly more so for those who would patiently and diligently try to understand his continuing attempts to interact.

George's productions of the back vowels [u], [u], *[o^{u}],* and [a] are on target. The front vowels do show a deviant pattern, however. Not only is the diphthong [e[1]] produced as a monophthong, but also the articulatory position of the vowel substitution for [e] is realised lower as *[i]*. This tendency to lower vowels is also noted in the other productions with front vowels, in which [i] becomes [1] and *[z]* becomes [ae].

American English Consonants

Four phonetic categories are used to transcribe consonants: (1) organ of articulation, (2) place of articulation, (3) manner of articulation, and (4) voicing features. Most textbooks state that only place, manner, and voicing are used to characterise individual consonants. However, they nevertheless often include the organ of articulation. For example, the term *lingual* as in *lingua-dental* or *lingua-palatal,* designates the active organ of articulation.

Organ of Articulation. Consonants are sounds characterized by the articulators creating a partial or total obstruction of the expiratory airstream. There are active and passive articulators. Active articulators, the so-called organs of articulation, are the parts within the vocal tract that actually move to achieve the articulator result. In describing the consonants of General American English, we are referring specifically to the movements of the lower lip and portions of the tongue. The structures actively involved in the articulation of the consonants of General American English and the resulting phonetic descriptors are contained in the table. The following figure displays the divisions of the tongue.

Place of Articulation. The place of articulation denotes the area within the vocal tract that remains motionless during consonant articulation, that is, the passive articulator; it is the part that the organ of articulation as active articulator approaches or contacts directly. The upper lip and teeth, the palate, and the velum are the main places of articulation when describing the consonants of General American English. The passive structures of articulation and their resulting phonetic descriptors are contained in the table. The following figure displays the structures of the oral cavity as organs and places of articulation.

Manner of Articulation. The manner of articulation refers to the type of constriction the organ and place of articulation produce for the realization of a particular consonant. There are various manners of articulation, ranging from complete closure for the production of stop-plosives to a very limited constriction of the vocal tract for the production of glides. The following manners of articulation are used to account phonetically for the consonants of General American English.

Stop-Plosives. During the production of stop-plosives, complete occlusion is secured at specific points in the vocal tract. Simultaneously, the velum is raised so that no air can escape through the nose. The expiratory air pressure builds up naturally behind this closure (stop); compression results, which is then suddenly released (plosive). Examples of stop-plosives are [p] and [b].

Fricatives. Fricatives result when organ and place of articulation approximate each other so closely that the escaping expiratory air-stream causes an audible friction. As with the stops, the velum is raised for all fricative sounds. Two examples of fricatives are [f] and [v]. Some fricatives, referred to as sibilants, have a sharper sound than others due to the presence of high-frequency components.

Nasals. These consonants are produced with the velum lowered so that the air can pass freely through the nasal cavity. However, there is complete occlusion within the oral cavity between organ and place of articulation. These sounds have been called nasal stops due to the closure in the oral cavity and the ensuing free air passage through the nasal cavity (. [m], [n], and [K] are the nasal speech sounds of General American English.

Affricates. For affricate sounds, two phases can be noted. First, the velum is raised as a complete closure is formed between organ and place of articulation. As a consequence of these articulatory conditions, expiratory air pressure builds up behind the blockage formed by the organ and place of articulation, the stop phase. Second the stop is then slowly (in comparison to the plosives) released orally, resulting in the friction portion of the speech sound. Affricates should not be viewed as a stop plus fricative combination similar to consonant blends or clusters, such as [ks], in which the stop portion is formed by a different organ and at a different place of articulation than the fricative portion. Rather, affricates are single uniform speech sounds characterised by a slow release of a stopping phase into a homorganic *(hom* = same) friction element. The two most prominent affricates of General American English are [tf] and [dj].

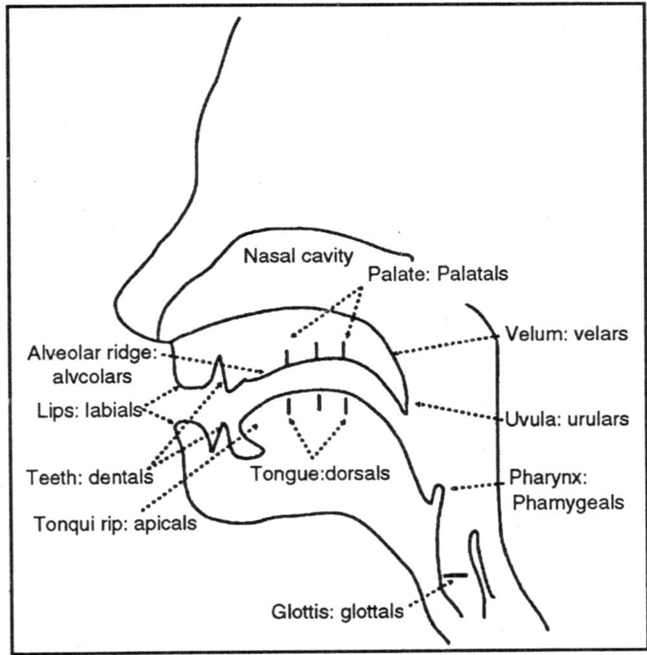

Glides. For the realization of glides, the constriction between organ and place of articulation is not as narrow as for fricatives. In addition to this relatively wide articulatory posture, glides are also characterized by a gliding movement of the articulators from a relatively constricted into a more open position. The sounds [w] and [j] are considered glides. According to the classification of the International Phonetic Alphabet (IPA), [w] and [j] are considered approximants. Approximants are consonants in which there is a much wider passage of air resulting in a smooth (as opposed to turbulent) airflow for these voiced sounds.

According to the symbols used by the International

Phonetic Association (IPA), the American English rhotics are officially transcribed as [ɹ], an upside down *r*, while the retrofl exed is characterized, an upside-down *r* with a retroflexed diacritic.

According to the IPA, the [r] symbol is officially reserved for the alveolar trilled "r" sound, which can be heard in Spanish, for example. Because trilled "r" sounds do not exist in General American English, and in order not to complicate matters unnecessarily, it is customary to use the [r] symbol for both the bunched and the retroflexed "r" sounds.

Rhotics. The phonetic characteristics of the rhotics are especially difficult to describe. First, there are at least two types of rhotic productions: *retroflexed* and *bunched*. Second, the actual forming of rhotics is highly context dependent. Thus, the production easily changes depending on the features of the surrounding sounds. In addition, the positioning of the tongue for individual speakers is highly variable. Generally the *retroflexed* rhotics are produced with the tongue tip in a retroflexed position *(retro* = back, *flex* = turn). The bunched rhotics, on the other hand, show an elevation of the whole corpus of the tongue toward the palate. Perhaps a better classification for [r] is the term *approximant,* which is used within the International Phonetic Alphabet. In this case, [r] is a central approximant. According to the International Phonetic Alphabet, there are two symbols used for the central rhotic approximants. The [ɹ] is a postalveolar approximant in which the tongue tip is raised and points directly upward toward the rear of the alveolar ridge.

Voicing. Voicing is the term used to denote the presence or absence of simultaneous vibration of the vocal cords resulting i. voiced or voiceless consonants. The voiced and voiceless consonants of General American English are summarized in the table.

Far more precision may often be necessary to describe how specific consonants are produced. However, this framework of organ of articulation, place of articulation, manner of articulation, and voicing provides a fairly accurate description of General American English consonants.

WHEN ORGAN, PLACE, MANNER, AND VOICING ARE NOT ENOUGH

In analyzing the articulatory requisites for the realization of [J], we find that it can be described—according to voicing, articulatory organ, place, and manner—as a voiceless coronal-prepalatal fricative. Although that is a generally satisfactory phonetic description, another production characteristic is lip rounding. Describing such an additional feature becomes necessary because some children with "sh" problems do not realize the rounding. In fact, the resulting aberrant production may be due entirely to the absence of this lip-rounding feature.

Table Phonetic Description: Voicing

Table Phonetic Description: Voicing		
Voicing	Phonetic Descriptor	Examples
With vocal fold vibration	Voiced	[b], [d], [g], [m], [n], [rj], [v], [z], [3], [5], [w], [j], [l], [r]
Without vocal fold vibration	Voiceless	[p], [t], [k], [f], [s], [J], [0], [m], [h]

The following phonetic descriptions classify the consonants of General American English according to the parameters of voicing, organ, place, and manner.

[p] voiceless bilabial stop-plosive

(Because both organ and place of articulation are the lower and upper lips, respectively, one should actually say labio-labial. However, the term *bilabial* is usually preferred.)

[b] voiced bilabial stop-plosive

[t] voiceless coronal-alveolar stop-plosive

[d] voiced coronal-alveolar stop-plosive

[k] voiceless postdorsal-velar stop-plosive

[g] voiced postdorsal-velar stop-plosive

[f] voiceless labio-dental fricative

[v] voiced labio-dental fricative

[s] voiceless apico-alveolar or predorsal-alveolar fricative

[s] (and [z]) can be produced in one of two ways: with the tongue tip up (i.e., as apico-alveolar fricative [sibilant]) or with the tongue tip resting behind the lower incisors (i.e., predorsal-alveolar fricative [sibilant]).

[z] voiced apico-alveolar or predorsal-alveolar fricative

[*f*] voiceless coronal-prepalatal or coronal-postalveolar fricative with lip rounding

[3] voiced coronal-prepalatal or coronal-postalveolar fricative with lip rounding

[è] voiceless apico-dental

The [è] and [ð] are typically produced with either the tongue tip resting behind the upper incisors (i.e., apico-dental) or with the tongue tip between the upper and lower incisors (i.e., interdental).

[ð] voiced apico-dental or interdental fricative

[m] voiced bilabial nasal

[n] voiced coronal-alveolar nasal

[K] voiced postdorsal-velar nasal

[w] voiced labial-velar glide or approximant

[M] voiceless labial-velar fricative

[j] voiced mediodorsal-mediopalatal glide

[l] voiced apico-alveolar lateral or lateral approximant

[r] voiced mediodorsal-mediopalatal rhotic approximant (bunched) or voiced apico-prepalatal rhotic approximant (retroflexed), officially [y].

Here, the term *apico* refers to the underside of the apex of the tongue. [h] voiceless unlocalized open consonant that is, an aspirate.

Although this sound is sometimes classified as a laryngeal or glottal fricative, in General American English, there is normally no constriction at the laryngeal, pharyngeal, or oral levels. [tf] voiceless coronal-alveolar stop portion followed by a voiceless coronal-prepalatal fricative portion

RHOTIC ERRORS VERSUS CENTRAL VOWELS WITH R-COLORING

Children with "r" problems, thus, rhotic consonant difficulties, often produce the central vowels with r- coloring

([>] and [»]) in error as well. However, that is not always the case.

Norm	->	Actual	Word	
Product		**Production**	**Example**	**Transcriptions**
Rhotics				
[tr]	->	[tw]	tree	[tri] —> [twi]
[br]	->	[bw]	bridge	[br? dj] —> [bw? 3]
[r]	->	[w]	ring	[r? ?] —> [w? ?]
[br]	->	[bw]	zebra	[zibr?] —> [zibw?]
[r]	->	[w]	garage	[g?r¨ 8] —> [di?w¨ b
[θr]	->	[θw]	thread	[θrεd] —> [θwεd]
[tr]	->	[tw]	treasure	[trε3^] —> [twε3^]
Central Vowels with R-Coloring				
[3-]	correct	[3-]	feather	*[fεð*]^[fεd*]*
[H	correct	[H	soldier	[sould3H -^ [so^u3H
Wz]	correct	[3-z]	scissors	[s? za-z] —> [s? za-z]
[3-]	correct	[3-]	birthday	[b^θde?] -^ [byde?]

On the one hand, Latoria has a [w] for substitution ([r] → [w]) for the rhotic consonant [r]. On the other, she can produce the central vowels with r-colouring accurately.

SOUNDS IN CONTEXT: COARTICULATION AND ASSIMILATION

Until now, this textbook has discussed articulatory characteristics of General American English speech sounds as discrete units. However, the articulators do not move from sound to sound in a series of separate steps. Speech consists of highly variable and overlapping motor movements. Sounds within a given phonetic context influence one another. For example, if the [s] production in *see* is contrasted to the one in *Sue*, it can be seen that [s] in *see* is produced with some spreading of the lips, whereas there is lip rounding in *Sue*. This difference is due to the influence of the following vowel articulations: [i], a vowel with lip spreading, facilitates this feature in the [s] production, whereas the lip rounding of [u] influences the production of [s] in *Sue*.

These types of modifications are grouped together under the term *coarticulation*. Coarticulation describes the concept that the articulators are continually moving into position for other segments over a stretch of speech. The result of coarticulation

is referred to as assimilation. The term assimilation refers to adaptive articulatory changes by which one speech sound becomes similar, sometimes identical, to a neighboring sound segment. Such a change may affect one, several, or all of a sound's phonetic constituents; that is, a sound may change its organ, place, manner, and/or voicing properties under the articulatory influence of another sound. Assimilation processes are perfectly natural consequences of normal speech production and are by no means restricted to developing speech in young children. Because the two segments become more alike, assimilatory processes are also referred to as *harmony processes.*

There are different *types* and *degrees* of assimilatory processes. In regard to the different types of assimilatory processes, the following should be noted:

- Assimilatory processes modifying directly adjacent sounds are called *contact* (or *contiguous) assimilations.* If at least one other segment separates the sounds in question, especially when the two sounds are in two different syllables, one speaks of *remote* (or *noncontiguous) assimilation.*

Manner of articulation is impacted when the [*l*] is changed from a lateral to a stop-plosive, similar to the [t] at the beginning of the word.

- Assimilations can be either *progressive* or *regressive.* In progressive assimilation, a sound segment influences a following sound. This is also referred to as *perseverative assimilation*. The previously noted contact assimilations for *jumping* and *skunk* and the remote assimilation for *telephone* are examples of progressive assimilation. A previously articulated sound influenced a following sound.

In regressive assimilation, a sound segment influences a preceding sound. If "is she" is pronounced, changing [s] into [ʒ], regressive assimilation is noted. Regressive assimilations are also known as *anticipatory* assimilations. The following are examples of progressive and regressive assimilation processes:

Organ, place, and manner of articulation are impacted as

[è] influences the previous segment [b]: This is regressive remote assimilation.

In regard to the different degrees of assimilatory influence, one distinguishes between phonemic assimilation and phonetic similitude. If an altered segment is perceived to be a different phoneme altogether, this is termed *phonemic assimilation. Phonetic similitude* occurs when the change in the segment is such that it is still perceived by speakers of a language as nothing more than a variation or allophone of the original segment.

Assimilation processes can also be total or partial. Total assimilation occurs when the changed segment and the source of the influence become identical. Partial assimilation exists when the changed segment is close to, but not identical with, the source segment.

The term *coalescence* is used when two neighboring segments are merged into a new and different segment. An example of coalescence would be the realization of *sandwich*. The bilabial features for the articulation of [w] have impacted the original coronal-alveolar nasal (regressive assimilation), which now is changed to a bilabial nasal [m].

Children at different stages of their speech language development tend to utilize assimilation processes in systematic ways. This is of obvious interest to clinicians whose task is to separate normal from impaired phonological development. In normally developing children and those with disordered phonology, syllable structure can impact their production possibilities. This will be discussed in the next section.

SYLLABLE STRUCTURE

If we are asked to break words down into component parts, syllables seem to be more natural than sounds. For example, speakers of unwritten languages will characteristically use syllable, not sound, divisions. They may even resist the notion that any further breakdown is possible. Also, preschool children use syllabification if they try to analyze a word. It is only after children are exposed to letters

and writing that they begin to understand the possibility of dividing words into sounds. Thus, syllables appear to be easily recognizable units.

Counting the number of syllables in a word is a relatively simple task. Probably all will agree on the number of syllables in the word *away* or *articulation,* for example. What we might disagree on are the beginning and end points of the syllables in question. To arrive at a consensus, it is first necessary to differentiate between written and spoken syllables.

If one consults a dictionary, written syllabification rules are found. We learn that the word *cutting* is to be divided cutting. However, differences may, and often do, exist between written and spoken syllables. The written syllabification rules for *cutting* do not reflect the way we would syllabify the word when speaking. The divisions would be more probable during normal speech. An awareness of existing differences between spoken and written syllable boundaries is important for speech-language specialists.

This is especially critical because a dictionary of rules for the boundaries of *spoken* syllables does not exist. Thus, two competent speakers of a given language may syllabify the same word in different ways. Words such as *hammer* and *window* would probably not cause problems. However, how should one syllabify *telephone.* That is, does belong to the second or to the first syllable? Variations in the syllabification of spoken words do indeed exist between speakers. To understand this, a look at the syllable structure might be a good way to begin.

Structurally, the syllable can be divided into three parts: *peak, onset,* and *coda*. The peak is the most prominent, acoustically most intense part of the syllable. Although vowels are clearly more prevalent as syllable peaks, consonants are not strictly excluded. Consonants that serve as the syllable peak are referred to as *syllabics.* A peak may stand alone, as in the fi rst syllable of the word *away,* or it can be surrounded by other sounds, as in *tan* or *bring.*

The onset of a syllable consists of all the segments prior to the peak, whereas the coda is made up of all the sound

segments of a syllable following its peak. The segments that compose the onset are also termed *syllable releasing* sounds, and those of the coda are termed *syllable arresting* sounds. Thus, the onset of *meet* [mit] is [m]; that is, [m] is the syllable releasing sound. The coda, or syllable arresting sound, of *meet is* [t]. This applies also to consonant blends within one syllable. The onset of *scratched* is [skr], its peak is [ae], and the coda [tʃt]. Not all syllables have onsets or codas. Both syllables of *today* [tu deʔ] lack a coda, whereas *off* [Qf] does not have an onset. The number of segments that an onset or a coda may contain is regulated by rules of the language in question. General American English syllables can have one to three segments in an onset (ray, stay, stray) and one to four segments in a coda (sit, sits, sixth, sixths).

The peak and coda together are referred to as the rhyme. Therefore, in the word *sun*, the onset is "s" and the rhyme is "un." Syllables that do not contain codas are called open or unchecked syllables. Examples of open, unchecked syllables are *do* [du], *glee* [gli], or the first syllable of *rebound*. Syllables that do have codas are called closed or checked syllable.

The use of specific syllable structures is often neglected when analyzing the speech characteristics of children. However, they do seem to play an important developmental role. A child's first words consist typically of open or unchecked syllables, such as [bQ] for *ball* or [m] for *milk*. If children start to produce closed syllables, they usually contain only single-segment codas. Similarly, two-syllable words at this stage of development consist usually of open syllables.

Syllable Structure: Clinical Implications

The syllable is also an important unit when assessing and treating children with articulatory or phonological disorders. Sometimes, the syllable unit can give us a more accurate picture of the child's articulatory capabilities than can individual sound productions. The ease of syllable production can be affected by at least three circumstances: (1) the *number of syllables* an utterance contains, (2) the *type of syllable* (open versus closed), and (3) the *degree of syllable stress* (stressed or unstressed). Generally, fewer syllables, open syllables, and stressed syllables usually facilitate accurate productions of specific target sounds.

The designs of most articulation tests document a striking lack of attention to these variables. Most assessment instruments focus on the beginning-initial, the middle-medial, and the end-final sound positions within words. At first glance, it may seem as if initial could be related to the syllable onset, medial to syllable peak, and final to syllable coda. However, this is not the case. For example, the word *window* may be used in an articulation test to assess the production of the word-medial [d] sound, while the word *bathtub* is used to test the word-medial [è] and [t] sounds. The elicitation of the *word pajamas* tests [d3] medially. From these examples, it appears that *medial* indicates anything between the beginning and the end of an utterance.

Is there any comparability between these "medial" positions? Let's examine the syllable structures of these three words:

"window"	[wn-do^{u}]	target [d]
1st syllable	stressed	onset-peak-coda
2nd syllable	unstressed	onset-peak
"bathtub"	[baeθ-tΛb]	target [θ] and [t]
1st syllable	stressed	onset-peak-coda
2nd syllable	unstressed	onset-peak-coda
"pajamas"	[pYd3aemYz]	target [d3]
1st syllable	unstressed	onset-peak
2nd syllable	stressed	onset-peak
3rd syllable	unstressed	onset-peak-coda

SUMMARY

This chapter presented an overview of the form and function of vowels and consonants of General American English. Both vowels and consonants were classified according to their articulatory production features and their linguistic functions. Phonetic descriptors were given to provide the clinician with a detailed account of articulatory action during norm production of vowels and consonants. These features can later be contrasted to those noted in the impaired sound realizations of children and adults with articulatory-phonological impairments.

In the second portion of this chapter, co-articulation, assimilation processes, and syllable structure were defined and examined. Coarticulation and resulting assimilatory processes were described as normal articulatory consequences that regularly occur in the speech of individuals. Assimilatory processes were defined according to the type and degree of sound modification. Examples were given of assimilatory processes in children as well as of the possible impact these processes could have on articulation test results.

The last section, on syllable structure, defined the parts of the syllable. Variations in syllable structure do not seem to be accounted for when testing individual sounds within most articulation tests. However, this may be a factor that could affect the articulatory proficiency of children and adults with impaired speech. An analysis of syllable structures would provide the clinician with additional knowledge when evaluating individuals with articulatory-phonological disorders.

CASE STUDY

The following sample is from Tina, age 3;8. fan

dig	[dɛq]	cat	[tæt]
house	[ha^{u}θ̩]	bath	[bæt]
knife	[naf]	red	[led]
duck	[dÅt]	ship	[sÇ¼p]
fan	[vɛn]	ring	[wiŋ]
yes	[wɛt]	thumb	[dΔm]
boat	[bot]	that	[zæt]
cup	[t^{u}p]	zip	[wip]

lamp	[wæmp]	key	[di]
goat	[dot]	win	[jin]

Compare the typical vowel productions to those noted in the sample according to (1) the portion of the tongue that is involved in the articulation (front, central, back) and (2) the tongue's position relative to the palate (high, mid, low).

THINK CRITICALLY

- Children often have trouble with the lip rounding associated with the sh-sounds ([/] and [3]). Which type of vowel contexts would promote lip rounding? Can you find five words that you could use to assist the lip rounding of [J]?
- dentify the following assimilation processes according to the following parameters: contact versus remote, progressive versus regressive, phonemic assimilation, phonetic similitude, or coalescence.

[nuspelpa-]
news [nuz] however newspaper
panty [psnti] ->[psni]
did you [did ju] -> [did3u]
incubate [inkjubelt] -> [irjkjubelt]
misuse [misjuz] ->[mijuz]

- Identify the following syllable structures according to (a) onset, peak, and coda and (b) closed or open syllables. For example: win.dow -4 [win.dow]

Therefore, all words should be two syllables in length, stress should be on the same syllable, and syllable structures should be comparable. Find six words that could be used for a 4year-old child that would test [k] under these conditions.

Index

A

B

C

D

E

F

T

U

V